Also by Astra Taylor

Examined Life: Excursions with Contemporary Thinkers

Occupy!: Scenes from Occupied America (coeditor)

THE PEOPLE'S PLATFORM

THE
PEOPLE'S
PLATFORM

TAKING BACK POWER AND CULTURE
IN THE DIGITAL AGE

ASTRA TAYLOR

METROPOLITAN BOOKS   HENRY HOLT AND COMPANY   NEW YORK

Metropolitan Books
Henry Holt and Company, LLC
Publishers since 1866
175 Fifth Avenue
New York, New York 10010
www.henryholt.com

Metropolitan Books® and m® are registered trademarks of
Henry Holt and Company, LLC.

Copyright © 2014 by Astra Taylor
All rights reserved.

Library of Congress Cataloging-in-Publication Data
Taylor, Astra.
The people's platform : taking back power and culture in the digital age / Astra Taylor.
p. cm.
Includes bibliographical references and index.
ISBN 978-0-8050-9356-8
1. Internet—Social aspects. 2. Virtual reality. 3. Equality. I. Title.
HM851.T39 2014
302.23'1—dc23 2012042645

Henry Holt books are available for special promotions and premiums. For details contact: Director, Special Markets.

First Edition 2014

Designed by Kelly S. Too

Printed in the United States of America
1 3 5 7 9 10 8 6 4 2

CONTENTS

THE PEOPLE'S PLATFORM

PREFACE

When I was twelve years old, while most of my peers were playing outside, I hunkered down in my family's den, consumed by the project of making my own magazine. Obsessed with animal rights and environmentalism, I imagined my publication as a homemade corrective to corporate culture, a place where other kids could learn the truth that Saturday morning cartoons, big-budget movies, and advertisements for "Happy Meals" hid from them. I wrangled my friends into writing for it (I know it's hard to believe I had any), used desktop publishing software to design it, and was thrilled that the father of one of my conspirators managed a local Kinkos, which meant we could make copies at a steep discount. Every couple of months my parents drove me to the handful of bookstores and food co-ops in Athens, Georgia, where I eagerly asked the proprietors if I could give them the latest issue, convinced that when enough young people read my cri de coeur the world would change.

It was a strange way to spend one's preadolescence. But equally strange, now, is to think of how much work I had to do to get it into readers' hands once everything was written and edited. That's how it went back in the early nineties: each precious copy could be accounted for, either given to a friend, handed out on a street corner, shelved at a local store, or mailed to the few dozen precious subscribers I managed to amass. And I, with access to a computer, a printer, and ample professional copiers, had it pretty easy compared to those who had walked a similar road just decades before me: a veteran political organizer told me how he and his friends had to sell blood in order to raise the funds to buy a mimeograph machine so they could make a newsletter in the early sixties.

When I was working on my magazine I had only vague inklings that the Internet even existed. Today any kid with a smartphone and a message has the potential to reach more people with the push of a button than I did during two years of self-publishing. New technologies have opened up previously unimaginable avenues for self-expression and exposure to information, and each passing year has only made it easier to spread the word.

In many respects, my adult work as an independent filmmaker has been motivated by the same concerns as my childhood hobby: frustration with the mainstream media. So many subjects I cared about were being ignored; so many worthwhile stories went uncovered. I picked up a camera to fill in the gap, producing various documentaries focused on social justice and directing two features about philosophy. On the side I've written articles and essays for the independent press, covering topics including disability rights and alternative education. When Occupy Wall Street took off in the fall of 2011, I became one of the coeditors of a movement broadsheet called the *Occupy! Gazette*, five crowd-funded issues in total, which my cohorts and I gave away for free on the Web and in print.

I'm a prime candidate, in other words, for cheering on the revolution that is purportedly being ushered in by the Internet. The digital transformation has been hailed as the great cultural leveler, putting the tools of creation and dissemination in everyone's hands and wresting control from long-established institutions and actors. Due to its remarkable architecture, the Internet facilitates creativity and communication in unprecedented ways. Each of us is now our own broadcaster; we are no longer passive consumers but active producers. Unlike the one-way, top-down transmission of radio or television and even records and books, we finally have a medium through which everyone's voice can supposedly be heard.

To all of this I shout an enthusiastic hurrah. Progressives like myself have spent decades decrying mass culture and denouncing big media. Since 1944, when Max Horkheimer and Theodor Adorno published their influential essay "The Culture Industry: Enlightenment as Mass Deception," critics have sounded the alarm about powerful corporate interests distorting our culture and drowning out democracy in pursuit of profit.

But while heirs to this tradition continue to worry about commercialism and media consolidation, there is now a countervailing tendency to assume that the Internet, by revolutionizing our media system, has rendered such concerns moot. In a digital world, the number of channels is theoretically infinite, and no one can tell anyone what to consume. We are the ultimate deciders, fully in charge of our media destinies, choosing what to look at, actively seeking and clicking instead of having our consumption foisted upon us by a cabal of corporate executives.

As a consequence of the Internet, it is assumed that traditional gatekeepers will crumble and middlemen will wither. The new orthodoxy envisions the Web as a kind of Robin Hood, stealing audience and influence away from the big and giving to the small. Networked technologies will put professionals and amateurs on an even playing field, or even give the latter an advantage. Artists and writers will thrive without institutional backing, able to reach their audiences directly. A golden age of sharing and collaboration will be ushered in, modeled on Wikipedia and open source software.

In many wonderful ways this is the world we have been waiting for. So what's the catch? In some crucial respects the standard assumptions about the Internet's inevitable effects have misled us. New technologies have undoubtedly removed barriers to entry, yet, as I will show, cultural democracy remains elusive. While it's true that anyone with an Internet connection can speak online, that doesn't mean our megaphones blast our messages at the same volume. Online, some speak louder than others. There are the followed and the followers. As should be obvious to anyone with an e-mail account, the Internet, though open to all, is hardly an egalitarian or noncommercial paradise, even if you bracket all the porn and shopping sites.

To understand why the most idealistic predictions about how the Internet would transform cultural production and distribution, upending the balance of power in the process, have not come to pass, we need to look critically at the current state of our media system. Instead, we celebrate a rosy vision of what our new, networked tools theoretically make possible or the changes they will hypothetically unleash. What's more, we need to look ahead and recognize the forces that are shaping the development and implementation of technology—economic forces in particular.

Writing critically about technological and cultural transformation means proceeding with caution. Writers often fall into one of two camps, the cheerleaders of progress at any cost and the prophets of doom who condemn change, lamenting all they imagine will be lost. This pattern long precedes us. In 1829, around the time advances in locomotion and telegraphy inspired a generation to speak rapturously of the "annihilation of space and time," Thomas Carlyle, the Victorian era's most irascible and esteemed man of letters, published a sweeping indictment of what he called the Mechanical Age.

Everywhere Carlyle saw new contraptions replacing time-honored techniques—there were machines to drive humans to work faster or replace them altogether—and he was indignant: "We war with rude Nature; and, by our resistless engines, come off always victorious, and loaded with spoils." Yet the spoils of this war, he anxiously observed, were not evenly distributed. While some raced to the top, others ate dust. Wealth had "gathered itself more and more into masses, strangely altering the old relations, and increasing the distance between the rich and the poor." More worrisome still, mechanism was encroaching on the inner self. "Not the external and physical alone is now managed by machinery, but the internal and spiritual also," he warned. "Men are grown mechanical in head and in heart, as well as in hand," a shift he imagined would make us not wiser but worse off.

Two years later, Timothy Walker, a young American with a career in law ahead of him, wrote a vigorous rebuttal entitled "Defense of Mechanical Philosophy." Where Carlyle feared the mechanical metaphor making society over in its image, Walker welcomed such a shift, dismissing Carlyle as a vaporizing mystic. Mechanism, in Walker's judgment, has caused no injury, only advantage. Where mountains stood obstructing, mechanism flattened them. Where the ocean divided, mechanism stepped across. "The horse is to be unharnessed, because he is too slow; and the ox is to be unyoked, because he is too weak. Machines are to perform the drudgery of man, while he is to look on in self-complacent ease." Where, Walker asked, is the wrong in any of this?

Carlyle, Walker observed, feared "that mind will become subjected to the laws of matter; that physical science will be built up on the ruins of our spiritual nature; that in our rage for machinery, we shall ourselves become machines." On the contrary, Walker argued, machines would free our minds by freeing our bodies from tedious labor, thus permitting all of humankind to become "philosophers, poets, and votaries of art." That "large numbers" of people had been thrown out of work as a consequence of technological change is but a "temporary inconvenience," Walker assured his readers—a mere misstep on mechanism's "triumphant march."

Today, most pronouncements concerning the impact of technology on our culture, democracy, and work resound with Carlyle's and Walker's sentiments, their well-articulated insights worn down into twenty-first-century sound bites. The argument about the impact of the Internet is relentlessly binary, techno-optimists facing off against techno-skeptics. Will the digital transformation liberate humanity or tether us with virtual chains? Do communicative technologies fire our imaginations or dull our senses? Do social media nurture community or intensify our isolation, expand our intellectual faculties or wither our capacity for reflection, make us better citizens or more efficient consumers? Have we become a nation of skimmers, staying in the shallows of incessant stimulation, or are we evolving into expert synthesizers and multitaskers, smarter than ever before? Are those who lose their jobs due to technological change deserving of our sympathy or our scorn ("adapt or die," as the saying goes)? Is that utopia on the horizon or dystopia around the bend?

These questions are important, but the way they are framed tends to make technology too central, granting agency to tools while sidestepping the thorny issue of the larger social structures in which we and our technologies are embedded. The current obsession with the neurological repercussions of technology—what the Internet is doing to our brains, our supposedly shrinking attention spans, whether video games improve coordination and reflexes, how constant communication may be addictive, whether Google is making us stupid—is a prime example. This focus ignores the business imperatives that accelerate media consumption and the market forces that encourage compulsive online engagement.

Yet there is one point on which the cheerleaders and the naysayers agree: we are living at a time of profound rupture—something utterly unprecedented and incomparable. All connections to the past have been rent asunder by the power of the network, the proliferation of smartphones, tablets, and Google glasses, the rise of big data, and the dawning of digital abundance. Social media and memes will remake reality—for better or for worse. My view, on the other hand, is that there is as much continuity as change in our new world, for good and for ill.

Many of the problems that plagued our media system before the Internet was widely adopted have carried over into the digital domain—consolidation, centralization, and commercialism—and will continue to shape it. Networked technologies do not resolve the contradictions between art and commerce, but rather make commercialism less visible and more pervasive. The Internet does not close the distance between hits and flops, stars and the rest of us, but rather magnifies the gap, eroding the middle space between the very popular and virtually unknown. And there is no guarantee that the lucky few who find success in the winner-take-all economy online are more diverse, authentic, or compelling than those who succeeded under the old system.

Despite the exciting opportunities the Internet offers, we are witnessing not a leveling of the cultural playing field, but a rearrangement, with new winners and losers. In the place of Hollywood moguls, for example, we now have Silicon Valley tycoons (or, more precisely, we have Hollywood moguls *and* Silicon Valley tycoons). The pressure to be quick, to appeal to the broadest possible public, to be sensational, to seek easy celebrity, to be attractive to corporate sponsors—these forces multiply online where every click can be measured, every piece of data mined, every view marketed against. Originality and depth eat away at profits online, where faster fortunes are made by aggregating work done by others, attracting eyeballs and ad revenue as a result.

Indeed, the advertising industry is flourishing as never before. In a world where creative work holds diminishing value, where culture is "free," and where fields like journalism are in crisis, advertising

dollars provide the unacknowledged lifeblood of the digital economy. Moreover, the constant upgrading of devices, operating systems, and Web sites; the move toward "walled gardens" and cloud
computing; the creep of algorithms and automation into every
corner of our lives; the trend toward filtering and personalization;
the lack of diversity; the privacy violations: all these developments
are driven largely by commercial incentives. Corporate power and
the quest for profit are as fundamental to new media as old. From a
certain angle, the emerging order looks suspiciously like the old one.

In fact, the phrase "new media" is something of a misnomer
because it implies that the old media are on their way out, as though
at the final stage of some natural, evolutionary process. Contrary to
all the talk of dinosaurs, this is more a period of adaptation than
extinction. Instead of distinct old and new media, what we have is
a complex cultural ecosystem that spans the analog and digital,
encompassing physical places and online spaces, material objects
and digital copies, fleshy bodies and virtual identities.

In that ecosystem, the online and off-line are not discrete realms,
contrary to a perspective that has suffused writing about the Internet since the word "cyberspace" was in vogue.[1] You might be reading this book off a page or screen—a screen that is part of a gadget
made of plastic and metal and silicon, the existence of which puts a
wrench into any fantasy of a purely ethereal exchange. All bits
eventually butt up against atoms; even information must be carried
along by something, by stuff.

I am not trying to deny the transformative nature of the Internet, but rather to recognize that we've lived with it long enough to
ask tough questions.[2] Thankfully, this is already beginning to happen. Over the course of writing this book, the public conversation
about the Internet and the technology industry has shifted significantly.[3] There have been revelations about the existence of a sprawling international surveillance infrastructure, uncompetitive business
and exploitative labor practices, and shady political lobbying initia-

tives, all of which have made major technology firms the subjects of increasing scrutiny from academics, commentators, activists, and even government officials in the United States and abroad.[4]

People are beginning to recognize that Silicon Valley platitudes about "changing the world" and maxims like "don't be evil" are not enough to ensure that some of the biggest corporations on Earth will behave well. The risk, however, is that we will respond to troubling disclosures and other disappointments with cynicism and resignation when what we need is clearheaded and rigorous inquiry into the obstacles that have stalled some of the positive changes the Internet was supposed to usher in.

First and foremost, we need to rethink how power operates in a post-broadcast era. It was easy, under the old-media model, to point the finger at television executives and newspaper editors (and even book publishers) and the way they shaped the cultural and social landscape from on high. In a networked age, things are far more ambiguous, yet new-media thinking, with its radical sheen and easy talk of revolution, ignores these nuances. The state is painted largely as a source of problematic authority, while private enterprise is given a free pass; democracy, fuzzily defined, is attained through "sharing," "collaboration," "innovation," and "disruption."

In fact, wealth and power are shifting to those who control the platforms on which all of us create, consume, and connect. The companies that provide these and related services are quickly becoming the Disneys of the digital world—monoliths hungry for quarterly profits, answerable to their shareholders not us, their users, and more influential, more ubiquitous, and more insinuated into the fabric of our everyday lives than Mickey Mouse ever was. As such they pose a whole new set of challenges to the health of our culture.

Right now we have very little to guide us as we attempt to think through these predicaments. We are at a loss, in part, because we have wholly adopted the language and vision offered up by Silicon Valley executives and the new-media boosters who promote their interests. They foresee a marketplace of ideas powered by profit-driven companies who will provide us with platforms to creatively express ourselves and on which the most deserving and popular will succeed.

They speak about openness, transparency, and participation, and these terms now define our highest ideals, our conception of what is good and desirable, for the future of media in a networked age. But these ideals are not sufficient if we want to build a more democratic and durable digital culture. Openness, in particular, is not necessarily progressive. While the Internet creates space for many voices, the openness of the Web reflects and even amplifies real-world inequities as often as it ameliorates them.

I've tried hard to avoid the Manichean view of technology, which assumes either that the Internet will save us or that it is leading us astray, that it is making us stupid or making us smart, that things are black or white. The truth is subtler: technology alone cannot deliver the cultural transformation we have been waiting for; instead, we need to first understand and then address the underlying social and economic forces that shape it. Only then can we make good on the unprecedented opportunity the Internet offers and begin to make the ideal of a more inclusive and equitable culture a reality. If we want the Internet to truly be a people's platform, we will have to work to make it so.

1

A PEASANT'S KINGDOM

I moved to New York City in 1999 just in time to see the dot-com dream come crashing down. I saw high-profile start-ups empty out their spacious lofts, the once ebullient spaces vacant and echoing; there were pink-slip parties where content providers, designers, and managers gathered for one last night of revelry. Although I barely felt the aftershocks that rippled through the economy when the bubble burst, plenty of others were left thoroughly shaken. In San Francisco the boom's rising rents pushed out the poor and working class, as well as those who had chosen voluntary poverty by devoting themselves to social service or creative experimentation. Almost overnight, the tech companies disappeared, the office space and luxury condos vacated, jilting the city and its inhabitants despite the irreversible accommodations that had been made on behalf of the start-ups. Some estimate that 450,000 jobs were lost in the Bay Area alone.[1]

As the economist Doug Henwood has pointed out, a kind of amnesia blots out the dot-com era, blurring it like a bad hangover. It seems so long ago: before tragedy struck lower Manhattan, before the wars in Afghanistan and Iraq started, before George W. Bush and then Barack Obama took office, before the economy collapsed a second time. When the rare backward glance is cast, the period is usually dismissed as an anomaly, an embarrassing by-product of irrational exuberance and excess, an aberrational event that gets chalked up to collective folly (the crazy business schemes, the utopian bombast, the stock market fever), but "never as something emerging from the innards of American economic machinery," to use Henwood's phrase.[2]

At the time of the boom, however, the prevailing myth was that the machinery had been forever changed. "Technological innovation," Alan Greenspan marveled, had instigated a new phase of productivity and growth that was "not just a cyclical phenomenon or a statistical aberration, but . . . a more deep-seated, still developing, shift in our economic landscape." Everyone would be getting richer, forever. (Income polarization was actually increasing at the time, the already affluent becoming ever more so while wages for most U.S. workers stagnated at levels below 1970s standards.)[3] The wonders of computing meant skyrocketing productivity, plentiful jobs, and the end of recessions. The combination of the Internet and IPOs (initial public offerings) had flattened hierarchies, computer programming jobs were reconceived as hip, and information was officially more important than matter (bits, boosters liked to say, had triumphed over atoms). A new economy was upon us.

Despite the hype, the new economy was never that novel. With some exceptions, the Internet companies that fueled the late nineties fervor were mostly about taking material from the off-line world and simply posting it online or buying and selling rather ordinary goods, like pet food or diapers, and prompting Internet users to behave like conventional customers. Due to changes in law and growing public enthusiasm for high-risk investing, the amount of money available to venture capital funds ballooned from $12 billion in 1996 to $106 billion in 2000, leading many doomed ideas to be propped up by speculative backing. Massive sums were committed to enterprises that replicated efforts: multiple sites specialized in selling toys or beauty supplies or home improvement products, and most of them flopped. Barring notable anomalies like Amazon and eBay, online shopping failed to meet inflated expectations. The Web was declared a wasteland and investments dried up, but not before many venture capitalists and executives profited handsomely, soaking up underwriting fees from IPOs or exercising their options before stocks went under.[4] Although the new economy evaporated, the experience set the stage for a second bubble and cemented a relationship between technology and the market that shapes our digital lives to this day.

As business and technology writer Sarah Lacy explains in her breathless account of Silicon Valley's recent rebirth, *Once You're Lucky, Twice You're Good*, a few discerning entrepreneurs extracted a lesson from the bust that they applied to new endeavors with aplomb after the turn of the millennium: the heart of the Internet experience was not e-commerce but e-mail, that is to say, connecting and communicating with other people as opposed to consuming goods that could easily be bought at a store down the street. Out of that insight rose the new wave of social media companies that would be christened Web 2.0.

The story Lacy tells is a familiar one to those who paid attention back in the day: ambition and acquisitions, entrepreneurs and IPOs. "Winning Is Everything" is the title of one chapter; "Fuck the Sweater-Vests" another. You'd think it was the nineties all over again, except that this time around the protagonists aspired to market valuations in the billions, not millions. Lacy admires the entrepreneurs all the more for their hubris; they are phoenixes, visionaries who emerged unscathed from the inferno, who walked on burning coals to get ahead. After the bust, the dot-coms and venture capitalists were "easy targets," blamed for being "silly, greedy, wasteful, irrelevant," Lacy writes. The "jokes and quips" from the "cynics" cut deep, making it that much harder for wannabe Web barons "to build themselves back up again." But build themselves back up a handful of them did, heading to the one place insulated against the downturn, Silicon Valley. "The Valley was still awash in cash and smart people," says Lacy. "Everyone was just scared to use them."

Web 2.0 was the logical consequence of the Internet going mainstream, weaving itself into everyday life and presenting new opportunities as millions of people rushed online. The "human need to connect" is "a far more powerful use of the Web than for something like buying a book online," Lacy writes, recounting the evolution of companies like Facebook, LinkedIn, Twitter, and the now beleaguered Digg. "That's why these sites are frequently described as addictive . . . everyone is addicted to validations and human connections."

Instead of the old start-up model, which tried to sell us things, the new one trades on our sociability—our likes and desires, our observations and curiosities, our relationships and networks—which is mined, analyzed, and monetized. To put it another way, Web 2.0 is not about users buying products; rather, users *are* the product. We are what companies like Google and Facebook sell to advertisers. Of course, social media have made a new kind of engagement possible: they have also generated a handful of enormous companies that profit off the creations and interactions of others. What is social networking if not the commercialization of the once unprofitable art of conversation? That, in a nutshell, is Web 2.0: content is no longer king, as the digital sages like to say; connections are.

Though no longer the popular buzzword it once was, "Web 2.0" remains relevant, its key tenets incorporated not just by social networking sites, but in just by all cultural production and distribution, from journalism to film and music. As traditional institutions go under—consider the independent book, record, and video stores that have gone out of business—they are being replaced by a small

number of online giants—Amazon, iTunes, Netflix, and so on—
that are better positioned to survey and track users. These behemoths "harness collective intelligence," as the process has been
described, to sell people goods and services directly or indirectly.
"The key to media in the twenty-first century may be who has the
most knowledge of audience behavior, not who produces the most
popular content," Tom Rosenstiel, the director of the Pew Research
Center's Project for Excellence in Journalism, explained.

> Understanding what sites people visit, what content they view,
> what products they buy and even their geographic coordinates
> will allow advertisers to better target individual consumers. And
> more of that knowledge will reside with technology companies
> than with content producers. Google, for instance, will know
> much more about each user than will the proprietor of any one
> news site. It can track users' online behavior through its Droid
> software on mobile phones, its Google Chrome Web browser, its
> search engine and its new tablet software. The ability to target
> users is why Apple wants to control the audience data that goes
> through the iPad. And the company that may come to know the
> most about you is Facebook, with which users freely share what
> they like, where they go and who their friends are.[5]

For those who desire to create art and culture—or "content," to use
that horrible, flattening word—the shift is significant. More and
more of the money circulating online is being soaked up by technology companies, with only a trickle making its way to creators or
the institutions that directly support them. In 2010 publishers of
articles and videos received around twenty cents of each dollar
advertisers spent on their sites, down from almost a whole dollar in
2003.[6] Cultural products are increasingly valuable only insofar as
they serve as a kind of "signal generator" from which data can be

mined. The real profits flow not to the people who fill the platforms where audiences congregate and communicate—the content
creators—but to those who own them.

The original dot-com bubble's promise was first and foremost about
money. Champions of the new economy conceded that the digital
tide would inevitably lift some boats higher than others, but they
commonly assumed that everyone would get a boost from the virtual effervescence. A lucky minority would work at a company that
was acquired or went public and spend the rest of their days relaxing
on the beach, but the prevailing image had each individual getting
in on the action, even if it was just by trading stocks online.

After the bubble popped, the dream of a collective Internet-
enabled payday faded. The new crop of Internet titans never bothered to issue such empty promises to the masses. The secret of
Web 2.0 economics, as Lacy emphasizes, is getting people to create
content without demanding compensation, whether by contributing code, testing services, or sharing everything from personal photos to restaurant reviews. "A great Web 2.0 site needs a mob of
people who use it, love it, and live by it—and convince their friends
and family to do the same," Lacy writes. "Mobs will devote more
time to a site they love than to their jobs. They'll frequently *build*
the site for the founders for free." These sites exist only because of
unpaid labor, the millions of minions toiling to fill the coffers of a
fortunate few.

Spelling this out, Lacy is not accusatory but admiring—
awestruck, even. When she writes that "social networking, media,
and user-generated content sites tap into—and exploit—core human
emotions," it's with fealty appropriate to a fiefdom. As such, her
book inadvertently provides a perfect exposé of the hypocrisy lurk-
ing behind so much social media rhetoric. The story she tells, after
all, is about nothing so much as fortune seeking, yet the question of

compensating those who contribute to popular Web sites, when it arises, is quickly brushed aside. The "mobs" receive something "far greater than money," Lacy writes, offering up the now-standard rationalization for the inequity: entertainment, self-expression, and validation.[7] This time around, no one's claiming the market will be democratized—instead, the promise is that culture will be. We will "create" and "connect" and the entrepreneurs will keep the cash.

This arrangement has been called "digital sharecropping."[8] Instead of the production or distribution of culture being concentrated in the hands of the few, it is the economic value of culture that is hoarded. A small group, positioned to capture the value of the network, benefits disproportionately from a collective effort. The owners of social networking sites may be forbidden from selling songs, photos, or reviews posted by individual users, for example, but the companies themselves, including user content, might be turned over for a hefty sum: hundreds of millions for Bebo and Myspace and Goodreads, one billion or more for Instagram and Tumblr. The mammoth archive of videos displayed on YouTube and bought by Google was less a priceless treasure to be preserved than a vehicle for ads. These platforms succeed because of an almost unfathomable economy of scale; each search brings revenue from targeted advertising and fodder for the data miners: each mouse click is a trickle in the flood.

Over the last few years, there has been an intermittent but spirited debate about the ethics of this economic relationship. When Flickr was sold to Yahoo!, popular bloggers asked whether the site should compensate those who provided the most viewed photographs; when the *Huffington Post* was acquired by AOL for $315 million, many of the thousands of people who had been blogging for free were aghast, and some even started a boycott; when Facebook announced its upcoming IPO, journalists speculated about what the company, ethically, owed its users, the source of its enormous valuation.[9] The same holds for a multitude of sites:

Twitter wouldn't be worth billions if people didn't tweet, Yelp would be useless without freely provided reviews, Snapchat nothing without chatters. The people who spend their time sharing videos with friends, rating products, or writing assessments of their recent excursion to the coffee shop—are they the users or the used?

The Internet, it has been noted, is a strange amalgamation of playground and factory, a place where amusement and labor overlap in confusing ways. We may enjoy using social media, while also experiencing them as obligatory; more and more jobs require employees to cultivate an online presence, and social networking sites are often the first place an employer turns when considering a potential hire. Some academics call this phenomenon "playbor," an awkward coinage that tries to get at the strange way "sexual desire, boredom, friendship" become "fodder for speculative profit" online, to quote media scholar Trebor Scholz.[10] Others use the term "social factory" to describe the Web 2.0, envisioning it as a machine that subsumes our leisure, transforming lazy clicks into cash. "Participation is the oil of the digital economy," as Scholz is fond of saying. The more we comment and share, the more we rate and like, the more economic value is accumulated by those who control the platforms on which our interactions take place.[11]

Taking this argument one step further, a frustrated minority have complained that we are living in a world of "digital feudalism," where sites like Facebook and Tumblr offer up land for content providers to work while platform owners expropriate value with impunity and, if you read the fine print, stake unprecedented claim over users' creations.[12] "By turn, we are the heroic commoners feeding revolutions in the Middle East and, at the same time, 'modern serfs' working on Mark Zuckerberg's and other digital plantations," Marina Gorbis of the Institute for the Future has written. "We, the armies of digital peasants, scramble for subsistence in digital manor economies, lucky to receive scraps of ad dollars here and there, but mostly getting by, sometimes happily, on social rewards—fun, social connections, online reputations. But when the commons are sold or traded on Wall Street, the vast disparities between us, the peasants, and them, the lords, become more obvious and more objectionable."[13]

Computer scientist turned techno-skeptic Jaron Lanier has staked out the most extreme position in relation to those he calls the "lords of the computing clouds," arguing that the only way to counteract this feudal structure is to institute a system of nano-payments, a market mechanism by which individuals are rewarded for every bit of private information gleaned by the network (an interesting thought experiment, Lanier's proposed solution may well lead to worse outcomes than the situation we have now, due to the twisted incentives it entails).

New-media cheerleaders take a different view.[14] Consider the poet laureate of digital capitalism, Kevin Kelly, cofounder of *Wired* magazine and longtime technology commentator. It is not feudalism and exploitation that critics see, he argued in a widely circulated essay, but the emergence of a new cooperative ethos, a resurgence of collectivism—though not the kind your grandfather worried about. "The frantic global rush to connect everyone to everyone, all the time, is quietly giving rise to a revised version of socialism," Kelly raves, pointing to sites like Wikipedia, YouTube, and Yelp.

Instead of gathering on collective farms, we gather in collective worlds. Instead of state factories, we have desktop factories connected to virtual co-ops. Instead of sharing drill bits, picks, and shovels, we share apps, scripts, and APIs. Instead of faceless politburos, we have faceless meritocracies, where the only thing that matters is getting things done. Instead of national production, we have peer production. Instead of government rations and subsidies, we have a bounty of free goods.

Kelly reassures his readers that the people who run this emerging economy are not left-wing in any traditional sense. They are "more likely to be libertarians than commie pinkos," he explains. "Thus, digital socialism can be viewed as a third way that renders irrelevant the old debates," transcending the conflict between "free-market individualism and centralized authority." Behold, then, the majesty of digital communitarianism: it's socialism without the state, without the working class, and, best of all, without having to share the wealth.

The sensational language is easy to mock, but this basic outlook is widespread among new-media enthusiasts. Attend any technology conference or read any book about social media or Web 2.0, whether by academics or business gurus, and the same conflation of communal spirit and capitalist spunk will be impressed upon you. The historian Fred Turner traces this phenomenon back to 1968, when a small band of California outsiders founded the *Whole Earth Catalog* and then, in 1985, the online community the Whole Earth 'Lectronic Link, the WELL, the prototype of online communities, and then *Wired*.

This group performed the remarkable feat of transforming computers from enablers of stodgy government administration to countercultural cutting edge, from implements of technocratic experts to machines that empower everyday people. They "reconfigured the status of information and information technologies," Turner explains, by contending that these new tools would tear down bureaucracy, enhance individual consciousness, and help build a new collaborative society.[15] These prophets of the networked age—led by the WELL's Stewart Brand and including Kelly and many other still-influential figures—moved effortlessly from the hacker fringe to the upper echelon of the Global Business Network, all while retaining their radical patina.

Thus, in 1984 Macintosh could run an ad picturing Karl Marx with the tagline, "It was about time a capitalist started a revolution"—and so it continues today. The online sphere inspires incessant talk of gift economies and public-spiritedness and democracy, but commercialism and privatization and inequality lurk beneath the surface.

This contradiction is captured in a single word: "open," a concept capacious enough to contain both the communal and capitalistic impulses central to Web 2.0 while being thankfully free of any social-ist connotations. New-media thinkers have claimed openness as the appropriate utopian ideal for our time, and the concept has caught on. The term is now applied to everything from education to culture to politics and government. Broadly speaking, in tech circles, open systems—like the Internet itself—are always good, while closed systems—like the classic broadcast model—are bad. Open is Google and Wi-Fi, decentralization and entrepreneurialism, the United States and Wikipedia. Closed equals Hollywood and cable television, cen-tral planning and entrenched industry, China and the *Encyclopaedia Britannica*. However imprecisely the terms are applied, the dichotomy of open versus closed (sometimes presented as freedom versus con-trol) provides the conceptual framework that increasingly underpins much of the current thinking about technology, media, and culture.

The fetish for openness can be traced back to the foundational myths of the Internet as a wild, uncontrollable realm. In 1996 John Perry Barlow, the former Grateful Dead lyricist and cattle ranger turned techno-utopian firebrand, released an influential manifesto, "A Declaration of the Independence of Cyberspace," from Davos, Switzerland, during the World Economic Forum, the annual meet-ing of the world's business elite. ("Governments of the Industrial World, you weary giants of flesh and steel, I come from Cyberspace, the new home of Mind. On behalf of the future, I ask you of the past to leave us alone. . . . You have no sovereignty where we gather.") Almost twenty years later, these sentiments were echoed by Google's Eric Schmidt and the State Department's Jared Cohen, who partnered to write *The New Digital Age*: "The Internet is the largest experiment involving anarchy in history," they insist. It is "the world's largest ungoverned space," one "not truly bound by terrestrial laws."

While openness has many virtues, it is also undeniably ambiguous. Is open a means or an end? What is open and to whom? Mark Zuckerberg said he designed Facebook because he wanted to make the world more "open and connected," but his company does everything it can to keep users within its confines and exclusively retains the data they emit. Yet this vagueness is hardly a surprise given the history of the term, which was originally imported from software production: the designation "open source" was invented to rebrand free software as business friendly, foregrounding efficiency and economic benefits (open as in open markets) over ethical concerns (the freedom of free software).[16] In keeping with this transformation, openness is often invoked in a way that evades discussions of ownership and equity, highlighting individual agency over commercial might and ignoring underlying power imbalances.

In the 2012 "open issue" of Google's online magazine *Think Quarterly*, phrases like "open access to information" and "open for business" appear side by side, purposely blurring participation and profit seeking. One article on the way "smart brands" are adapting to the digital world insists that as a consequence of the open Web, "consumers have more power than ever," while also outlining the ways "the web gives marketers a 24/7 focus group of the world," unleashing a flood of "indispensable" data that inform "strategic planning and project development." Both groups are supposedly "empowered" by new technology, but the first gets to comment on products while the latter boosts their bottom line.

By insisting that openness is the key to success, whether you are a multinational corporation or a lone individual, today's digital gurus gloss over the difference between humans and businesses, ignoring the latter's structural advantages: true, "open" markets in some ways serve consumers' buying interests, but the more open people's lives are, the more easily they can be tracked and exploited by private interests.[17] But as the technology writer Rob Horning has observed, "The connections between people are not uniformly reciprocal." Some are positioned to make profitable use of what they glean from the network; others are more likely to be taken advantage of, giving up valuable information and reaping few benefits. "Networks," Horning writes, "allow for co-optation as much as cooperation."[18]

Under the rubric of open versus closed, the paramount concern is access and whether people can utilize a resource or platform without seeking permission first. This is how Google and Wikipedia wind up in the same camp, even though one is a multibillion-dollar advertising-funded business and the other is supported by a nonprofit foundation. Both are considered "open" because they are accessible, even though they operate in very different ways. Given that we share noncommercial projects on commercial platforms all the time online, the distinction between commercial and noncommercial has been muddled; meanwhile "private" and "public" no longer refer to types of ownership but ways of being, a setting on a social media stream. This suits new-media partisans, who insist that the "old debates" between market and the state, capital and government, are officially behind us. "If communism vs. capitalism was the struggle of the twentieth century," law professor and open culture activist Lawrence Lessig writes, "then control vs. freedom will be the debate of the twenty-first century."[19]

No doubt, there is much to be said for open systems, as many have shown elsewhere.[20] The heart of the Internet is arguably the end-to-end principle (the idea that the network should be kept as flexible, unrestricted, and open to a variety of potential uses as possible). From this principle to the freely shared technical protocols and code that Tim Berners-Lee used to create the World Wide Web, we have open standards to thank for the astonishing growth of the online public sphere and the fact that anyone can participate without seeking permission first.[21]

Open standards, in general, foster a kind of productive chaos, encouraging innovation and invention, experimentation and engagement. But openness alone does not provide the blueprint for a more equitable social order, in part because the "freedom" promoted by the tech community almost always turns out to be of the Darwinian variety. Openness in this context is ultimately about promoting competition, not with protecting equality in any traditional sense; it has little to say about entrenched systems of economic privilege, labor rights, fairness, or income redistribution. Despite enthusiastic commentators and their hosannas to democratization, inequality is not exclusive to closed systems. Networks reflect and exacerbate imbalances of power as much as they improve them.

The tendency of open systems to amplify inequality—and new-media thinkers' glib disregard for this fundamental characteristic—was on vivid display during a talk at a 2012 installment of the TEDGlobal conference convened under the heading "Radical Openness." Don Tapscott, self-proclaimed "thought leader" and author of influential books including *Growing Up Digital* and *Wikinomics*, titled his presentation "Four Principles for the Open World": collaboration, transparency, sharing, and empowerment.

Tapscott told the story of his neighbor Rob McEwen, a banker turned gold mine owner, the former chairman and CEO of Goldcorp Inc. When staff geologists couldn't determine where the mineral deposits at one of his mines were located, McEwen turned to the Web, uploading data about the company's property and offering a cash reward to anyone who helped them hit pay dirt. "He gets submissions from all around the world," Tapscott explained. "They use techniques that he's never heard of, and for his half a million dollars in prize money, Rob McEwen finds 3.4 billion dollars worth of gold. The market value of his company goes from 90 million to 10 billion dollars, and I can tell you, because he's my neighbor, he's a happy camper."

This is Tapscott's idea of openness in action: a banker-turned-

CEO goes from rich to richer (of course, there was no mention of the workers in the mine and the wages they were paid for their effort, nor an acknowledgment of Goldcorp's lengthy record of human rights and environmental violations).[22] For Tapscott, McEwen's payoff is a sign of a bold new era, an "age of promise fulfilled and of peril unrequited," to use his grandiloquent phrase. "And imagine, just consider this idea, if you would," he concluded. "What if we could connect ourselves in this world through a vast network of air and glass? Could we go beyond just sharing information and knowledge? Could we start to share our intelligence?" The possibility of sharing any of the windfall generated as a consequence of this collective wisdom went unmentioned.

A similar willful obliviousness to the problems of open systems undercuts the claims of new-media thinkers that openness has buried the "old debates." While Lawrence Lessig convincingly makes the case that bloated intellectual property laws—the controlling nature of copyright—often stifle creative innovation from below, his enthusiasm for the free circulation of information blinds him to the increasing commodification of our expressive lives and the economic disparity built into the system he passionately upholds.

"You can tell a great deal about the character of a person by asking him to pick the great companies of an era," Lessig declares in *Remix: Making Art and Commerce Thrive in the Hybrid Economy*, and whether they root for the "successful dinosaurs" or the "hungry upstarts." Technology, he continued, has "radically shifted" the balance of power in favor of the latter. Proof? "The dropouts of the late 1990s (mainly from Stanford) beat the dropouts of the middle 1970s (from Harvard). Google and Yahoo! were nothing when Microsoft was said to dominate." This, it seems, is what it means to have moved beyond the dichotomy of market and state into the realm of openness—that we must cheerlead the newly powerful from the sidelines for no better reason than that they are new.

Even if the players weren't from Stanford and Harvard (two

institutions where Lessig has held prominent appointments), the statement would still be unsettling. Who could possibly construe a contest between the dropouts of these elite and storied institutions as one between underdogs and an oppressor? And why should we cheer Amazon over local bookstores, Apple over independent record labels, or Netflix over art house cinemas, on the basis of their founding date or their means of delivery? The dinosaurs and upstarts have more in common than Lessig cares to admit.

As Woodrow Wilson famously said, "That a peasant may become king does not render the kingdom democratic." Although new-media celebrants claim to crusade on behalf of the "yeoman creator," they treat the kings of the digital domain with unwavering reverence, the beneficence of their rule evident in the freedom that their platforms and services allow. Praising the development of what he calls "hybrid economies," where sharing and selling coexist, Lessig argues that advances in advertising will provide adequate support for the creation and dissemination of culture in a digital age. "As if by an invisible hand," the ways we access culture will dramatically change as the dinosaurs "fall to a better way of making money" via hypertargeted marketing.

Lessig is deeply concerned about control of culture and appalled that a generation has been criminalized for downloading copyrighted content, yet he ignores the problem of commercialism and is sanguine about the prospect of these same youth being treated as products, their personal data available for a price.[23] Though the reviled traditional broadcast model evolved the way it did to serve the interests of advertisers, Internet enthusiasts brush away history's warnings, confident that this time will be different.

Going against the grain of traditional media critics, Lessig and others believe that the problem is not commercialism of culture but control. The long-standing progressive critique of mass media identified the market as the primary obstacle to true cultural democracy. When General Electric acquired NBC, for example, the CEO assured shareholders that the news, a commodity just like "toasters, lightbulbs, or jet engines," would be expected to make the same profit margin as any other division. But art and culture, the critical line of thought maintains, should be exempt, or at least shielded, from the revenue-maximizing mandates of Wall Street, lest vital forms of creativity shrivel up or become distorted by the stipulations of merchandising—an outlook that leads to advocating for regulations to break up conglomerates or for greater investment in public media.

Internet enthusiasts, in contrast, tend to take a laissez-faire approach: technology, unregulated and unencumbered, will allow everyone to compete in a truly open digital marketplace, resulting in a richer culture and more egalitarian society. Entertainment companies become the enemy only when they try to dictate how their products are consumed instead of letting people engage with them freely, recontextualizing and remixing popular artifacts, modifying and amending and feeding them back into the semiotic stream.

When all is said and done, the notion of a hybrid economy turns out to be nothing more than an upbeat version of digital sharecropping, a scenario in which all of us have the right to remix sounds and images and spread them through networks that profit from our every move. The vision of cultural democracy upheld by new-media thinkers has us all marinating in commercial culture, downloading it without fear of reprisal, repurposing fragments and uploading the results to pseudo-public spaces—the privately owned platforms that use our contributions for their own ends or sell our attention and information to advertisers. Under this kind of open system, everything we do gets swept back into a massive, interactive mash-up in the cloud, each bit parsed in the data mine, invisible value extracted by those who own the backend.

In a way, this is the epitome of what communications scholar Henry Jenkins calls "convergence culture"—the melding of old and new media that the telecom giants have long been looking forward to, for it portends a future where all activity flows through their pipes. But it also represents a broader blurring of boundaries: communal spirit and capitalist spunk, play and work, production and consumption, making and marketing, editorializing and advertising, participation and publicity, the commons and commerce. The "old rhetoric of opposition and co-optation" has been rendered obsolete, Jenkins assures us.[24] But if there is no opposition—no distinction between noncommercial and commercial, public and private, independent and mainstream—it is because co-optation has been absolute.

Though she now tours under her own name, the Portland-based musician Rebecca Gates long fronted the Spinanes, a band that, in the nineties and early aughts, released three albums on the influential Sub Pop label. She had, in many ways, the classic indie rock experience, playing clubs around the country, sleeping on couches, getting aired on college radio and MTV's *120 Minutes*. Sub Pop provided advances for the band to make records and tour support, and though the albums never sold enough copies to recoup, the label made it possible for Gates to devote herself to her craft. Then, after a hiatus of ten years, Gates finished a new record and went back on the road, but this time she self-released her music, taking advantage of the low cost of digital distribution. Gates was cautiously optimistic that she could end up better off than under the old model—that the enterprise may be more sustainable and satisfying—even if she sold fewer copies in the end.

Gates thought a lot about the new opportunities offered by technology as part of a project undertaken in partnership with the Future of Music Coalition, a nonprofit that advocates for the rights of independent artists, lobbying for everything from health care to community radio. She led an ambitious survey of working musicians to see how they had actually fared as the recording industry transforms. "It's really easy to get hung up on success stories," Gates told me, referencing appealing anecdotes about creators who "made it" by leaving their record labels and going viral online or by giving their music away and relying on touring income or T-shirt sales. Gates discovered it was hard to generalize about people's experiences. "I've seen hard data for people who are in successful bands, quote unquote, festival headlining bands, who would make more money in a good retail job," she said.

"There's this myth that's not quite a myth that you don't need intermediaries anymore," Gates continued. But it is harder than it seems for artists like Gates to bypass the giants and go solo, directing traffic to their own Web sites, though that's what many artists would prefer to do. "Let's imagine your record is done, that somehow you paid for production and you're in the clear—then immediately you're in a situation where you are dealing with iTunes, which takes thirty percent, and if you are small and you go through a brokerage, which you sometimes have to do, you can lose fifty percent." Artists who do work with labels, big or small, often end up getting less from each digital sale.

A similar arrangement applies to streaming services such as Pandora and Spotify, which have come under fire from a range of working musicians for their paltry payouts. The four biggest major labels have an equity stake in Spotify and receive a higher royalty rate than the one paid to independent artists and labels (one independent songwriter calculated that it would take him 47,680 plays on Spotify to earn the profit of the sale of one LP[25]). "As far as I can tell, there's been this replication of the old model," Gates said. "There's a large segment of the tech platforms that are simply a replacement for any sort of old label structures except that now they don't give advances."

During this crucial moment of cultural and economic restructuring, artists themselves have been curiously absent from a conversation dominated by executives, academics, and entrepreneurs.

Conference after conference is held to discuss the intersection of music and new media, Gates notes, but working musicians are rarely onstage talking about their experiences or presenting their ideas, even as their work is used to lure audiences and establish lucrative ventures, not unlike the way books and CDs have long been sold as loss leaders at big chains to attract shoppers. The cultural field has become increasingly controlled by companies "whose sole contribution to the creative work," to borrow Cory Doctorow's biting expression, "is chaining children to factories in China and manufacturing skinny electronics" or developing the most sophisticated methods for selling our data to advertisers.

It wasn't supposed to be this way. One natural consequence of Web-based technologies was supposed to be the elimination of middlemen, or "disintermediation." "The great virtue of the Internet is that it erodes power," the influential technologist Esther Dyson said. "It sucks power out of the center, and takes it to the periphery, it erodes the power of institutions over people while giving to individuals the power to run their lives."[26] The problem, though, is that disintermediation has not lived up to its potential. Instead, it has facilitated the rise of a new generation of mediators that are sometimes difficult to see. As much as networked technology has dismantled and distributed power in more egalitarian ways, it has also extended and obscured power, making it less visible and, arguably, harder to resist.

The disruptive impact of the Web has been uneven at best. From one angle, power has been sucked to the periphery: new technologies have created space for geographically dispersed communities to coalesce, catalyzed new forms of activism and political engagement, and opened up previously unimaginable avenues for self-expression and exposure to art and ideas. That's the story told again and again. But if we look from another angle and ask how, precisely, the power of institutions has been eroded, the picture becomes murkier.

Entrenched institutions have been strengthened in many ways. Thanks to digital technologies, Wall Street firms can trade derivatives at ever-faster rates, companies can inspect the private lives of prospective and current employees, insurance agencies have devised new methods to assess risky clients, political candidates can marshal big data to sway voters, and governments can survey the activities of citizens as never before. Corporate control—in media as in other spheres—is as secure as ever. In profound ways, power has been sucked in, not out.

In the realm of media and culture, the uncomfortable truth is that the information age has been accompanied by increasing consolidation and centralization, a process aided by the embrace of openness as a guiding ideal. While the old-media colossi may not appear to loom as large over our digital lives as they once did, they have hardly disappeared. Over the previous decade, legacy media companies have not fallen from the Fortune 500 firmament but have actually risen. In early 2013 they surprised analysts by reporting skyrocketing share prices: Disney and Time Warner were up 32 percent, CBS 40.2 percent, Comcast a shocking 57.6 percent.[27]

These traditional gatekeepers have been joined by new online gateways, means of accessing information that cannot be avoided. A handful of Internet and technology companies have become as enormous and influential as the old leviathans: they now make up thirteen of the thirty largest publicly traded corporations in the United States.[28] The omnipresent Google, which, on an average day, accounts for approximately 25 percent of all North American consumer Internet traffic, has gobbled up over one hundred smaller firms, partly as a method of thwarting potential rivals, averaging about one acquisition a week since 2010; Facebook now has well over one billion users, or more than one in seven people on the planet; Amazon controls one-tenth of all American online commerce and its swiftly expanding cloud computing services host the data and traffic of hundreds of thousands of companies located in almost two hundred countries, an estimated one-third of all Internet users accessing Amazon's cloud at least once a day; and Apple, which sits on almost $140 billion in cash reserves, jockeys with Exxon Mobil for the title of the most valuable company on earth, with a valuation exceeding the GDP (gross domestic product) of most nations.[29]

Instead of leveling the field between small and large, the open Internet has dramatically tilted it in favor of the most massive players. Thus an independent musician like Rebecca Gates is squeezed from both sides. Off-line, local radio stations have been absorbed by Clear Channel and the major labels control more of the music market than they did before the Internet emerged. And online Gates has to position herself and her work on a monopolists' platform or risk total invisibility.

Monopolies, contrary to early expectations, prosper online, where winner-take-all markets emerge partly as a consequence of Metcalfe's law, which says that the value of a network increases exponentially by the number of connections or users: the more people have telephones or have social media profiles or use a search engine, the more valuable those services become. (Counterintuitively, given his outspoken libertarian views, PayPal founder and first Facebook investor Peter Thiel has declared competition overrated and praised monopolies for improving margins.[30]) What's more, many of the emerging info-monopolies now dabble in hardware, software, and content, building their businesses at every possible level, vertically integrating as in the analog era.

This is the contradiction at the center of the new information system: the more customized and user friendly our computers and mobile devices are, the more connected we are to an extensive and opaque circuit of machines that coordinate and keep tabs on our activities; everything is accessible and individualized, but only through companies that control the network from the bottom up.[31] Amazon strives to control both the bookshelf and the book and everything in between. It makes devices, offers cloud computing services, and has begun to produce its own content, starting various publishing imprints before expanding to feature film production.[32] Google is taking a similar approach, having expanded from search into content, operating system design, retail, gadget manufacturing, robotics, "smart" appliances, self-driving cars, debit cards, and fiber broadband.

More troublingly, at least for those who believed the Internet upstarts would inevitably vanquish the establishment dinosaurs, are the ways the new and old players have melded. Condé Nast bought Reddit, Fox has a stake in Vice Media, Time Warner bet on Maker Studios (which is behind some of YouTube's biggest stars), Apple works intimately with Hollywood and AT&T, Facebook joined forces with Microsoft and the major-label-backed Spotify, and Twitter is trumpeting its utility to television programmers. Google, in addition to cozying up to the phone companies that use its Android operating system, has struck partnership deals with entertainment companies including Disney, Paramount, ABC, 20th Century Fox, and Sony Pictures while making numerous overtures to network and cable executives in hopes of negotiating a paid online television service.[33]

Google has licensing agreements with the big record companies for its music-streaming service and holds stake alongside Sony and Universal in Vevo, the music video site that is also the most viewed "channel" on YouTube.[34] YouTube has attempted to partly remake itself in television's image, investing a small fortune in professionally produced Web series, opening studios for creators in New York, Los Angeles, and London, and seeking "brand safe" and celebrity-driven content to attract more advertising revenue.[35] "Top YouTube execs like to say they're creating the next generation of cable TV, built and scaled for the web," reports *Ad Age*. "But instead of 500-odd channels on TV, YouTube is making a play for the 'next 10,000,' appealing to all sorts of niches and interest groups."[36]

Though audiences may be smaller as a consequence of this fragmentation, they will be more engaged and more thoroughly monitored and marketed to than traditional television viewers.[37] As Lessig predicted, the "limitations of twentieth-century advertising" are indeed being overcome. As a consequence, the future being fashioned perpetuates and expands upon the defects of the earlier system instead of forging a new path.

Meanwhile, the captains of industry leading the charge toward mergers and acquisitions within the media sphere cynically invoke the Internet to justify their grand designs. Who can complain, they shrug, if one fellow owns a multibillion-dollar empire when anyone can start a Web site for next to nothing? The subject of antitrust investigations in Europe and the United States, Google executives respond to allegations that the company abuses its dominance in search to give its own services an advantage by insisting that on the Internet "competition is one click away."

Such is Rupert Murdoch's view of things as well. Not long before the phone-hacking scandal brought down his tabloid *News of the World*, Murdoch made a bid for BSkyB, a move that would have given him control of over half of the television market in the UK. He assured the British House of Lords that concerns about ownership and consolidation were "ten years out of date" given the abundance of news outlets for people to choose from online. The House of Lords, however, was not convinced, as a lengthy report to Parliament made clear: "We do not accept that the increase of news sources invalidates the case for special treatment of the media through ownership regulation. We believe that there is still a danger that if media ownership becomes too concentrated the diversity of voices available could be diminished."[38]

In the United States, however, even the core attribute of the Internet's openness, so disingenuously deployed by the likes of Murdoch, is under threat. The nation's leading cable lobbying group has a phalanx of full-time staff campaigning against Net neutrality—the idea that government regulation should ensure that the Internet stay an open platform, one where service providers cannot slow down or block certain Web sites to stifle competition or charge others a fee to speed up their traffic.

Ironically, the effort is headed by ex-FCC (Federal Communications Commission) chairman Michael Powell, who, in 2003, began his abdication of his role as public servant by publishing an op-ed in which he argued against government intervention in the media marketplace. "The bottomless well of information called the Internet" makes ownership rules simply unnecessary, a throwback to "the bygone era of black-and-white television," Powell wrote, positively invoking the very attributes of the Internet he is now paid handsomely to undermine. (In 2013 the revolving door came full circle when Tom Wheeler became Chairman of the FCC; Wheeler once stood at the helm of the same lobbying organization Powell now presides over.)[39]

Based on the principle of common carriage—rules first established under English common law and applied initially to things like canals, highways, and railroads and later to telegraph and telephone lines—advocates of Net neutrality seek to extend this tradition to our twenty-first-century communications system, prohibiting the owners of a network from abusing their power by discriminating against anyone's data, whether by slowing or stopping it or charging more to speed it up. They hope to defend the openness of the Internet by securing federal regulation that would guarantee that all bits, no matter who is sending or receiving them, are treated equally. The images and text on your personal Web site, they maintain, should be delivered as swiftly as Amazon or CNN's front page.

Telecom companies have something different in mind. AT&T, Verizon, Time Warner, Comcast, and others recognize that they could boost revenue significantly by charging for preferential service—adding a "fast lane" to the "information superhighway," as critics have described their plan. Service providers, for example, could ban the services of rivals outright, decide to privilege content they own while throttling everything else, or start charging content providers to have their Web sites load faster, prioritizing those who pay the most—all three scenarios putting newcomers and independents at a substantial and potentially devastating disadvantage while favoring the already consolidated and well capitalized.

The Internet is best thought of as a series of layers: a physical layer, a code layer, and a content layer. The bottom "physical," or ISP (Internet service provider) layer, is made up of the cables and routers through which our communications travel. In the middle is the "code" or "applications," which consists of the protocols and software that make the lower layer run. On top of that is the "content," the information we move across wires and airwaves and see on our screens. The telecommunications companies, which operate the physical layer, are fundamental to the entire enterprise. Common carriers—"mediating institutions" essential to social functioning—are sometimes called "public callings," a term that underscores the responsibility that comes with such position and power.

In his insightful book *The Master Switch*, Tim Wu, originator of the term "Net neutrality," explains why this may be the biggest media and communications policy battle ever waged. "While there were once distinct channels of telephony, television, radio, and film," Wu writes, "all information forms are now destined to make their way increasingly along the master network that can support virtually any kind of data traffic." Convergence has raised the stakes. "With every sort of political, social, cultural, and economic transaction having to one degree or another now gone digital, this proposes an awesome dependence on a single network, and no less vital need to preserve its openness from imperial designs," Wu warns. "This time *is* different: with everything on one network, the potential power to control is so much greater."

While we like to imagine the Internet as a radical, uncontrollable force—it's often said the system was designed to survive a nuclear attack—it is in fact vulnerable to capture by the private interests we depend on for access. In 2010, rulings by the FCC based on a controversial proposal put forth by Verizon and Google established network neutrality on wired broadband but failed to extend the common carrier principle to wireless connections; in other words, network neutrality rules apply to the cable or DSL service you use at home but not to your cell phone. In 2013, Google showed further signs of weakening its resolve on the issue when it began to offer fiber broadband with advantageous terms of service that many observers found violate the spirit of Net neutrality.[40]

Given the steady shift to mobile computing, including smartphones, tablets, and the emerging Internet-of-things (the fact that more and more objects, from buildings to cars to clothing, will be networked in coming years), the FCC's 2010 ruling was already alarmingly insufficient when it was made. Nevertheless, telecommunications companies went on offense, with Verizon successfully challenging the FCC's authority to regulate Internet access in federal appeals court in early 2014. But even as the rules were struck down, the judges acknowledged concerns that broadband providers represent a real threat, describing the kind of discriminatory behavior they were declaring lawful: companies might restrict "end-user subscribers' ability to access the *New York Times* website" in order to "spike traffic" to their own news sources or "degrade the quality of the connection to a search website like Bing if a competitor like Google paid for prioritized access."[41]

Proponents of Net neutrality maintain that the FCC rules were in any case riddled with loopholes and the goal now is to ground open Internet rules and the FCC's authority on firmer legal footing (namely by reclassifying broadband as a "telecommunications" and not an "information" service under Title II of the Communications Act, thereby automatically subjecting ISPS to common carrier obligations.) Opponents contend that Net neutrality would unduly burden telecom companies, which should have the right to dictate what travels through their pipes and charge accordingly, while paving the way for government control of the Internet. As a consequence of the high stakes, Net neutrality—a fight for the Internet as an open platform—has become a cause célèbre, and rightly so. However arcane the discussion may sometimes appear, the outcome of this battle will profoundly affect us all, and it is one worth fighting for.

Yet openness at the physical layer is not enough. While an open network ensures the equal treatment of all data—something undoubtedly essential for a democratic networked society—it does not sweep away all the problems of the old-media model, failing to adequately address the commercialization and consolidation of the digital sphere. We need to find other principles that can guide us, principles that better equip us to comprehend and confront the market's role in shaping our media system, principles that help us rise to the unique challenge of bolstering cultural democracy in a digital era. Openness cannot protect us from, and can even perpetuate, the perils of a peasant's kingdom.

2

FOR LOVE OR MONEY

Not that many years ago, Laura Poitras was living in Yemen, alone, waiting. She had rented a house close to the home of Abu Jandal, Osama bin Laden's former bodyguard and the man she hoped would be the subject of her next documentary. He put her off when she asked to film him, remaining frustratingly elusive. Next week, he'd tell her, next week, hoping the persistent American would just go away.

"I was going through hell," Poitras said, sitting in her office a few months after the premiere of her movie *The Oath*, the second in her trilogy of documentaries about foreign policy and national security after September 11. "I just didn't know if it was going to be two years, ten years, you know?" She waited, sure there was a story to be told and that it was extraordinary, but not sure if she'd be allowed to tell it. As those agonizing months dragged on, she did her best to be productive and pursued other leads. During Ramadan Poitras was invited to the house of a man just released from Guantánamo, whom she hoped to interview. "People almost had a heart attack that I was there," Poitras recounts. "I didn't film. I was shut down, and I was sat with the women. They were like, 'Aren't you afraid that they're going to cut your head off?'"

Bit by bit Abu Jandal opened up. Poitras would go home with only three or four hours of footage, but what she caught on tape was good enough to keep her coming back, a dozen times in all. "I think it probably wasn't until a year into it that I felt that I was going to get a film," Poitras said. A year of waiting, patience, uprootedness, and uncertainty before she knew that her work would come to anything.

With the support of PBS and a variety of grants, *The Oath* took almost three years to make, including a solid year in the editing room. The film's title speaks of two pledges: one made by Jandal and others in al-Qaeda's inner circle promising loyalty to bin Laden and another made by an FBI agent named Ali Soufan, who interrogated Abu Jandal when he was captured by U.S. forces. "Soufan was able to extract information without using violence," Poitras has said, and he testified to Congress against violent interrogation tactics. "One of his reasons is because he took an oath to the Constitution. In a broad sense, the film is about whether these men betrayed their loyalties to their oaths."[1]

"I always think, whenever I finish a film, that I would never have done that if I had known what it would cost emotionally, personally." The emotional repercussions of disturbing encounters can be felt long after the danger has passed; romantic relationships are severed by distance; the future is perpetually uncertain. Poitras, however, wasn't complaining. She experiences her work as a gift, a difficult process but a deeply satisfying one, and was already busy planning her next project, about the erosion of civil liberties in the wake of the war on terror.

In January 2013 she was contacted by an anonymous source that turned out to be Edward Snowden, the whistle-blower preparing to make public a trove of documents revealing the National Security Administration's massive secret digital surveillance program. He had searched Poitras out, certain that she was someone who would understand the scope of the revelations and the need to proceed cautiously. Soon she was on a plane to Hong Kong to shoot an interview that would shake the world and in the middle of another film that would take her places she never could have predicted at the outset.[2]

No simple formula explains the relationship between creative effort and output, nor does the quantity of time invested in a project correlate in any clear way to quality—quality being, of course, a slippery and subjective measure in itself. We can appreciate obvious skill, such as the labor of musicians who have devoted decades to becoming masters of their form, but it's harder to assess work that is more subjective, more oblique, or less polished.

Complex creative labor—the dedicated application of human effort to some expressive end—continues despite technological innovation, stubbornly withstanding the demand for immediate production in an economy preoccupied with speed and cost cutting. We should hardly be surprised: aesthetic and communicative impulses are, by their very nature, indifferent to such priorities. A vase isn't any more useful for being elaborately glazed. Likewise, a film is not necessarily any more informative for its demanding production qualities. We can't reduce the contents of a novel to a summary of the plot, nor whittle down philosophical insight to a sound bite without something profound being lost along the way.

Cultural work, which is enhanced by the unpredictability of the human touch and the irregular rhythms of the imagination and intelligence, defies conventional measures of efficiency. Other trades were long ago deprived of this breathing room, the singular skill of the craftsperson automated away by the assembly line, much as the modern movement in architecture, to take one of many possible examples, has cut back on hand-finished flourishes in favor of standardized parts and designs.

For better or worse, machines continue to encroach on once protected territory. Consider the innovations aimed to optimize intrinsically creative processes—software engineered to translate texts, monitor the emotional tone of e-mails, perform research, recommend movies and books, "to make everything that's implicit in a writer's skill set explicit to a machine," as an executive of one start-up describes its effort.[3] Algorithms designed to analyze and intensify the catchiness of songs are being used to help craft and identify potential Top 40 hits. These inventions, when coupled with steadily eroding economic support for arts and culture, underscore the fact that no human activity is immune to the relentless pressure to enlist technology to the cause of efficiency and increased productivity.[4]

The problem isn't with technology or efficiency, per se. Efficiency can be a remarkable thing, as in nature where nothing is wasted, including waste itself, which nurtures soil and plant and animal life. But the kind of efficiency to which techno-evangelists aspire emphasizes standardization, simplification, and speed, not diversity, complexity, and interdependence. And efficiency often masquerades as a technically neutral concept when it is in fact politically charged.

Instead of connoting the best use of scarce resources to attain a valued end, efficiency has become a code word promoting markets and competition over the public sphere, and profitability above all.[5] Music, author and engineer Christopher Steiner predicts in *Automate This*, will become more homogenized as executives increasingly employ bots to hunt for irresistible hooks. "Algorithms may bring us new artists, but because they build their judgment on what was popular in the past, we will likely end up with some of the same kind of forgettable pop we already have."[6]

There's no denying the benefits the arts have reaped from technological innovation. Writing is a technology par excellence, one that initially aroused deep distrust and suspicion. Likewise, the book is a tool so finely honed to suit human need that we mistake it for something eternal and immutable.[7] Every musical instrument— from the acoustic guitar to the timpani to synthesizers—is a contrived contraption. Without advances in chemistry and optics we would have no photography; without turntables, no hip-hop. I owe my career as a documentarian to the advent of digital video. New inventions make unimaginable art possible. No doubt, with emerging technologies, we stand on the brink of expressive forms still inconceivable.

Nonetheless, the arts do not benefit from technological advancement in the way other industries do: a half century ago it took pretty much the same amount of time and labor to compose a novel, produce a play, or conduct an orchestra as it takes today. Even with the aid of a computer and access to digital archives, the task of researching and constructing, say, a historical narrative remains obstinately demanding. For filmmakers the costs of travel, payments to crew, and money to support time in the field and the editing room persist despite myriad helpful innovations. Technology may enable new expressive forms and distribution may be cheaper than in the past, but the process of making things remains, in many fundamental respects, unchanged. The arts, to use the language of cultural economics, depend on a type of labor input that cannot be replaced by new technologies and capital.

In the mid-sixties, two Princeton economists, William Baumol and William Bowen, made the groundbreaking argument that economic growth actually creates a "cost disease" where labor-intensive creative productions are concerned, the relative cost of the arts increasing in comparison to other manufactured goods. Baumol and Bowen's analysis focused specifically on live performance, but their basic insight is applicable to any practice that demands human ingenuity and effort that cannot be made more efficient or eliminated through technological innovation. (Explaining Baumol and Bowen's dilemma in the *New Yorker*, James Surowiecki notes that there are, in effect, two economies in existence, one that is becoming more productive while the other isn't. In the first camp, we have the economy of computer manufacturing, carmakers, and Walmart bargains; in the second, the economy of undergraduate colleges, hair salons, auto repair, and the arts. "Cost disease isn't anyone's fault. . . . It's just endemic to businesses that are labor-intensive," Surowiecki explains.)[8]

To put it in the jargon proper to the economic analysis, the arts suffer from a "productivity lag," where productivity is defined as physical output per work hour. Baumol and Bowen's famous example is a string quartet: today it takes the same number of people the same amount of time to perform a composition by Mozart as it did in the 1800s, a fact that yields an exasperating flat line next to the skyward surge of something like computer manufacturing, which has seen productivity increases of 60 percent per year. "That the tendency for costs to rise and for prices to lag behind is neither a matter of bad luck nor mismanagement," Baumol and Bowen explain in their seminal study. "Rather, it is an inescapable result of the technology of live performance, which will continue to contribute to the widening of the income gaps of the performing organizations."

Analyzing the predicament faced by the labor-intensive arts, they hypothesized two cures to the cost disease. The first remedy was social subsidy, and in fact their work played an important role in energizing the push for increased funding for cultural institutions in the United States. The second cure was tied to a more general economic prediction, one infused with the optimism of the era. It may be the unfortunate fate of the arts to stagnate in terms of productivity growth, Baumol and Bowen maintained, but increased productivity in other sectors would help buoy creators. In their view, rising wages and—more important—an increase in free time would give the American people ample opportunities to create and enjoy art.[9]

In a digital age, however, art and culture face a core contradiction, since copies can be made with the push of a button. Like the live performances Baumol and Bowen discuss, most creative endeavors have high fixed costs. While the hundredth or thousandth or millionth digital copy of Poitras's first documentary, *My Country, My Country*, about a Sunni family trying to survive in war-torn Iraq, costs virtually nothing, the first copy cost her nearly four hundred thousand dollars.

When copies can be made and distributed across the globe in an instant, the logic of supply and demand pushes the price down to nothing. Yet when human imagination and exertion are essential to the creative process, the cost of cultural production only rises. It's a paradox that cannot be wished away. Baumol and Bowen identified "an ever-increasing gap" between the operating costs of labor-intensive creative products and their earned income. In a digital economy, this gap becomes a yawning cavern.

To new-media utopians, monetary concerns are irrelevant. In recent years a bevy of popular technologists, scholars, and commentators have united to paint an appealing picture of a future where the cultural field, from entertainment to academia, is remade as a result of digital technologies that allow individuals to create and collaborate at no cost. Before the Internet, the story goes, people needed to be part of a massive bureaucracy and have a big budget to do something like make a movie. Now anyone with a mobile phone can shoot a video and upload it to a global distribution platform. Before the Internet, a small number of specialists were hired to compose an encyclopedia. Now volunteers scattered across the globe can create one more comprehensive than any the world has ever known. And so on.

An amateur paradise is upon us, a place where people are able to participate in cultural production for the pleasure of it, without asking permission first. Social media have enabled a new paradigm of collaboration. The old closed, hierarchical, institutional model is being replaced by a decentralized, networked system open to all. Barriers to entry have been removed, gatekeepers have been demolished, and the costs of creating and distributing culture have plummeted. New tools not only have made cultural production more efficient but have equalized opportunity.

NYU professor Clay Shirky, perhaps the leading proponent of this view, calls this process "social production." Harvard's Yochai Benkler uses the term "peer production," business writer Jeff Howe calls it "crowdsourcing," and Don Tapscott and his coauthor Anthony D. Williams say "wikinomics." Whatever term they use, the commentators agree that a revolution is unfolding, with the potential to transform not just culture but also politics and the economy. They put social production on a pedestal, holding it up as more egalitarian, ethical, and efficient than the old model it is said to supersede.

Tapping the deep vein of American populism, new-media thinkers portray the amateur ethos flourishing online as a blow against the elitism and exclusivity of the professions, their claims to expertise and authority, and the organizations they depend on, and there's something appealing about this view.[10] The professional class is not blameless by any means: it has erected often arbitrary barriers in the form of credentialing and licensing and has often failed to advance the public good while securing its own position.

The professions, as many others have observed, have served as a kind of "class fortress," excluding talented, motivated people in service of monopolistic self-preservation. ("Institutions will try to preserve the problem to which they are the solution" is known in tech circles as the Shirky principle.) It is this aspect of professionalism that outrages Internet apostles, who celebrate the liberation from professionals who claim special knowledge and cheer the fact that authority is shifting from "faraway offices to the network of people we know, like, and respect."[11]

More far-reaching, mass amateurization is said to reveal something profound about human nature. Social media, enthusiasts contend, prove that long-dominant assumptions were wrong. The abundance of user-generated content, no matter how silly or derivative, reveals an intrinsic creative drive. While most of us probably didn't need the Internet to show us that human beings share an irrepressible urge to create and share—an "art instinct"—for some this truism is a revelation.

It follows, by this logic, that if people are intrinsically motivated to produce culture, and technology enables them to act on this motivation effortlessly and affordably and without financial reward, then amateurs are less compromised than compensated professionals and thus superior. "Amateurs," Shirky writes, "are sometimes separated from professionals by skill, but always by motivation; the term itself derives from the Latin amare—'to love.' The essence of amateurism is intrinsic motivation: to be an amateur is to do something for the love of it."

Making a similar case, Yochai Benkler likens cultural creation to blood drives: the quality of donations increases when organizers stop paying.[12] "Remember, money isn't always the best motivator," Benkler said, reiterating the point during a TED Talk touching on similar themes. "If you leave a fifty-dollar check after dinner with friends, you don't increase the probability of being invited back. And if dinner isn't entirely obvious, think of sex."[13]

So it won't matter if some people's operating costs end up exceeding their earned income. A well-received academic monograph about the impact of online file sharing on music production, published under the auspices of Harvard Business School, echoes these insights, allaying any suspicion one might have that lack of income could inhibit the world's creative output. The authors argue that a decline in "industry profitability" won't hurt production because artists' unique motivations will keep them churning out music even if they are operating at a loss. "The remuneration of artistic talent differs from other types of labor in at least two important respects. On the one hand, artists often enjoy what they do, suggesting they might continue being creative even when the monetary incentives to do so become weaker. In addition, artists receive a significant portion of their remuneration not in monetary form." To quote the professors, "many of them enjoy fame, admiration, social status, and free beer in bars."[14]

Another paper, published with the romantic title "Money Ruins Everything," comes to a similar conclusion. Its authors, a team of social scientists, were stunned by what they found online: throngs of people who, instead of engaging in cost-benefit analysis, "produce content for the love of it, for the joy of expressing themselves, because it is fun, to demonstrate that they are better at it than others, or for a host of other non-commercial motivations." The very existence of creators who "produce content for the love of it and are prepared to work for free—or even to lose money to feed their desire to create" upends traditional models of media production. If you want insight into the culture of the future, they say, just look at Wikipedia, the open source software community, and popular photo-sharing services. There are millions of people who contribute user-generated content without promise of remuneration or reward.

This distinction between love and money seems self-evident and uncomplicated. If the choice is between a powerful record mogul and a teenager uploading a video of himself singing in his bedroom, or the inanity of a high-grossing nightly cable news host versus some insightful commentary on a personal Web site, who wouldn't side with the little person? But the distinction is deceptive. What sounds like idealism, upon further reflection, reveals itself to be the opposite. For one thing, it is deeply cynical to deny professionals any emotional investment in their work. Can we really argue that creative professionals—filmmakers, writers, architects, graphic designers, and so on—do not care deeply about what they do? And what about doctors, teachers, and scientists?

The corollary of Benkler's and Shirky's argument is that only those who despise their work deserve to be paid for their efforts.[15] It's worth pointing out that these men—despite their enthusiasm for social production—release their books with conventional publishers and hold positions at elite academic institutions. Surely they do not believe their work as professional writers, researchers, and teachers is suspect because they were compensated. There is a note of truth in the idea that adversity fuels creativity, but when reduced to an economic truism—a decline in industry profitability won't hurt artistic production because artists will work for beer—the notion rings not just hollow but obscene.

These tidily opposed categories of professional and amateur are ones into which few actually existing creative people perfectly fit. And the consequences of the digital upheaval are far more equivocal than the Shirkys and Benklers acknowledge. While the economics of the Web might apply to remixing memes or posting in online forums, the costs and risks associated with creative acts that require leaving one's computer have hardly collapsed.

Where will this new paradigm leave projects like *The Oath*? Following Shirky's logic, Laura Poitras is one of those professionals who should be overthrown by noble amateurs, her labor-intensive filmmaking process a throwback to another era, before creativity was a connected, collective process. The Internet might be a wonderful thing, but you can't crowdsource a relationship with a terrorist or a whistle-blower.

Makers of art and culture have long straddled two economies, the economy of the gift and the economy of the market, as Lewis Hyde elegantly demonstrated in his book *The Gift: Creativity and the Artist in the Modern World*. Unlike other resources, Hyde explained, culture is passed from person to person, between whom it forms "feeling-bonds," an initiation or preservation of affection. A simple purchase, on the other hand, forges no necessary connection, as any interaction at a cash register makes clear. Thus culture is a gift, a kind of glue, a covenant, but one that, unlike barter, obliges nothing in return. In other words, the fruits of creative effort exist to be shared. Yet the challenge is how to support this kind of work in a market-based society. "Invariably the money question comes up," writes Hyde. "Labors such as mine are notoriously non-remunerative, and your landlord is not interested in your book of translations the day your rent comes due."

The fate of creative people is to exist in two incommensurable realms of value and be torn between them—on one side, the purely economic activity associated with the straightforward selling of goods or labor; on the other, the fundamentally different, elevated form of value we associate with art and culture. It is this dilemma that led Baudelaire to ruefully proclaim that the "prostitution of the poet" was "an unavoidable necessity."

Yet the challenge of maintaining oneself in a world of money is hardly a problem unique to the creatively inclined. This dilemma may not trouble those who choose to pursue wealth above all else, but most people seek work that feeds both the spirit and the belly. Likewise, the cultural realm is not the only sphere in which some essential part cannot be bought or sold. Teaching, therapy, medicine, science, architecture, design, even politics and law when practiced to serve the public good—certainly the gift operates within these fields as well. The gift can even be detected in supposedly menial jobs where people, in good faith, do far more than meager wages require of them. Creative people are not the only ones who struggle desperately to balance the contradictory demands of the gift and the market. But culture is the domain where this quandary is often most visible and acknowledged. Culture is one stage on which we play out our anxieties about the impact of market values on our inner lives. As we transition to a digital age, this anxiety is in full view.

———

The supposed conflict between amateurs and professionals sparked by the Internet speaks to a deep and long-standing confusion about the relationship between work and creativity in our society. Artists, we imagine, are grasshoppers, singing while ants slog away—or butterflies: delicate and flighty creatures who, stranded in a beehive, have the audacity to demand honey. No matter how exacting or extensive the effort a project requires, if the process allows for some measure of self-realization, it's not unpleasant or self-sacrificing enough to fit our conception of work as drudgery. We tend to believe that the labor of those who appear to love what they do does not by definition qualify as labor.

We have succumbed, as the essayist Rebecca Solnit put it to me, to the "conventionalized notion of work as the forty hours of sub-mission to another's purpose snipped out of your life (and leaving a hole in your heart and mind)." Along the way we ignore the fact that many people, not only members of the vaunted "professional" class, love their jobs. "A lot of builders and firemen really enjoy them-selves. Bakers and cooks can be pretty happy, and so can some farm-ers and fishermen." Nor should we romanticize creative labor, she noted: "Most artists don't love all parts of their work—I hate all the administration, the travel, the bad posture, the excess solitude, and the uncertainty about my own caliber and my future."

In the 1951 classic *White Collar*, sociologist C. Wright Mills pre-sented a powerful alternative to the stark dichotomies of amateurs versus professionals. Examining the emerging category of office worker, Mills advocated, instead, for what he called the Renaissance view of work, a process that would allow for not only the creation of objects but the development of the self—an act both mental and manual that "confesses and reveals" us to the world. The problem, as Mills saw it, was that development of the self was trivialized into "hobbies"—they were being amateurized, in other words—and so relegated to the lesser realm of leisure as opposed to the realm of legitimate labor.[16]

"Each day men sell little pieces of themselves in order to try to buy them back each night and week end with the coin of fun," wrote Mills, despairing of a cycle that splits us in two: an at-work self and an at-play self, the person who produces for money and the person who produces for love.[17] New-media thinkers believe social production and amateurism transcend the old problem of alienated labor by allowing us to work for love, not money, but in fact the unremunerated future they anticipate will only deepen a split that many desperately desire to reconcile.

Innovations and invention were expected to bring about humankind's inevitable release from alienated labor. The economist John Maynard Keynes once predicted that the four-hour workday was close at hand and that technical improvements in manufacturing would allow ample time for people to focus on "the art of life itself." Into the 1960s experts agonized over the possibility of a "crisis of leisure time," which they prophesized would sweep the country—a crisis precipitated not for want of time off but by an excess of it.

In 1967, testimony before a Senate subcommittee indicated that "by 1985 people could be working just 22 hours a week or 27 weeks a year or could retire at 38." Over the ensuing decades countless people have predicted that machines would facilitate the "end of work" by automating drudgery and freeing humans to perform labor they enjoy ("Let the robots take the jobs, and let them help us dream up new work that matters," concludes one *Wired* cover story rehashing this old idea).[18]

New-media thinkers do not pretend this future has come to pass, but in *Cognitive Surplus* Clay Shirky presents what can be read as a contemporary variation on this old theme, explaining how the cumulative free time of the world's educated population—an estimated trillion hours a year—is being funneled into creative, collaborative projects online.[19] Time is something Shirky claims we have a growing abundance of thanks to two factors: steadily increasing prosperity and a decline of television viewing. The Web, he argues, challenges us to stop thinking of time as "individual minutes to be whiled away" and imagine it, instead, as a "social asset that can be harnessed."[20]

Projects like Wikipedia, message boards, and the latest viral memes are creative paradigms for a new age: entertaining, inclusive, easy to make, and efficient—the accumulation of tidbits of attention from thousands of people around the world. Much of the art and culture of the future, he wagers, will be produced in a similar manner, by pooling together spare moments spent online. Our efforts shall be aggregated, all the virtual crumbs combining to make a cake. Institutions will be supplanted as a consequence of the deployment of this surplus.[21]

Shirky's contributions reveal not how far we've progressed in pursuit of "the art of life" but how much ground has been lost since Keynes, how our sense of what's possible has been circumscribed despite the development of new, networked wonders. Today's popular visionary imagines us hunched over our computers with a few idle minutes to spare, our collective clicks supposed to substitute for what was once the promise of personal creative development—the freedom to think, feel, create, and act with the whole of one's being.

In addition to other problematic aspects of his argument, Shirky's two foundational assertions—that television watching is down and that free time has increased over recent decades—are both unfounded. Despite competition from the Internet, television viewing has generally risen over recent years, with the average American taking in nearly five hours of video each day, 98 percent through a traditional TV set. "Americans," a 2012 Nielsen report states, "are not turning off."[22]

According to economists, with the exception of those who suffer from under- and unemployment, work hours have actually risen.

Those lucky enough to be fully employed are, in fact, suffering from "time impoverishment." Today the average citizen works longer hours for less money than he or she once did, putting in an extra four and a half weeks a year compared to 1979. Married couples with children are on the job an extra 413 hours, or an extra ten weeks a year, combined.[23] Adding salt to the wounds, the United States is the only industrialized nation where employers are not required by law to provide workers any paid vacation time.[24]

The reason the prophecies of Mills and Keynes never came to pass is obvious but too often overlooked: new technologies do not emerge in a vacuum free of social, political, and economic influences. Context is all-important. On their own, labor-saving machines, however ingenious, are not enough to bring about a society of abundance and leisure, as the Luddites who destroyed the power looms set to replace them over two centuries ago knew all too well. If we want to see the fruits of technological innovation widely shared, it will require conscious effort and political struggle. Ultimately, outcomes are shaped as much by the capabilities of new technologies as by the wider circumstances in which they operate.

Baumol and Bowen, for example, made their rosy predictions against the backdrop of a social consensus now in tatters. When they wrote their report in the sixties, the prevailing economic orthodoxy said that both prosperity and risk should be broadly spread. Health care, housing, and higher education were more accessible to more people than they had ever been. Bolstered by a strong labor movement, unemployment was low and wages high by today's standards. There was talk of shortened workweeks and guaranteed annual income for all. As a consequence of these conditions, men and women felt emboldened to demand more than just a stable, well-compensated job; they wanted work that was also engaging and gratifying.

In the fifties and sixties, this wish manifested in multiple ways, aiming at the status quo from within and without. First came books like *The Organization Man* and *The Lonely Crowd*, which voiced widespread anxieties about the erosion of individuality, inwardness, and agency within the modern workplace. Company men revolted against the "rat race." Conformity was inveighed against, mindless acquiescence condemned, and affluence denounced as an anesthetic to authentic experience. Those who stood poised to inherit a gray flannel suit chafed against its constraints. By 1972 blue-collar workers were fed up, too, with wildcat strikers at auto factories protesting the monotony of the assembly line. The advances of technology did not, in the end, liberate the worker from drudgery but rather further empowered those who owned the machines. By the end of the 1970s, as former labor secretary Robert Reich explains,

> a wave of new technologies (air cargo, container ships and terminals, satellite communications and, later, the Internet) had radically reduced the costs of outsourcing jobs abroad. Other new technologies (automated machinery, computers, and ever more sophisticated software applications) took over many other jobs (remember bank tellers? telephone operators? service station attendants?). By the '80s, any job requiring that the same steps be performed repeatedly was disappearing—going over there or into software.[25]

At the same time the ideal of a "postindustrial society" offered the alluring promise of work in a world in which goods were less important than services. Over time, phrases like "information economy," "immaterial labor," "knowledge workers," and "creative class" slipped into everyday speech. Mental labor would replace the menial; stifling corporate conventions would give way to diversity and free expression; flexible employment would allow them to shape their own lives.

These prognostications, too, were not to be. Instead the increase of shareholder influence in the corporate sector accelerated the

demand for ever-higher returns on investment and shorter turnaround. Dismissing stability as the refusal to innovate (or rather cut
costs), business leaders cast aspersions on the steadying tenets of the
first half of the twentieth century, including social provisions and
job security. Instead of lifetime employment, the new system valo-
rized adaptability, mobility, and risk; in the place of full-time employment, there were temporary contracts and freelance instability. In
this context, the wish for expressive, worthwhile work, the desire to
combine employment and purpose, took on a perverse form.

New-media thinkers, with their appetite for disintermediation
and creative destruction, implicitly endorse and advance this transformation. The crumbling and hollowing out of established cultural
institutions, from record labels to universities, and the liberation of
individuals from their grip is a fantasy that animates discussions of
amateurism. New technologies are hailed for enabling us to "organize without organizations," which are condemned as rigid and suf-
focating and antithetical to the open architecture of the Internet.

However, past experience shows that the receding of institutions
does not necessarily make space for a more authentic, egalitarian
existence: if work and life have been made more flexible, people have
also become unmoored, blown about by the winds of the market; if
old hierarchies and divisions have been overthrown, the price has
been greater economic inequality and instability; if the new system
emphasizes potential and novelty, past achievement and experience
have been discounted; if life has become less predictable and prede-
termined, it has also become more precarious as liability has shifted
from business and government to the individual. It turns out that
what we need is not to eliminate institutions but to reinvent them,
to make them more democratic, accountable, inclusive, and just.

More than anyone else, urbanist Richard Florida, author of *The Rise
of the Creative Class*, has built his career as a flag-bearer for the idea

that individual ingenuity can fill the void left by declining institutions. Like new-media thinkers, with whom he shares a boundless admiration for all things high tech and Silicon Valley, he also shuns "organizational or institutional directives" while embracing the values meritocracy and openness. In Florida's optimistic view, the demise of career stability has unbridled creativity and eliminated alienation in the workplace. "To some degree, Karl Marx had it partly right when he foresaw that the workers would someday control the means of production," Florida declares. "This is now beginning to happen, although not as Marx thought it would, with the proletariat rising to take over factories. Rather, more workers than ever control the means of production, because it is inside their heads; they are the means of the production."[26]

Welcome to what Florida calls the "information-and-idea-based economy," a place where "people have come to accept that they're on their own—that the traditional sources of security and entitlement no longer exist, or even matter." Where earlier visionaries prophesied a world in which increased leisure allowed all human beings the well-being and security to freely cultivate their creative instincts, the apostles of the creative class collapse labor into leisure and exploitation into self-expression, and they arrogate creativity to serve corporate ends.

"Capitalism has also expanded its reach to capture the talents of heretofore excluded groups of eccentrics and nonconformists," Florida writes. "In doing so, it has pulled off yet another astonishing mutation: taking people who would once have been bizarre mavericks operating at the bohemian fringe and setting them at the very heart of the process of innovation and economic growth." According to Florida's theory, the more creative types colorfully dot an urban landscape, the greater a city's "Bohemian Index" and the higher the likelihood of the city's economic success.

It's all part of what he calls the "Big Morph"—"the resolution of the centuries-old tension between two value systems: the Protestant

work ethic and the Bohemian ethic" into a new "creative ethos."
The Protestant ethic treats work as a duty; the Bohemian ethic, he
says, is hedonistic. Profit seeking and pleasure seeking have united,
the industrialist and the bon vivant have become one. "Highbrow
and lowbrow, alternative and mainstream, work and play, CEO and
hipster are all morphing together today," Florida enthuses.[27]

What kind of labor is it, exactly, that people will perform in this
inspired Shangri-la? Florida's popular essays point the way: he applauds
a "teenage sales rep re-conceiving a Vonage display" as a stunning
example of creative ingenuity harnessed for economic success; later he
announces, anecdotally, that an "overwhelming" number of students
would prefer to work "lower-paying temporary jobs in a hair salon"
than "good, high-paying jobs in a machine tool factory." Cosmetology
is "more psychologically rewarding, creative work," he explains.[28]

It's tempting to dismiss such a broad definition of creativity as
out of touch, but Florida's declarations illuminate an important trend
and one that helped set the terms for the ascension of amateurism. It
is not that creative work has suddenly become abundant, as Florida
would have us believe; we have not all become Mozarts on the floor
of some big-box store, Frida Kahlos at the hair salon. Rather, the
point is that the psychology of creativity has become increasingly
useful to the economy. The disposition of the artist is ever more in
demand. The ethos of the autonomous creator has been repurposed
to serve as a seductive facade for a capricious system and adopted as
an identity by those who are trying to make their way within it.

Thus the ideal worker matches the traditional profile of the enthusiastic virtuoso: an individual who is versatile and rootless, inventive
and adaptable; who self-motivates and works long hours, tapping
internal and external resources; who is open to reinvention, emphasizing potential and promise opposed to past achievements; one who
loves the work so much, he or she would do it no matter what, and
so expects little compensation or commitment in return—amateurs
and interns, for example.

The "free" credo promoted by writers such as Chris Anderson and other new-media thinkers has helped lodge a now rung on an ever-lengthening educational and career ladder, the now obligatory internship. Like artists and culture makers of all stripes, interns are said to be "entrepreneurs" and "free agents" investing in their "personal brands." "The position of interns is not unlike that of many young journalists, musicians, and filmmakers who are now expected to do online work for no pay as a way to boost their portfolios," writes Ross Perlin, author of the excellent book *Intern Nation*. "If getting attention and building a reputation online are often seen as more valuable than immediate 'monetization,' the same theory is being propounded for internships in the analog world—with exposure, contacts, and references advanced as the prerequisite, or even plausible alternative, to making money."[29]

As Perlin documents in vivid detail, capitalizing on desperate résumé-building college students and postgraduates exacerbates inequality. Who can afford to take a job that doesn't pay but the relatively well off? Those who lack financial means are either shut out of opportunities or forced to support themselves with loans, going into debt for the privilege of working for free.

Creativity is invoked time and again to justify low wages and job insecurity. Across all sectors of the economy, responsibility for socially valuable work, from journalism to teaching and beyond, is being off-loaded onto individuals as institutions retreat from obligations to support efforts that aren't immediately or immensely profitable. The *Chronicle of Higher Education* urges graduate students to imagine themselves as artists, to better prepare for the possibility of impoverishment when tenure-track jobs fail to materialize: "We must think of graduate school as more like choosing to go to New York to become a painter or deciding to travel to Hollywood to become an actor. Those arts-based careers have always married hope and desperation into a tense relationship."[30] In a similar vein, NPR reports that the "temp-worker lifestyle" is a kind of "performance art," a statement that conjures a fearless entertainer mid-tightrope or an acrobat hurling toward the next trapeze without a safety net—a thrilling image, especially to employers who would prefer not to provide benefits.[31]

The romantic stereotype of the struggling artist is familiar to the musician Marc Ribot, a legendary figure on the New York jazz scene who has worked with Marianne Faithfull, Elvis Costello, John Zorn, Tom Waits, Alison Krauss, Robert Plant, and even Elton John. Ribot tells me he had an epiphany watching a "great but lousy" made-for-TV movie about Apple computers. As he tells it, two exhausted employees are complaining about working eighteen-hour days with no weekends when an actor playing Steve Jobs tells them to suck it up—they're not regular workers at a stodgy company like IBM but *artists*.

"In other words art was the new model for this form of labor," Ribot says, explaining his insight. "The model they chose is musicians, like Bruce Springsteen staying up all night to get that perfect track. Their life does not resemble their parents' life working at IBM from nine to five, and certainly doesn't resemble their parents' pay structures—it's all back end, no front end. All transfer of risk to the worker." (In 2011 Apple Store workers upset over pay disparities were told, "Money shouldn't be an issue when you're employed at Apple. Working at Apple should be viewed as an experience.")[32]

In Ribot's field this means the more uncertain part of the business—the actual writing, recording, and promoting of music—is increasingly "outsourced" to individuals while big companies dominate arenas that are more likely to be profitable, like concert sales and distribution (Ticketmaster, Amazon, iTunes, and Google Play, none of which invests in music but reaps rewards from its release). "That technological change is upon us is undeniable and irreversible," Ribot wrote about the challenges musicians face as a consequence of digitization. "It will probably not spell the end of music as a commodity, although it may change drastically who is profiting off whose music. Whether these changes will create a positive future for producers or consumers of music depends on whether musicians can organize the legal and collective struggle necessary to ensure that those who profit off music in any form pay the people who make it."

Ribot quotes John Lennon: "You think you're so clever and classless and free." Americans in general like to think of themselves as having transcended economic categories and hierarchies, Ribot says, and artists are no exception. During the Great Depression artists briefly began to think of themselves as workers and to organize as such, amassing social and political power with some success, but today it's more popular to speak of artists as entrepreneurs or brands, designations that further obscure the issue of labor and exploitation by comparing individual artists to corporate entities or sole proprietors of small businesses.

If artists are fortunate enough to earn money from their art, they tend to receive percentages, fees, or royalties rather than wages; they play "gigs" or do "projects" rather than hold steady jobs, which means they don't recognize the standard breakdowns of boss and worker. They also spend a lot of time on the road, not rooted in one place; hence they are not able to organize and advocate for their rights.

What's missing, as Ribot sees it, is a way to understand how the economy has evolved away from the old industrial model and how value is extracted within the new order. "I think that people, not just musicians, need to do an analysis so they stop asking the question, 'Who is my legal employer?' and start asking, 'Who works, who creates things that people need, and who profits from it?'" These questions, Ribot wagers, could be the first step to understanding the model of freelance, flexible labor that has become increasingly dominant across all sectors of the economy, not just in creative fields.

are told that a war is being waged between the decaying institutions of the off-line world and emerging digital dynamos, between closed industrial systems and open networked ones, between professionals who cling to the past and amateurs who represent the future. The cheerleaders of technological disruption are not alone in their hyperbole. Champions of the old order also talk in terms that reinforce a seemingly unbridgeable divide.

Unpaid amateurs have been likened to monkeys with typewriters, gate-crashing the cultural conversation without having been vetted by an official credentialing authority or given the approval of an established institution. "The professional is being replaced by the amateur, the lexicographer by the layperson, the Harvard professor by the unschooled populace," according to Andrew Keen, obstinately oblivious to the failings of professionally produced mass culture he defends.

The Internet is decried as a province of know-nothing narcissists motivated by a juvenile desire for fame and fortune, a virtual backwater of vulgarity and phoniness. Jaron Lanier, the technologist turned skeptic, has taken aim at what he calls "digital Maoism" and the ascendance of the "hive mind." Social media, as Lanier sees it, demean rather than elevate us, emphasizing the machine over the human, the crowd over the individual, the partial over the integral. The problem is not just that Web 2.0 erodes professionalism but, more fundamentally, that it threatens originality and autonomy.

Outrage has taken hold on both sides. But the lines in the sand are not as neatly drawn as the two camps maintain. Wikipedia, considered the ultimate example of amateur triumph as well as the cause of endless hand-wringing, hardly hails the "death of the expert" (the common claim by both those who love the site and those who despise it). While it is true that anyone can contribute to the encyclopedia, their entries must have references, and many of the sources referenced qualify as professional. Most entries boast citations of academic articles, traditional books, and news stories. Similarly, social production does not exist quite outside the mainstream. Up to 85 percent of the open source Linux developers said to be paradigmatic of this new age of volunteerism are, in fact, employees of large corporations that depend on nonproprietary software.[33]

More generally, there is little evidence that the Internet has precipitated a mass rejection of more traditionally produced fare. What we are witnessing is a convergence, not a coup. Peer-to-peer sites—estimated to take up half the Internet's bandwidth—are overwhelmingly used to distribute traditional commercial content, namely mainstream movies and music. People gather on message boards to comment on their favorite television shows, which they download or stream online. The most popular videos on YouTube, year after year, are the product of conglomerate record labels, not bedroom inventions. Some of the most visited sites are corporate productions like CNN. Most links circulated on social media are professionally produced. The challenge is to understand how power and influence are distributed within this mongrel space where professional and amateur combine.

Consider, for a moment, Clay Shirky, whose back-flap biography boasts corporate consulting gigs with Nokia, News Corp, BP, the U.S. Navy, Lego, and others. Shirky embodies the strange mix of technological utopianism and business opportunism common to many Internet entrepreneurs and commentators, a combination of populist rhetoric and unrepentant commercialism. Many of amateurism's loudest advocates are also business apologists, claiming to promote cultural democracy while actually advising corporations on how to seize "collaboration and self-organization as powerful new levers to cut costs" in order to "discover the true dividends of collective capability and genius" and "usher their organizations into the twenty-first century."[34]

The grassroots rhetoric of networked amateurism has been harnessed to corporate strategy, continuing a nefarious tradition. Since

the 1970s populist outrage has been yoked to free-market ideology
by those who exploit cultural grievances to shore up their power
and influence, directing public animus away from economic elites
and toward cultural ones, away from plutocrats and toward professionals. But it doesn't follow that criticizing "professionals" or
"experts" or "cultural elites" means that we are striking a blow against
the real powers; and when we uphold amateur creativity, we are not
necessarily resolving the deeper problems of entrenched privilege or
the irresistible imperative of profit. Where online platforms are concerned, our digital pastimes can sometimes promote positive social
change and sometimes hasten the transfer of wealth to Silicon Valley
billionaires.

Even well-intentioned celebration of networked amateurism
has the potential to obscure the way money still circulates. That's
the problem with *PressPausePlay*, a slick documentary about the
digital revolution that premiered at a leading American film festival. The directors examine the ways new tools have sparked a
creative overhaul by allowing everyone to participate—or at least
everyone who owns the latest Apple products. That many of the
liberated media makers featured in the movie turn out to work in
advertising and promotion, like celebrity business writer Seth
Godin, who boasts of his ability to turn his books into bestsellers
by harnessing the power of the Web, underscores how the hype
around the cultural upheaval sparked by connective technologies
easily slides from making to marketing. While the filmmakers
pay tribute to DIY principles and praise the empowering potential
of digital tools unavailable a decade ago, they make little mention
of the fact that the telecommunications giant Ericsson provided
half of the movie's seven-hundred-thousand-dollar budget and promotional support.[35]

We should be skeptical of the narrative of democratization by
technology alone. The promotion of Internet-enabled amateurism
is a lazy substitute for real equality of opportunity. More deeply,

it's a symptom of the retreat over the past half century from the ideals of meaningful work, free time, and shared prosperity—an agenda that entailed enlisting technological innovation for the welfare of each person, not just the enrichment of the few.

Instead of devising truly liberating ways to harness machines to remake the economy, whether by designing satisfying jobs or through the social provision of a basic income to everyone regardless of work status, we have Amazon employees toiling on the warehouse floor for eleven dollars an hour and Google contract workers who get fired after a year so they don't have to be brought on full-time. Cutting-edge new-media companies valued in the tens of billions retain employees numbering in the lowly thousands, and everyone else is out of luck. At the same time, they hoard their record-setting profits, sitting on mountains of cash instead of investing it in ways that would benefit us all.

The zeal for amateurism looks less emancipatory—as much necessity as choice—when you consider the crisis of rising educational costs, indebtedness, and high unemployment, all while the top 1 percent captures an ever-growing portion of the surplus generated by increased productivity. (Though productivity has risen 23 percent since 2000, real hourly pay has effectively stagnated.)[36] The consequences are particularly stark for young people: between 1984 and 2009, the median net worth for householders under thirty-five was down 68 percent while rising 42 percent for those over sixty-five.[37] Many are delaying starting families of their own and moving back in with Mom and Dad.

Our society's increasing dependence on free labor—online and off—is immoral in this light. The celebration of networked amateurism—and of social production and the cognitive surplus—glosses over the question of who benefits from our uncompensated participation online. Though some internships are enjoyable and useful, the real beneficiary of this arrangement is corporate America, which reaps the equivalent of a two-billion-dollar annual subsidy.[38]

And many of the digital platforms to which we contribute are highly profitable entities, run not for love but for money.

Creative people have historically been encouraged to ignore economic issues and maintain indifference to matters like money and salaries. Many of us believe that art and culture should not succumb to the dictates of the market, and one way to do this is to act as though the market doesn't exist, to devise a shield to deflect its distorting influence, and uphold the lack of compensation as virtuous. This stance can provide vital breathing room, but it can also perpetuate inequality. "I consistently come across people valiantly trying to defy an economic class into which they were born," Richard Florida writes. "This is particularly true of the young descendants of the truly wealthy—the capitalist class—who frequently describe themselves as just 'ordinary' creative people working on music, film or intellectual endeavors of one sort or another."

How valiant to deny the importance of money when it is had in abundance. "Economic power is first and foremost a power to keep necessity at arm's length," the French sociologist Pierre Bourdieu observed. Especially, it seems, the necessity of talking honestly about economics.

Those who applaud social production and networked amateurism, the colorful cacophony that is the Internet, and the creative capacities of everyday people to produce entertaining and enlightening things online, are right to marvel. There is amazing inventiveness, boundless talent and ability, and overwhelming generosity on display. Where they go wrong is in thinking that the Internet is an egalitarian, let alone revolutionary, platform for our self-expression and development, that being able to shout into the digital torrent is adequate for democracy.

The struggle between amateurs and professionals is, fundamentally, a distraction. The tragedy for all of us is that we find ourselves in a world where the qualities that define professional work—stability, social purpose, autonomy, and intrinsic and extrinsic rewards—are scarce. "In part, the blame falls on the corporate elite," Barbara Ehrenreich wrote back in 1989, "which demands ever more bankers and lawyers, on the one hand, and low-paid helots on the other." These low-paid helots are now unpaid interns and networked amateurs. The rub is that over the intervening years we have somehow deceived ourselves into believing that this state of insecurity and inequity is a form of liberation.

3

WHAT WE WANT

Today it is standard wisdom that a whole new kind of person lives in our midst, the digital native—"2.0 people" as the novelist Zadie Smith dubbed them. Exalted by techno-enthusiasts for being hyper-connected and sociable, technically savvy and novelty seeking—and chastised by techno-skeptics for those very same traits—this new generation and its predecessors are supposedly separated by a gulf that is immense and unbroachable. Self-appointed experts tell us that "today's students are no longer the people our educational system was designed to teach"; they "experience friendship" and "relate to information differently" than all who came before.[1]

Reflecting on this strange new species, the skeptics are inclined to agree. "The cyber-revolution is bringing about a different magnitude of change, one that marks a massive discontinuity," warns the literary critic Sven Birkerts. "Pre-Digital Man has more in common with his counterpart in the agora than he will with a Digital Native of the year 2050." It is not just cultural or social references that divide the natives from their pre-digital counterparts, but "core phenomenological understandings." Their very modes of perception and sense making, of experiencing the world and interpreting it, Birkerts claims, are simply incomprehensible to their elders. They are different creatures altogether.[2]

The tech-enthusiasts make a similarly extreme case for total generational divergence, idolizing digital natives with fervor and ebullience equal and opposite to Birkerts's unease. These natives, born and raised in networked waters, surf shamelessly, with no need for privacy or solitude. As described by Nick Bilton in his book *I Live in the Future and Here's How It Works*, digital natives prefer media in "bytes" and "snacks" as opposed to full "meals"—defined as the sort of lengthy article one might find in the *New Yorker* magazine. Digital natives believe "immediacy trumps quality."[3]

They "unabashedly create and share content—any type of content," and, unlike digital immigrants, they never suffer from information overload. People who have grown up online also do not read the news. Or rather, we are told, for them the news is whatever their friends deem interesting, not what some organization or authoritative source says is significant. "This is the way I navigate today as well," Bilton, technology writer for the *New York Times*, proudly declares. "If the news is important, it will find me."[4] (Notably, Bilton's assertion was contradicted by a Harvard study that found eighteen-to twenty-nine-year-olds still prefer to get their political news from established newspapers, print or digital, than from the social media streams of their friends.)[5]

These two poles of opinion typify an ongoing debate about the way technology is transforming a younger generation's relationship to traditional cultural forms, a debate that gets especially vehement around the question of journalism's future—a topic with the profoundest of implications for the public sphere and health of democracy. In the popular imagination, either the Internet has freed us from the stifling grip of the old, top-down mass media model, transforming consumers into producers and putting citizens on par with the powerful, or we have stumbled into a new trap, a social media hall of mirrors made up of personalized feeds, "filter bubbles," narcissistic chatter, and half-truths. Young people are invoked to lend credence to both views: in the first scenario, they are portrayed as empowered and agile media connoisseurs who, refusing to passively consume news products handed down from on high, insist on contributing to the conversation; in the second, they are portrayed as pliant and ill-informed, mistaking what happens to interest them for what is actually important.

The fact that two hundred thousand undergraduates are now majoring in journalism in the United States—a number that has risen 35 percent over the past decade despite rising tuition costs and a rapidly shrinking job market—implies the possibility of a different situation altogether. Presumably, many of these students still see some utility in traditional journalism and hope to devote themselves to the cause of investigating things that matter at substantial length. The critic Lawrence Weschler turned melancholic when reflecting on the fate of students who take his popular course on the art of the long essay. "They come into my office crying hot tears," he told me, "when they realize there's nothing they'd rather do with their lives."

Yet the likelihood of these students getting a job writing long assignments is slim to none, and that has as much to do with economic realities as with technological innovation or the rewiring of their brains and the attenuation of their attention spans—with opportunity, in other words, as much as inclination. If the economics of the Web favor aggregation and link baiting, shocking headlines and quickly consumable trifles, future media makers will inevitably produce exactly that.

The optimists on one side, the skeptics on the other, those who laud the next generation and those who scorn it—oddly, both camps end up making the same mistake. The imagination and ambitions of an entire cohort have been preemptively and presumptuously denied. The naysayers and the celebrants stand ready to write the obituary for human beings who look beneath the surface, who care about the world beyond their immediate surroundings, who pay attention to that which is complex and outside them. One camp applauds the caricature while the other chides it, but both agree that the emerging media landscape accurately reflects what digital natives want. Neither recognizes the persistence of individuals who do not conform to this mold, nor do they bother wondering how to carve out and sustain a cultural space in which a wider variety of capabilities might flourish.

A few days after the first massive pro-democracy demonstration in Egypt in early 2011, Andrew Burton got on a plane heading to Cairo. He landed late the night of February 1 and slept at the airport, rising at dawn to head into the city. Walking around Tahrir Square with his camera in hand, he found his morning went smoothly. He got his bearings and took pictures of protesters, who were friendly and welcoming. But when Burton headed out from his hotel later that afternoon, the press were reporting clashes between the pro-democracy activists and Mubarak's supporters, many of whom were hired thugs and plainclothes cops. Moving through the crowd, Burton felt the tension twisting the air.

When Burton stopped to photograph a man painting slogans over antigovernment graffiti, he was grabbed from behind and his lens covered. He pulled away and, unsure of what to do, tried to head back to his hotel, but an angry crowd gathered around him and began to attack. A group of men rushed to his aid, taking most of the blows and pushing Burton down an alley until his back was up against an army tank. His shirt was ripped and strange hands plunged into his pockets. Then Burton felt someone get a grip under his armpits and lift him upward, dumping him into the tank where he found himself surrounded by fourteen soldiers, his age and smiling. "They scooted over, and made a place for me to sit. Everything was quiet—the transition from an angry mob scene to a cramped

interior happened very, very quickly," he later recounted. "The soldiers were joking, laughing, making fun of me; they didn't seem to
care too much about what was going on outside." He took cover for
the next few hours, making small talk in broken English and sharing food. When things calmed down a general flagged a taxi that
took him back to his hotel.

Burton is an ambitious and talented young photographer, barely
a year out of college when we met, someone who defies all the easy
stereotypes of his generation. He makes "content," has a Web site,
and sends out social media updates, but for him these are ways of
engaging deeply with the issues he cares about, a means of focusing
on them, not flitting across the surface. The trip to Egypt was his
first to a conflict zone, one made on his own dime in hopes that an
outlet would pick up his photographs, which Bloomberg News eventually did. When we met a few weeks later, he was hatching plans to
travel to Tunisia to document the nation's first democratic election;
he had no idea that within days he would be in Japan shooting the
triple crisis of earthquake, tsunami, and nuclear meltdown that shook
the region.

"I'm not much of an adrenaline junkie or a speed demon. There
are a lot of war photographers who just get dare-devilish," Burton
says. Instead, as someone who minored in international relations
and politics, he's more interested in exploring social movements and
the complex interactions between government and the governed; it
just happens that conflict is how those issues most visibly manifest
themselves. "But when I was in Egypt I missed a lot of that. I failed
in that sense. Instead I got more nuanced, quiet moments that other
photographers may have missed. It was day six, so I wasn't going to
get anything totally new," he recalls with a hint of regret. "But
there were little things, like the subway to Tahrir Square, which
wasn't running, which people had turned into a kind of makeshift
dump. There was the whole financial district, which was totally
shut down. Or I shot these mini-businesses that kept people fed or

were set up to charge cell phones. Just how people got by. There's a kind of industry pressure, or maybe it's personal pressure, to get exciting images of conflict and violence, but they're not always the most interesting."

The industry to which he refers, Burton admits, is shrinking, and photojournalism, long an uncertain venture, is considered a dying profession by many. He sees himself and his peers trying to squeak through the door, holding on to threads. He knows veteran photographers who complain of new pressures, saying that magazines like *National Geographic* used to give them six months to a year to complete an assignment and that they now are expected to turn things over in a matter of weeks or a couple of months.

To most freelancers, even a few weeks of steady focus sounds luxurious, since the demands on them are even more intense. Burton self-financed his trips to the Beijing Olympics, Egypt, and Japan and was lucky to find news organizations that, after the fact, licensed his photos to *USA Today* or the Associated Press, which meant he earned a couple of hundred bucks a day, allowing him to break even or make a small profit after expenses. (Due to dwindling budgets, established news organizations are turning to freelance writers as well as photographers to cover hazardous international beats, sometimes paying as little as seventy dollars for a story filed from the front lines.)[6]

On top of money problems are the personal risks that come with going solo in a crisis zone. "One photo editor told me to remember that even when I'm freelancing for an organization, no one will have my back. If I get shot, the editors buying my photos don't help me because I'm not staff," Burton says. Burton recently read *The Forever War*, journalist Dexter Filkins's account of reporting from Baghdad in 2003 for the *New York Times*, which took out an insurance policy for Filkins and his fellow journalists that cost fourteen thousand dollars a month, not to mention the armored car that cost a quarter of a million dollars and the security adviser who cost a thousand dollars a day. Burton contrasts that with the story of João Silva, a photographer who was on contract with the paper (a position between freelance and staff) in Afghanistan. In 2010 he stepped on a land mine while accompanying American soldiers patrolling an area near the town of Arghandab and lost both his legs. Silva was fortunate that the *Times* volunteered to pay for his medical expenses, but the point is that the paper wasn't required to.

Despite all the hype about the Web enabling people to cut out middlemen and fly solo, Burton made clear during our first conversation that his dream was getting a staff position with a wire service or a newspaper or simply securing some sort of institutional support. "We're expected to be society's eyes and ears," Burton said, but fewer and fewer organizations can justify the expense. "I have really dark days, like when I go a week without getting any work and I just think, fuck this. I can't do it. Realistically, it's impossible. Will I be able to eat, have a savings account, have a family?" It's a labor of love: "It has to be your passion."

In the summer of 2013 Burton, to his great relief, squeaked through the door. He was offered a staff position at Getty Images, which he happily accepted. The job meant financial stability, health insurance, and the peace of mind that comes from knowing the organization would stand behind him should he run into trouble documenting something dangerous or controversial.

There are people who find other ways to make a living taking photographs, Burton acknowledged, though the alternatives to reportage make him deeply ambivalent. He's got friends who shoot weddings or fashion spreads. "You can also work for an NGO," he told me. "More people are doing that, which is basically the same thing as working for a corporation, but you don't feel as bad about it." And as is the case for all creative fields with business models in crisis, advertising, public relations, and other corporate projects beckon.

There's a case to be made that Burton and others like him should content themselves with being hobbyists. To use an analogy dear to new-media thinkers, it's as though they are trying to break into the buggy whip business when cars are flying off the assembly line. Anyone with a cell phone can take a picture and publish it online, and millions upon millions do, every day. It's getting increasingly unrealistic, according to this line of thought, to expect to be hired to do something like making images, which are so ubiquitous.

In one possible future, people like Burton and I will be obsolete; we won't need dedicated photographers and documentary filmmakers because everyone will simply chronicle their own lives, streaming it all for the world to watch. This may sound far-fetched, but consider that some of the most searing and powerful images of recent conflicts were not taken by professional photographers (like Robert Capa during World War II or Eddie Adams in Vietnam) but shot off the cuff. They were shocking candids injudiciously produced by perpetrators of violence as they tortured prisoners in Abu Ghraib or proudly flanked mutilated Afghan civilians, not compositions by outside observers.

In all their raw cruelty, these photos made the despicable aspects of war palpable in a way that the work of professional shooters fails to do. They were immediate, disorienting, and deeply disturbing. Similarly, we've been captivated by footage shot by civilians who happened to be on the scene during moments of political upheaval, terrorism, and natural disasters. The effect is often more authentic and gripping than anything an outsider could produce. Nonetheless, depending on idiocy (people's misjudgments about how the images they produce and share will be received), ego (their conviction that their own lives are worth broadcasting), or chance (hoping that they happen to be standing beside the Hudson River when a plane lands in it or in the room when someone goes on a rampage) for our collective enlightenment is a risky proposition.

Most people would probably agree that there are things we need to see and situations where we can't count on bystanders to point and shoot or guilty parties to incriminate themselves. Yet many influential new-media thinkers argue that the prospect should be eagerly embraced. In the future they anticipate, legacy news organizations will wither away and be replaced by a wired citizenry, collectively creating and rating user-generated content using collaborative filtering mechanisms, evolving a distribution system more inclusive and engaging than what came before. The line between reporter and reader will blur as a growing number of people create, curate, and circulate content. If journalism continues to exist as such, it will be less about going out gathering facts and reporting from the field and more about "curating" other people's contributions and guiding a conversation, the shift focusing from content to the connections it produces.

Jeff Jarvis, a self-proclaimed Internet triumphalist, represents this strand of thinking taken to its logical extreme. He believes we are witnessing a massive epistemological shift, the veritable end of the Gutenberg era, with its dependence on print and corresponding emphasis on authorship, linearity, fixity, and closure. Digital technology, he says, disrupts such modes of knowing and the institutions that supported them, unleashing an information flow to which anyone can contribute, empowering the "people formerly known as readers," and ushering in a democratized age of information gathering.

"We no longer need companies, institutions, or government to organize us," Jarvis declares, adopting his standard insurgent tone. The future, Jarvis likes to say, is not *institutional* but *entrepreneurial*. The Burtons of the world should be able to go it alone, and if they can't make it, it's because they're not innovative enough. (Jarvis, for all his blather, does not live by his own advice. Like many new-media thinkers, he's employed by an academic department and publishes his books and articles through traditional channels. "Dog's gotta eat," he's fond of saying.)

Not content to condemn institutions to the dustbin of history,

Jarvis goes even further: our very definition of news, he insists, is radically changing, becoming hyper-local and hyper-personal. "You're hungry and you want a burrito," Jarvis exclaimed during one of his frequent stump speeches. "I think it's a wonderful thing and it's also a definition of news. There's a really good burrito place here. That's news." No longer will editors and journalists deliver the "products" they think people should have (the Gutenberg era). Instead, news will be a "process" and the people will decide for themselves what classifies.

Anyone who resists this redefinition, who dares to speak of quality or duty—who, like Burton, believe there are things people *ought* to see—are doomed elitists, arrogant know-it-alls who don't respect the wisdom of the crowd. "The whole notion of 'long-form journalism' is writer-centered, not public-centered," Jarvis tweeted, sounding suspiciously like Rupert Murdoch, who has scoffed at the idea of in-depth reporting as "a higher calling, of blah blah responsibility, of reverential bullshit."

The reduction of news to whatever we happen to want to know in the moment is terrifying. What about politics, poverty, foreign policy, and all of the other problems that plague us? But when challenged on the issue of importance, new-media thinkers are quick to point out the shortcomings of traditional news-gathering organizations, and they have plenty of material to draw on. After a series of historic failures—from the credulous reporting on the nonexistent weapons of mass destruction in Iraq to the business press missing the story of the subprime mortgage scandal and the financial crash until well after the fact—public trust in the media is at a two-decade low, with 63 percent of poll respondents saying that news stories are often inaccurate.[7]

If the political left and right are united in one thing, it's their hatred of the mainstream media, the dreaded MSM, and generally for good reason. Coverage is often shallow and sensational; spectacle trumps substance. Given that professionals appear to have been asleep at the wheel while our country fell into crisis, it's hardly surprising that people are open to the possibility that passionate amateurs could do a superior job. And yet, ironically, the mainstream media's blunders only prove how badly we need a vibrant and robust watchdog press.

After all, the powers that be are hardly trembling at the prospect of the demise of accountability journalism. Political leaders and corporate titans would much prefer to conduct their work away from prying eyes. "Newspapers may have done their jobs poorly," as the critic Thomas Frank put it, "but the answer is hardly to renounce the job itself." The solution to the failures of journalism is more and better journalism. Commonsensical as that may be, it's a solution that has gone untried, for reasons rooted in journalism's long decline.

The story has been told many times, but it's worth summarizing briefly. The seeds of the decline were sowed years ago. Though it's hard to believe now, newspapers were once the envy of the business world. Through the eighties and nineties, 20, 30, even 40 percent returns on investment were not uncommon, triple the norm for U.S. industry over the same period. Dollar signs in their eyes, chains devoured up local papers, consolidating and centralizing to maximize shareholder value, sometimes purchasing vibrant independent publications just to kill off competition.

The overlords of monopoly journalism became increasingly disconnected from the communities they were supposed to serve. And when profits plateaued, they gutted themselves to maintain growth, trimming staff, reducing reporting budgets, and publishing fluff. Today, newspaper chiefs prefer to point fingers at new technology or distracted readers or even their own staff, but the erosion of standards and depth owes more to their long greedy binge than to the Internet or the rise of blogging or social media.

The tenure of Sam Zell, a Wall Street–approved real estate mogul who as owner of the Tribune Company (which then included the *Los Angeles Times*, the *Chicago Tribune*, and other newspapers) drove it into bankruptcy, has become a parable of misguided corporate leadership. At a public gathering he become irate when one of his employees expressed concern that his papers were abandoning their obligation to keep communities informed about things that matter. Zell accused her of "classic journalistic arrogance" and told her to "fuck off."

When the Internet came on the scene, newspapers were primed to respond with cost-cutting techniques honed in prior decades to drive up profits: firing editors, writers, photographers, fact-checkers, and pruning other news-gathering expenses. Almost overnight, when content started circulating freely online, print sales began to decline precipitously and advertising rates went into free fall. Between 2006 and 2011, U.S. print advertising revenues fell by 55 percent; Craigslist alone wiped out about twenty billion dollars from classified revenue. Publications began to experience the paradox of falling profits even as audiences grew. In 2012, for example, digital readership was up but print advertising revenue losses outpaced digital gains by a factor of ten to one.[8]

In the UK, the *Guardian* saw its audience explode online, up 40 percent between 2012 and 2013 alone, yet the paper, along with its sister publication the *Observer*, still lost almost $50 million.[9] Subsidized by its parent company's more lucrative holdings, the *Guardian* is in an enviable position compared to its competitors and, by aggressively courting an international audience, the company has seen its digital revenue rise.

But for most publications, Web-based advertising will never make up for the losses. In 2010, for example, the newspaper industry took in only $3 billion of Web-based ad earnings compared to $22.8 billion from print advertising, though half of the people the industry reached accessed its products online.[10] For a variety of reasons—including the problem of near-limitless inventory and the automation of ad sales—digital advertising brings in a fraction of its print counterpart, which means publications have to attract thirty online readers to replace one paid subscriber. Making matters worse, while the digital ad market is booming overall, digital ad sales for newspapers have essentially flatlined since 2006.[11] (This is partly what is driving the adoption of metered paywalls as a source of revenue, though they seem to work only for the handful of publications that have a global brand or specialize in financial reporting.)

Digital dimes, the experts are fond of saying, have replaced analog dollars—and as more people start reading on mobile devices, where advertisements don't display well, instead of on their home computers, those dimes will turn into pennies. The impact of the shift to mobile will be "apocalyptic," predicts Michael Wolff, a writer who has straddled the legacy media and start-up worlds. "There is no way even a stripped-down, aggregation-based, unpaid citizen-journalist staffed newsroom can support itself in a mobile world," he warns.[12] Thus, ironically, print editions, despite their antiquated reputations, remain the primary profit centers for many companies, funding much of the news we access online.

Hit by a double whammy of technological change and a global recession, publishers across the country have cut staff, slashed sections, or closed shop.[13] Owners instituted the imprudent strategy of eviscerating their own product to save it. Cities that had multiple dailies now have one or, sometimes, none. More and more Americans now live in what former newspaper editor Tom Stites calls "news deserts," places where original reporting, print or digital, has completely dried up—a problem particularly acute within minority and rural communities.[14] Since 2000, American newsrooms have shrunk by a full 30 percent, with costly investigative units, Washington bureaus, and foreign desks always among the first things to go. In the early nineties a paper like the *Oakland Tribune* employed over a hundred reporters; now it has under a dozen. There are fewer full-time newsroom professionals working today than there were in 1978, when there were one hundred million fewer citizens.[15]

A recent study found 44.7 percent fewer reporters working in the Bay Area than a decade ago.[16] Nationwide, the number of full-time reporters covering state capitals was cut almost in half between 2003 and 2009, creating a vacuum of oversight proven to encourage and enable corruption.[17] Over recent years almost two hundred newsrooms have been closed, and many have been cut in half. Though we are drowning in data, we actually know less and less about what is happening in our own backyards and abroad.

Since 1998 at least twenty papers and companies have cut their foreign bureaus entirely, leaving only a handful of American newspapers that maintain stables of reporters; in 2003 thirteen papers and chains employed reporters dedicated to foreign affairs in Washington, D.C., a number that has dwindled to six.[18] According to research conducted by reporter Jill Carroll for Harvard University, the entire U.S. media, print and broadcast combined, supported a mere 141 foreign correspondents overseas in 2006, a shockingly meager number for a global superpower.[19] Instead of the age of openness and transparency that new-media thinkers anticipate, much will lie shrouded in darkness, out of sight and mind. What we don't know can and does hurt us, as we have seen in debacle after debacle, the truth revealed only after the damage has been done.

Faced with this devastation, the cheerleaders of new media counter that a combination of volunteerism, technological savvy, and market economics will lead, as a matter of course, to the best possible outcome. Innovation will make up for any losses as if by magic: old inefficiencies will vanish, crowdsourcing—allowing readers to assist with reporting for free—will provide cheaper content, and algorithms will sort through mountains of data to extract interesting stories. By properly harnessing new tools, the newsrooms of the future will be able to do more with less, or they will simply cease to exist.

"Maybe media won't be a job at all, but will instead be a hobby. There is no law that says that industries have to remain at any given size," former *Wired* editor in chief Chris Anderson reflected in a 2009 interview with *Der Spiegel*. "Once there were blacksmiths and there were steel workers, but things change. The question is not should journalists have jobs. The question is can people get the information they want, the way they want it?" On that front, Anderson, the quintessential techno-optimist, saw no cause for alarm. "The marketplace will sort this out," he concluded.

And yet the market, in many ways, is what got us into this mess. It was the market that hungered for higher and higher profits and lower production costs, decreeing that investigative reporters and foreign correspondents were not worth the investment. It was the market that encouraged conglomerates to assimilate their competitors. It was also the market that devalued still-solvent newspapers when it became clear that the old astronomical returns were untenable and the prospects for growth limited.

A study of eleven publicly traded newspaper companies released in 2012 revealed that, despite declining revenue, all experienced continued, albeit reduced, annual profits—not enough, however, to prevent stock prices from plunging. Wall Street's insistence that earnings rise, year after year, and the expectation that print will, inevitably, be phased out has led to what scholars have called a "virtual freefall in share prices," driving down stock prices by 80 percent on average in one year alone. The market has actually sped up the demise of companies that might have had a fighting chance at survival.[20]

At the same time, the market has found value in surprising places. Plenty of sectors connected to the news business are thriving as never before. The "disruption" of the news industry, to use a favorite new-media buzzword, has been uneven at best. The gossip mills are going strong, in print and online. Financial news is prospering in digital form, for it caters to affluent specialists eager to pay a premium for a split-second advantage. Advertising and public relations are flourishing. Meanwhile, television, against all predictions to the contrary, will not soon be vanquished by interactive technologies.

The mudslinging, partisan heart of cable news also beats hard and fast, with viewership holding steady and projected revenue rising despite some bumps along the way.[21]

Across the board, commercial broadcasters are doing comparatively well. In addition to subscribers' fees for cable networks, stable income from conventional advertisers, and savings from staff cutbacks and cheap content (talking heads and reality programming), they have the Supreme Court to thank. Its 2010 ruling in *Citizens United v. Federal Election Commission* struck down a century of campaign finance regulations, allowing station executives to fatten their coffers with billions in political ad revenues—a "lifeline" that will likely expand over time.[22] Between 2002 and 2010 there was a 250 percent increase in the number of TV commercials for House, Senate, and gubernatorial candidates—and, given the rising demand for space, the ads cost more, not less. "Whereas in the 1990s the average commercial TV station received about 3 percent of its revenues from campaign ads," Robert McChesney and John Nichols reported in the *Nation* in 2010, "this year campaign money could account for as much as 20 percent."[23]

Industry analysts salivated as the 2012 election approached, the projected windfall set to rise from 2008's $2.8 billion to $5 billion. "No one loves a good political brawl like a U.S. broadcast company. The fiercer the fight, the more money broadcasters can expect from campaign advertising—particularly in an era when political rhetoric grows more heated every day," enthused a 2011 Moody's Investors Service report. Cable has found a new cash cow that it can milk for years to come. This the market has sorted out.

Against this backdrop, journalism's plight appears all the starker. As the historian Paul Starr has noted, "Public goods are notoriously under-produced in the marketplace, and news is a public good." The fact is, a mass market for serious reporting has never actually existed; in the United States readers have never paid anywhere near the actual price of news production. Instead, newspapers, by bundling the crossword puzzle and the real estate classifieds with the metro section and stories about world events, assembled a mass audience that could be sold to advertisers, who provided, on average, about 80 percent of revenues.[24]

In-depth reporting is an "ancillary benefit" of this process, an unprofitable enterprise subsidized in a decidedly roundabout fashion. But this model is now falling apart. The Internet, by unbundling the different functions of the newspaper and allowing readers to go direct, has certainly made things more efficient—we can now download as many crossword puzzles as we desire, go to Craigslist to find an apartment, and visit the local blog or the foreign news aggregator to read about what's happening in the world. But it has eliminated the cross-subsidies that kept journalism afloat and, by doing so, exposed a form of market failure.

Stephen Janis, a reporter who has made the move from print to the Web, was one of the victims of the newspaper industry's collapse, losing his job at the *Baltimore Examiner* when it folded in 2009. While the layoffs have been painful, Janis believes the shakedown of the newspaper industry will be a healthy thing overall, challenging journalists to become more relevant.

With two of his ex-coworkers he founded the *Investigative Voice*, an online news site that aimed to provide the kind of nitty-gritty beat coverage that no one wants to invest in anymore. For a time it was a shining example of what many hope our new-media future will be: it combined the best of old-school shoe leather journalism and exploited the Internet as a quick and affordable distribution platform. The editors carved out rare middle ground between print traditionalists and new-media futurists.

For example, rather than dropping the finished story at once, Janis would let his investigations unspool piece by piece online, a technique he calls "episodic investigative journalism." "Where print kind of creates this situation where you've got to have the whole story and it's static," Janis explained, "the Internet allows you to keep posting and posting and updating, and building on what people call and tell you." Readers weren't exactly reporters, but they made suggestions and sometimes acted as sources. At the *Investigative Voice* Janis covered drug dealing within the government, racism in the police department, homicides and prostitution, corporate corruption—everything you would expect of the city mythologized in *The Wire*, a television series Janis says is not cynical enough, however sordid and authentic it seems to viewers.

One major multipart story was initiated by a long-cultivated source who called Janis late one night to tell him that a man employed by the city had just been arrested for molesting a woman while impersonating a police officer, pulling her over using flashing lights and then fondling her in her car before she escaped. Janis dug up evidence that the guy was on parole, and a close examination of records showed that he had been paid a salary and overtime during his stint in jail. Janis published what he had uncovered, which led to more tips.

"Through each continuous story, it became worse and worse," Janis told me. "I found out they were falsifying sick leave and supervisors never checked on him, that he had been sentenced to eighteen months in prison for sexually abusing a minor, which was another horrible tale. . . . And then we found out he was still working in schools, fixing leaks and stuff." Janis's detective work prompted Baltimore's inspector general to open a department-wide probe, and the city solicitor ordered a citywide review of personnel policies related to criminal convictions and the employment of sex offenders in jobs that bring them into contact with the public.

But the big challenge the *Investigative Voice* faced—and one that plagues other projects like it—isn't technological. It's the lack of human capital. "Reporters do not have any special privileges other than the first amendment. If you're willing to do the work and you're good at it, I think the Web gives you an opportunity to be relevant," Janis told me. "But you have to do the work, and the work is the hard part. So many stories I get come from hanging around city hall at a useless hearing and someone comes up and gives me a tip, or from going to a crime scene. That kind of stuff is the hardest thing to pull off if you're kind of an independent amateur or you're someone who has a job working nine-to-five."

Janis himself is a well-known reporter with a lot of connections. But even he encountered resistance when he continued to show up at city hall after losing his newspaper job. "You have to really push your organization, your relevance," which can be hard for a novice or a free agent to do. "People aren't going to automatically trust you," Janis explained. "Why would they? Particularly people like cops who are incredibly paranoid and could get into a lot of trouble, or politicians." Janis is skeptical that we can expect amateurs to adequately cover this space, partly because everything happens during regular work hours when most people are unavailable. I asked him if he'd ever seen a blogger at city hall and he laughed. Often, there aren't even press reporters.

Devoted to the mission of serving as broad a community as possible, *Investigative Voice* made its articles available for free. The afternoon I met Janis, he was pleased because he had just sold an ad for the site, a rare occurrence. A handful of subscriptions were sold to people who believed in the enterprise, but that has brought in only a trickle measurable in hundreds of dollars. While wealthy individuals from the technology sector have recently been investing in high-profile journalism outlets (Facebook's Chris Hughes with the *New Republic*, Amazon's Jeff Bezos with the *Washington Post*, and eBay's Pierre Omidyar with his online start-up), capital has not been flowing to small- and medium-sized efforts, which are sinking. Many now argue that foundation funding is the only option if we want investigative reporting to survive.

Nationwide there are a few shining examples of Web-based nonprofits that are held up as the saviors of the industry and hailed by new-media thinkers as emblematic of journalism's bright digital-first future—Voice of San Diego, MinnPost, and ProPublica, to name a few. These experiments, which produce and distribute excellent public interest journalism, are laudable, but they are also minuscule compared to the estimated $1.6 billion in annual reporting and editing capacity that has been lost since 2005. *Mother Jones* recently tallied the funds available to what it called "marquee" nonprofit journalism projects and found that they have around $100 million combined at their disposal, or about half of what the *New York Times* spends on news gathering annually (or a tenth of what Apple spends on advertising).[25]

There's simply no way this model can match the money previously generated by the commercial sector.[26] "The nonprofits are really cool and they're great. I've done work for lots of them. I think that they're wonderful," said A. C. Thompson, a ProPublica staffer who spent over three years investigating police misconduct after Hurricane Katrina. "But the truth of the matter is, there's not enough philanthropic money in U.S. foundations to cover the shortfall in journalism and reporting resources."

Janis was equally skeptical about going the nonprofit route. The problem, he pointed out, is that most donors only want to invest in "gimmicks," not actual reporting. ("They ask, 'Oh are you tweeting?' Tweeting is delivery. It's like spending all your time worrying what your delivery boy or girl is doing with the newspaper on their bike!") Funding organizations also tend to make one initial seed grant and move on, rarely committing to the long haul, which is why many otherwise promising community news start-ups have already gone under.[27] In a 2012 *Columbia Journalism Review* report on three well-funded nonprofit digital news organizations founded in 2009, only one, the Texas Tribune, had survived. "There aren't that many sites like *Investigative Voice*," Janis explained. "because it's very time-consuming, and people get tired real quickly."

Almost a year later, Janis wasn't tired of his job, but he was tired of being broke. "I didn't have the capital or ability to viably fund it to keep me out of poverty. It became impossible to keep reporting. My income was so low, it was terrifying." He accepted a position with the local Fox affiliate, where he could continue his investigations and also make enough money to live and see a doctor once in a while. His colleagues pushed forward with *Investigative Voice* but eventually were forced to call it quits as well.

"It's really too bad," Janis reflected. "The site was completely relevant. I had access to people and developed more sources working there than I had anywhere else. And people really liked the independence of our coverage. They liked that it was real and were upset when we shut down. It worked as a social model, but the business model was totally broken." Those two models, Janis continued, have completely diverged. "There's this divide between what the community needs and wants to read and what they are willing to pay for. There's a missing social contract. I think those two things can be married, but it's going to be a long time before it's figured out."

Nick Davies is a prominent journalist who has been outspoken about the shortcomings of his chosen profession. An award-winning investigative reporter who brokered the *Guardian*'s collaboration with WikiLeaks to publish the Afghanistan war logs and broke the phone-hacking scandal that prompted an ongoing investigation into Rupert Murdoch's empire, his 2008 book *Flat Earth News* (subtitled *An Award-Winning Reporter Exposes Falsehood, Distortion and Propaganda in the Global Media*) exhaustively documents how contemporary journalism has been corrupted by ever-intensifying commercial pressure.[28]

When clear returns are demanded, risks cannot be taken. Stories need to be "quick to cover" and "safe to publish," free of controversy and full of quotes from official sources. They must avoid problems that require deep background or ideas that require lengthy explanation. These low standards, coupled with the fact there are more people working in public relations than there are journalists in both the UK and the United States (where the ratio is about four to one and climbing), leave the news media highly susceptible to manipulation.[29]

Old-fashioned fellow that he is, Davies explained to me that he believes the job of journalist is to report new information and check facts but, surveying the media landscape, he sees very little reporting or fact checking going on. Recruiting a team of researchers from Cardiff University's school of journalism to analyze the British press, Davies found that "a massive 60 per cent of these quality-print stories consisted wholly or mainly of wire copy and/or PR material, and a further 20 per cent contained clear elements of wire copy and/or PR to which more or less other material had been added. With 8 per cent of the stories, they were unable to be sure about their source. That left only 12 per cent of stories where the researchers could say that all the material was generated by the reporters themselves."

Davies dubs the 88 percent of material cobbled from wire copy and press releases "churnalism," and that, combined with the forces that collude to create it, he says, is what ails us. "Taken together, these data portray a picture of journalism in which any meaningful independent journalistic activity by the press is the exception rather than the rule," the Cardiff researchers conclude. "We are not talking about investigative journalism here, but the everyday practices of news judgment, fact-checking, balance, criticizing and interrogating, sources, etc., that are, in theory, central to routine, day-to-day journalism."[30] And what of those wire copy scribes—those industrious providers of the raw material everyone else recycles? Most of them work for Press Association, the British version of the Associated Press, where they crank out up to ten stories a day, often spending no more than an hour per piece.

The commercial pressure, corporate corruption, government distortion, and celebrity scandals that contort our public discourse are enough to make anyone wish for a massive media overthrow. It's no wonder, then, that people find solace in the idea of an amateur utopia, a public sphere where the unsavory issue of money is side-stepped and pure-hearted citizen journalists work unsullied. Davies dismisses the vision. "The fact is that reporting is difficult—it involves real skills, some of them quite obscure; it needs resources and time; it also, I think, needs to be accountable." There might be some very good stuff published under the auspices of citizen journalism, Davies acknowledges. "But the dangers are clear."

Idealizing citizen journalists, imagining them as necessarily agenda-less and untainted, is one such danger. But the problem, as Davies knows, goes deeper than the overblown battle of amateurs versus professionals, journalists versus bloggers, print versus digital, old media versus new, or analog immigrants versus digital natives. Writers working on the Web have broken enough big stories—forcing the resignation of an attorney general here, bringing down a congressman there—to prove that legacy organizations do not have a monopoly on impact. And as far as arguments about quality, perusing any newsstand puts the paper-based argument quickly to rest: countless scandalmongering publications have long proven that the quality of reporting has nothing to do with some intrinsic property of the page.

The problem with the utopian ideal is that the economic demands that bedeviled writers under the old-media model have been carried over, and compounded, by the digital transformation. What writers need, whatever format their work comes in, is a reprieve from churnalism's demand for more stories, more scoops, more stuff. They need the time and space to take the long view. Above all, they need the freedom to follow ideas that don't pan out. Investigative reporting is a leap of faith, one that often means coming back empty-handed.

"I spent three days last week pursuing a lead which turned out to be false. That's not uncommon," Davies told me. "The source was well meaning. Several other well-meaning sources even confirmed it. But, down at the bottom of the barrel, it turned out they were wrong, they were simply recycling an attractive rumor. What investigative reporters need most of all is to work for an organization that will give them the time and resources and support to dig deep and will be grateful when they discover that a story is false, because we got to the truth."

Investigative reporting is resource-intensive work, dependent on massive outlays of time and money. A. C. Thompson took over a year to write his first piece on vigilante killings after Hurricane Katrina and the resulting police cover-ups. To get the first two thousand words, he drove hundreds of miles tracking down potential witnesses and convincing them to speak about what had happened (many had since evacuated to other states and some didn't want to risk putting themselves in harm's way), visiting courthouse after courthouse to dig through city records (seven in all), and negotiating for countless hours with a corrupt New Orleans coroner who refused outright to comply with requests (a six-month, ten-thousand-dollar lawsuit eventually did the trick). A similarly lengthy investigation backed by ProPublica involved a budget that easily reached half a million dollars.[31]

The promise of the Internet was that it would allow for more of an investment in this kind of work. The Organisation for Economic Co-operation and Development estimates that physical production and distribution costs take up about 52 percent of newspaper budgets.[32] Delivering news electronically, in theory, could produce savings that could be recycled back into the newsroom and used to sustain real reporting. But unfortunately that is not what has happened. As Davies notes, "So far, media owners have shown every sign of grasping electronic delivery as yet another chance to cut costs and increase revenue without putting anything back into journalism."

Consider the New Orleans Times-Picayune, which cooperated with Thompson and ProPublica for a series of reports on Katrina's aftermath, as a case in point. Instead of building on that success, absentee owners downsized operations to wring immediate gains. Though the paper was profitable and despite public outcry, owners laid off half the staff and shifted the majority of operations to an anemic and unattractive Web site, while briefly making New Orleans the largest city not to have a daily paper in print—a risky proposition in a region where 36 percent of the population do not have home Internet access.[33]

The uncomfortable truth is that the online world has only accelerated churnalism's already rapid pace. We have become accustomed to instant updates, video streams, and live blogging and tweeting. The pressure to react, to comment, and to attract clicks means journalists are working more quickly than ever before, counting seconds in their race against the clock.

Writing in the *Columbia Journalism Review*, Dean Starkman denounced what he calls "the hamster wheel"—the obsession with "motion for motion's sake," which yields "volume without thought." The *Wall Street Journal*, Starkman notes, produced as many stories—twenty-one thousand—in the first six months of 2010 as it did over the course of an entire year only a decade ago, not counting Web-only material, while the number of journalists employed by the paper dropped by 13 percent (and the *Journal* has fared far better than most papers thanks to its focus on valuable financial information).

Starkman quotes a memo from the *Journal*'s managing editor at the time, Robert Thomson, introducing a system called "URGENT" that would induce his underlings to produce at an even more frantic clip: "Even a headstart of a few seconds is priceless for a commodities trader or a bond dealer—that same story can be repurposed for a range of different audiences, but its value diminishes with the passing of time." In an "age of digitally compressed content," he warned, there is no other way—slower forms of news gathering must be sent to the "knackery." Thus the hamster wheel involves not just racing ahead but leaving behind, abandoning, as Starkman says, "investigations you will never see, good work left undone, public service not performed."

In 2010 the Pew Research Center's Project for Excellence in Journalism (PEJ) published a study on the "news ecosystem" in Baltimore. The findings echoed similar studies of news production in other cities. "As the economic model that has subsidized professional journalism collapses, the number of people gathering news in traditional television, print and radio organizations is shrinking markedly," the report's introduction states. "What, if anything, is taking up that slack?"

Examining news production over the course of one week, researchers found that while the number of outlets had mushroomed online, "much of the 'news' people receive contains no original reporting." A full 95 percent of the stories that did contain new information came from the traditional media, in particular the only local daily paper, the *Sun*. Sources such as local Web sites, blogs, and Twitter functioned primarily as "an alert system and a way to disseminate stories from other places," contributing, above all, to the breaking of news more quickly. "This faster dissemination of news," the PEJ study reported, "was tied to three other trends."

As news is posted faster, often with little enterprise reporting added, the official version of events is becoming more important. We found official press releases often appear word for word in first accounts of events, though often not noted as such.

In the growing echo chamber online, formal procedures for citing and crediting can get lost. We found numerous examples of Web sites carrying sections of other people's work without attribution and often suggesting original reporting was added when none was. We found elements of this in several major stories we traced.

And sometimes old stories that were already obsolete were posted or linked to after events had changed and the original news site had updated them.

The Pew researchers confirmed Nick Davies's findings: the seeming abundance of Web sites to visit doesn't necessarily give us more to choose from. Meanwhile, the local papers that are setting the terms and tone of coverage—namely the *Sun* and a handful of specialty print publications focused on business and law—offer substantially less than they did only a few years ago.

"For all of 2009, for instance, the *Sun* produced 32% fewer stories on any subject than it did in 1999, and 73% fewer stories than in 1991, when the company still published an evening and morning paper with competing newsrooms," the Pew researchers warned. "And a comparison of one major story during the week studied— about state budget cuts—found newspapers in the area produced only one-third as many stories in 2009 as they did the last time the state made a similar round of budget cuts in 1991, and the Baltimore *Sun* one seventh as many." Those numbers aren't particularly surprising given that the once venerable *Sun*, during Sam Zell's reign, slashed its editorial division in 2009, with over sixty people laid off.

Stephen Janis saw the Pew report's bleak portrait as strikingly accurate. "It's true, ninety percent of the Internet start-ups are reposting, repurposing, aggregating, or they'll write a little paragraph or post a link to something else," he said. Immediately after the *Examiner* folded, Janis worked briefly for Raw Story, a Web-only publication that describes itself as an "investigative news nexus."

"Before I knew it I was sitting on my couch all day, trolling government listservs trying to geek out some kind of micro-scoop," Janis recounted with a shake of his head. "They wanted me to write up something that happened on a television show, and they wanted it posted in nine minutes because they wanted to get it out first, before anyone else. I would take five minutes to get a photograph, and I'd be getting messages on my instant message thing from my managing editor saying, 'What the hell are you doing?'" Janis laughed at the memory. "I wasn't fast enough. I also decided there's no point in it. That's not the way I report. I use people out in the world to give me a little bit of a clue." This is how the hamster wheel runs: "You find this little micro alteration of the story and you post something on it really quick."

Indeed, the *Huffington Post*, with its multiple international editions, boasts of publishing over twelve hundred items per day, more than three times as many as the *New York Times*, the nation's largest newsroom (and that's not including blog posts). Back in 2010, when the site's output was little over half the current rate, Jeff Bercovici, a media analyst at *Forbes*, marveled at the quantity: "On a per-capita basis, each Huffpo staffer produces 10 times as many pieces of content as a *Times* staffer."[34]

To make those numbers, the *Huffington Post* writers have to work quickly, repurposing, or aggregating content from other sources, condensing articles into a few paragraphs, or framing video clips with short statements. These posts are presented alongside contributions from a stable of thousands of uncompensated bloggers, predictably lowbrow slide shows (a format favored by Web sites dependent on page views for advertising revenue since each new photo counts as a click), and, as the Cardiff researchers suggested, warmed-over press releases.

Bercovici's description of the site's strategy constitutes a textbook example of digital churnalism: "If you want to understand Huffpo's rocket-like growth, you have to look at things like its aggressive search engine optimization, its cutting-edge social integration, and its highly efficient, ever-evolving publishing platform, which helps editors whip out stories at breakneck pace and supplies them with the feedback to maximize their traffic in real time."[35]

Days before AOL's $315 million purchase of the *Huffington Post* was announced, a document known as the "AOL Way" was leaked online. Fifty-eight pages detailed an editorial strategy based on increasing output from thirty-three thousand to fifty-five thousand stories monthly and upping page views to seven thousand per piece to ensure profitability (seven thousand page views are needed to break even on an article where the writer is paid twenty-five dollars; the report noted how editors could keep track of the money made by each article down to the penny).

Editors were ordered to pursue subjects based on four criteria: traffic potential, revenue potential, edit quality, and turnaround time. Staffers, meanwhile, were required to double their yield, turning out around ten stories per day. To ensure success, editors had to "identify in-demand topics" by watching trending subjects on search engines and social media. "Use editorial insight & judgment to assign topics," the report advised. "Ex: 'Macaulay Culkin' & 'Mila Kunis' are trending because they broke up—write a story about Macaulay Culkin and Mila Kunis." Combining two trending themes makes links twice as enticing.

The next step on the path to success is pairing irresistible content with search engine optimized headlines, or "SEO winning titles," as the report put it, in the style of the one example proffered: "LADY GAGA GOES PANTLESS IN PARIS." Following the announcement of AOL's acquisition, word circulated that Arianna Huffington would adjust the system to make space for higher "content quality." But a *Huffington Post* headline from before the purchase—"Taylor Momsen Goes Pantsless, Curses on Morning Television" [*sic*]—showed that the strategy was not too far from her own.[36]

New-media gossip juggernaut Gawker also pays tribute to churnalism's animating spirits: shortness, sensationalism, superficiality, and speed. Though writers sometimes buck the trend to post sharp and sardonic opinion pieces and the occasional stand-alone reported essay, the overwhelming majority of what goes up on the site is composed under the glow of a large, prominently placed screen that keeps real-time tabs on the number of views, comments, and "uniques" (new visitors, who are even more valuable than page views to advertisers), metrics that determine staff bonuses and advancement.

In a profile published in the *Atlantic*, Gawker's founder, Nick Denton, told veteran journalist James Fallows that he believes his market-minded approach can solve journalism's business woes, at least where subjects such as "gossip, technology, sex talk, and so on" are concerned. "But not the worthy topics. Nobody wants to eat the boring vegetables. Nor does anyone want to pay to encourage people to eat their vegetables," Denton declared. "But, anyway, look at me. I used to cover political reform in post-communist Eastern Europe, which had been my subject at Oxford. And now I tell writers that the numbers (i.e., the audience) won't support any worthiness. We can't even write stories about moguls like Rupert Murdoch or Barry Diller unless it involves photographs of them cavorting with young flesh. (I used to enjoy those stories in the old days, before web metrics.)"[37]

Fallows, who once wrote a scathing indictment of commercial media, *Breaking the News*, recognizes Denton as a new breed of media mogul, a man who, though not particularly admirable, is at least honest about his approach: he makes no grandiose claims or appeals to the public good. Denton's paradigm, Fallows predicted, will prevail (the eight Web sites comprising the Gawker's American network already generate more traffic than the online versions of the *Washington Post* and *USA Today*).[38] "His enterprises, and his rationale for them, present a distillation of the model toward which the news business is trending," Fallows writes. The media of the Gawker age deliver what customers "want" rather than what they "should" have. Like Nick Bilton and Jeff Jarvis, Fallows sees the future as inevitably shaped by distinction.

The distinction reaches its apotheosis in online content farms. If you have ever asked the Internet anything—like how to make a soufflé or what causes an ingrown toenail—chances are that you have stumbled across their wares. Demand Media, founded in 2006, and its imitators have published millions of items over the years. Content farms do not produce writing anyone cares deeply about—instead, they rely on data about what people are searching for and determine how much advertisers will pay to reach them. Algorithms craft assignments out of Web queries, and a database coordinates thousands of freelance writers who spit out formulaic and search-optimized articles for as little as a few dollars a pop.[39]

"While more traditional media companies focus on supplying experiences they believe consumers might like, we're unapologetically dedicated to delivering the ones they already demand," Demand Media's "manifesto" declares.

That approach—the brazen appeal to audience and advertisers—won the company an initial valuation of $1.5 billion when it hit the public market, putting the mill on par with the *New York Times*, whose traffic it then exceeded. Though Google has since chastised Demand Media and other content farms for spamming the Web with "low quality" material and tweaked its algorithms to demote such offerings, the search giant and Demand Media eventually struck up a lucrative partnership to provide material to YouTube.[40]

Just as content farms are engineered to game search engines, an increasing number of sites are designed to game social networks. No one does this better than Jonah Peretti, cofounder of the *Huffington Post* and mastermind of the Web site BuzzFeed, a compendium of instantly digestible gags, top ten lists, and branded content with some pallid political reporting thrown in. The reigning king of "contagious media," Peretti is perhaps the only person who can reasonably claim to have cracked the viral code, reaching upward of 130 million people a month and earning the backing of leading venture capitalists as a result.

He did it by optimizing BuzzFeed posts for sharing on Facebook in particular, which now rivals search referrals as a driver of Web traffic. "Our technology powers the social distribution of content, detects what is trending on the web, and connects people in realtime with the hottest content of the moment," BuzzFeed's "about" section boasts. Partnering with companies such as General Electric and Taco Bell, BuzzFeed's integrated style of advertising "helps good things win the online popularity contest" and "accelerate sharing."

The recipe for reaching what Peretti calls the "Bored at Work Network" is relatively straightforward: content should be "easy to understand, easy to share, and includes a social imperative"; it should not be too weighty ("It is hard to make viral media especially for serious topics"); the maker should spend at least as much time planning how to promote the material as she did making it ("Focus on the mechanics of how an idea spreads, not just the idea itself"); and the maker should be ready to sacrifice quality for popularity ("The best ideas don't always win" and "Quality is not a growth strategy").

If nothing else, we should remember the concept of the Bored at Work Network when alarms are sounded about our diminishing attention spans and ever more distracted natures. Changes in our media consumption habits are often the consequence of changing circumstances and opportunities. Just as suburbanization helped kill afternoon newspapers, which had traditionally been purchased in city centers and read on bus or train rides home, and boost radio, broadcast through car stereos during the daily commute, there has been a corresponding shift from watching news on television or reading the paper in the relative quiet of home to the ability to consume news and entertainment on our devices wherever we happen to be, including the office. That people are increasingly drawn toward media they can process in stolen moments on the job is not a sign of some fundamental spiritual degradation, nor proof of technology's inevitably ruinous influence on our intellectual faculties.

Forward-thinking entrepreneurs are busy thinking beyond immediacy and looking toward the next phase of the Internet's evolution. We're moving past real time, the technologists promise, to something even more compelling (un-real time, perhaps?). Soon enough we'll live in a world where search engines not only answer our questions but tell us what questions we want to ask.

"We don't need you to type at all. We know where you are. We know where you've been. We can more or less know what you're thinking about," Google's Eric Schmidt has said. Search technology is already becoming predictive, offering you results before you've even looked for them based on what they know about you, your routines, and your social relationships (which is quite a lot). The media of the future will anticipate our needs and forecast our interests, reading our collective unconscious and fulfilling our desires before the pangs of longing have been fully felt.

Giving people what they want reduces us to consumers instead of treating us like citizens, consumers who are on the prowl for the predictable and comfortable. What we want winds up being suspiciously like what we've already got, more of the same—the cultural equivalent of a warm bath. But the mistake new-media boosters make is to equate our spur-of-the-moment searches and fleeting fancies with deep-seated needs and desires. Just because we sometimes use the Internet to find restaurant recommendations or share cute animal pictures doesn't mean restaurants and cute animals are all that we care about.

Wharton Business School professor Katherine Milkman has examined what she calls the "want/should conflict," making the connection between cultural and edible products even more explicit than Gawker's Nick Denton. Wants for Milkman are things like "junk foods" and "lowbrow films," while shoulds are "healthy" and "highbrow." Analyzing consumer habits in a paper titled "Highbrow Films Gather Dust: Time-Inconsistent Preferences and Online DVD Rentals," Milkman, with coauthors Todd Rogers and Max Bazerman, shows that when people make choices for the distant future, they are more likely to pick "should" movies, like documentaries, while in the now we prefer "want" films full of action and adventure.

Evidence of this "time inconsistent preference" or "present bias," as it's called, was also found to apply to online grocery shopping: the further in advance an order was placed, the more healthy items people bought. As the essay on film rentals put it, "The tendency to put off options preferred by our *should* selves (e.g. saving, eating vegetables) in favor of options preferred by our *want* selves (e.g. spending, eating ice cream) is stronger for decisions that will take effect immediately than decisions that will take effect in the future." We have, in effect, multiple selves and they want different things. As Milkman has said in one of her talks: Next week I'll watch *Born into Brothels* and eat an apple; tonight I'll watch *Spider-Man* and eat M&Ms.

When I first read Milkman's paper, it was with the creeping shame of a vegetable maker, a server of steamed broccoli cinema while my more successful colleagues prepare tastier fare. But on a second reading, the real meaning of her analysis became clear. The shoulds are not things that people don't want but rather things they *want to want*. And the Internet offers both: not quite the cultural equivalent of a junk food court, it resembles more a strange place where carrot sticks might be mixed in among the Milk Duds. For a creator it's a hard place to compete when others approach the Web like those unscrupled marketers who put the cartoon-endorsed cereal on the low shelf for toddlers to see, all to set off a page view feeding frenzy.

Still, the categories of want and should are too tidy. In our insistence on the division between virtue and delight, we have forgotten one of the messages contained in Horace's famous *Ars Poetica*. Poetry, Horace said, should be *"dulce et utile,"* sweet *and* useful, entertaining *and* edifying, pleasure *and* duty. It's this sense of pleasure and duty that motivates someone like Andrew Burton, whose notion of photojournalism as a window to view the wider world stands in stark contrast to the vision of hyper-personalized news streams.[41]

Those news streams will say a lot about us—who our friends are, as Bilton predicts, or that we are hungry for a burrito, as Jarvis imagines—while Burton still believes that the media should also aim to provide a lens for seeing otherness. Where one side puts the self and its immediate passions front and center, the other is turned outward, intent on acknowledging the stubborn persistence of perspectives and experiences that aren't our own. The news, in this second instance, can never be reduced to something as simple as "what we want" because when we cast our gaze toward the beyond, there is no way to know what we'll see.

There are reasons to doubt that what we want is only obvious or solipsistic. As Maria Popova, founder and editor of the erudite Web site Brain Pickings, has observed, the dominant way knowledge and information are organized online pushes us toward the already familiar instead of broadening our horizons: "An algorithm can only work with existing data. It can only tell you what you might like, based on what you have liked."[42]

There's also a persistent chronology bias built into most platforms, the most recent posts consistently rising to the top, privileging newness over other worthy qualities (another example is the way Twitter algorithms favor novelty of terms to determine what's trending). Popova willfully subverts both of these tendencies on her site, a wide-ranging and thoughtfully curated repository of unexpected gems that are sometimes decades or even centuries old, and has earned a dedicated following for her efforts.

Similarly, for all the talk about content needing to be quick and timely to lure readers, the material that was the most timeless got the strongest response on the *Investigative Voice* Web site while it existed. For example, Janis told me of his "dispatch" series where he spent three days at a time in various neighborhoods interviewing locals with an eye toward providing a more complex narrative about the social and economic serration and corrupt criminal justice system that have put Baltimore on the map. What Janis has seen in the reaction to these pieces is "the exact opposite of the common wisdom." Months later they still attracted readers and inspired discussion despite the absence of a news hook.

"The mantra of the Web is about capturing eyeballs by embel-

lishing sites with bells and whistles to draw in multitudes of visitors," Janis wrote in an essay for Harvard's Nieman Journalism Lab
that touched on the shortcomings of that approach, contrasting the
engagement model where reporting cuts deep instead of going wide.
None of the undergraduate students Janis regularly speaks to wants
to go into the eyeball business, he told me; they all envision a higher
calling.

While students may not want to spend their days chasing eyeballs, that's what the market will likely demand that they do. Instead
of exploring important topics at necessary length, they'll get a job
shortening the work of others, collecting links from across the Web,
cutting and condensing the material into bite-size chunks. It's what
one media blogger, fresh out of college, calls working in the salt
mines of the aggregator.

"Yes, it's gross in many ways and could be considered a form of
bottom-feeding," he admits. "As a child of this moment myself, and
defensive as it may seem, I have to say: the kids are not to blame."
Resistance to this new order may not be futile, but it is not easy. "To
date, I have made roughly 1,107 times more money linking to thinly
sourced reports about Lindsay Lohan than I have reporting any original news. . . . But once you factor in money spent on schooling, the
earnings I've received outside of aggregation-oriented writing positions is still in the bloodiest shade of red imaginable. It's unlikely
the numbers will ever even out."[43]

4

UNEQUAL UPTAKE

Not long after WikiLeaks released its enormous cache of classified diplomatic cables, making the private observations of jaded attachés public for all to see, I spent a Saturday afternoon at a quickly assembled conference trying to make sense of the implications. The conversation hinged on the tangled theme of media, technology, and politics. Does WikiLeaks represent a new kind of transnational investigative journalism? Has the Web made us all reporters? Is transparency an unambiguous good? Should all information be free, to everyone, everywhere? The United States government had been caught off its guard and the audience was electrified by the possibilities of networked people power.

Onstage a series of panelists including Arianna Huffington, Douglas Rushkoff, Esther Dyson, and Andrew Keen gave short presentations, their remarks occasionally punctuated by questions from the floor. "Information flow is corrosive to institutions, whether it's record labels or a state ministry," Mark Pesce, a regular commenter on technology, rapturously proclaimed from a large screen on the stage, his head beamed in over a choppy video connection. Our

being "hyper-connected" has made us "hyper-empowered," he continued, a state of affairs that will lead, inevitably, to "hyper-democracy."
Fighting back against mighty monolithic institutions seemed so
easy. We all had the tools: computers and mobile phones, Internet
access, social networks. "We are passing from a world organized
around power-to-power transactions to one based on peer-to-peer
engagement," Jeff Jarvis, the event's moderator, proclaimed, inspired
by Assange's example.

As the panelists waxed on, I thought back to my recent trip to
the Gulf Coast in the midst of the Deepwater Horizon disaster, when
the oil was gushing out of the ocean floor at a dizzying rate. Floating
on a skiff between the islands of grass that make up the bayou, some
locals pointed out the channels that prospectors had been cutting
for decades through the wetlands in search of petroleum, eroding
the coast and choking the trees, endangering those who live farther
inland by eliminating nature's best defense against storms. We
watched grimy birds pecking their way across toxic shores and saw
dolphins shimmying through reeking water, the mist leaving a
grinding, metallic taste on our tongues, a noxious reminder of the
two million gallons of dispersants dumped into the ocean. "Thanks
for coming to help us get our story out there," people said to my
friend, who was reporting on the spill for a literary magazine.

Were the people I met in Louisiana citizens of Pesce's hyper-
democracy? Was I, hyper-empowered with my smartphone and
social media contacts? That's not how I felt down south, where my
impotence was thrown into unpleasant relief by the enormity of the
unfolding catastrophe.

Some days after that boat ride, we visited an organization serving one of the region's Vietnamese communities. Many of them had
come to New Orleans as refugees and their lives had been turned
upside down a second time by the spill; their jobs disappeared overnight. Standing in the courtyard, we made small talk with two men
who looked like journalists. After some cajoling, it came out that

they worked for BP making media that showed the "positive" side of the crisis, short reports that were heavily promoted on YouTube and across the Web.

They were part of the company's spectacular public relations campaign, which included purchasing popular search terms like "oil spill" from Google to ensure their links were at the top of all results. One analyst estimated the company spent upwards of ten thousand dollars a day to maintain its prominent position in online searches, in addition to the almost one hundred million dollars it allocated to an advertising blitz in the three months after the disaster.

In many ways, the disaster in the Gulf was remarkably visible (although a quickly imposed ruling barred anyone from going within sixty-five feet of any response vessels or booms on the water or beaches, under threat of civil penalty of up to forty thousand dollars and a Class D felony punishable by up to fifteen years in jail). It was a media event for the new age: thousands of us sat glued to streaming footage of the oil rushing from its source; we forwarded videos of the burning rig, black smoke choking the sky; Stephen Colbert's pithy comment—"In honor of oil-soaked birds, 'tweets' are now 'gurgles' "—became the most retweeted of the year.

But sitting in the boat, I realized just how profoundly the decks were stacked against independent truth tellers—and not only because we were self-financed and especially vulnerable to bullying regulations. Deep investigations into questions about what had caused the blowout, the devastation of the local ecosystem and economy, the health risks associated with fuel and dispersants, and the work needed to be done monitoring the four thousand oil platforms and twenty-seven thousand old oil wells, many of them leaking, were well beyond the scope of any individual.

Even Julian Assange had been unable to act independently, joining up with major news organizations like the *New York Times* and the *Guardian* to release the thousands of cables. WikiLeaks had been organized initially around the premise that the public would sift through and interpret raw data, collaboratively writing necessary analysis, making sense of the issues and evidence without professional censors and meddling middlemen.

That turned out to be "not at all true," Assange lamented. "Media are the only channels that have the motivation and resources required to have a real impact." It wasn't that the WikiLeaks mastermind had lost faith in people to think for themselves; rather, he recognized that they lacked the time the task required and the power to legitimize and publicize the results. Motivation and resources, time and power—these are assets that are not evenly distributed, even if the Internet has removed many of the old barriers to entry. They are inequalities that we must take into account when we talk about the network's "level playing field."

The desire to transcend earthly inequality has suffused discussions of the Internet for decades. Early techno-utopians long ago declared that even the atom was "past" and promised the "tyranny of matter" overthrown.[1] The terrestrial and corporeal, they confidently predicted, would soon be abandoned for the weightless Web. Unencumbered by our fleshy selves and released from the material conditions that constrain them, everyone would be made equal by binary code, free to participate as peers on an open network.

"We are creating a world that all may enter without privilege or prejudice accorded by race, economic power, military force, or station of birth. Ours is a world that is both everywhere and nowhere, but it is not where bodies live," John Perry Barlow wrote in his influential Declaration of the Independence of Cyberspace. "The caste system is an artifact of the world of atom," Nicholas Negroponte declared. Before he reinvented himself as a techno-skeptic, the virtual reality pioneer Jaron Lanier concurred. "The Web was built by millions of people simply because they wanted it, without need, greed, fear, hierarchy, authority figures, ethnic identification, advertising, or any other form of manipulation," he enthused. New-media enthusiasts have stuck with this attitude. In *The Wealth of Networks* Yochai Benkler proclaims, "We can live a life more authored by our own will and imagination than by the material and social conditions in which we find ourselves."

It's an inspiring idea, but it's not true. Material and social conditions have not given way to will and imagination. Neither the body nor its social context has become irrelevant. The disparities of the off-line world have not been upended and we do not have equal access to the tools of creative production and capacity to attract an audience.

Despite proclamations to the contrary, the online and off-line worlds are not separate; the digital is not distinct from "real life," a realm where analog prejudices are abandoned. While the Internet offers marginalized groups powerful and potentially world-changing opportunities to meet and act together, new technologies also magnify inequality, reinforcing elements of the old order. Networks do not eradicate power: they distribute it in different ways, shuffling hierarchies and producing new mechanisms of exclusion.

Even as social stratifications have been challenged by the digital transformation, new pecking orders have taken root. There's a troubling segmentation of populations in terms of the tools, time, and know-how needed to participate in virtual life; familiar prejudices exist online without vital checks and balances; there's an increasing bias toward what scholars call "homophily" (the inclination to seek out the familiar) with a corresponding threat to diversity. Moreover, a winner-take-all, jackpot economy has emerged, with audiences and the attendant rewards directed to a surprisingly small range of sources. These trends belie the claim of a more democratic culture.

When you have a laptop at home and a smartphone in your pocket, it can be easy to forget that not everyone is online. Globally, most of the population is not. In the United States, one-third of households lack broadband access. The rate at which the gap is closing has slowed in recent years, with rural communities, low-income people, and minorities left behind. While Latinos and African Americans have gained some ground thanks to mobile technology, wireless smartphones are inferior substitutes for wired connections.

"While we still talk about 'the' Internet, we increasingly have two separate access marketplaces: high-speed wired and second-class wireless," law professor Susan Crawford explained in an op-ed. "High-speed access is a superhighway for those who can afford it, while racial minorities and poorer and rural Americans must make do with a bike path." Mobile connections cost more, are subject to data caps, and are less open, adaptable, and generative. Handheld devices simply can't compare to personal computers if you want to do a long-distance learning program, fill out a résumé, start a business, program an app, write a long essay, or edit a feature-length film.[2]

Digital democracy requires that these gulfs be closed. Yet research shows that simply making sure everyone is able to log on to the Internet is not enough. Conversations about technology tend to focus on connectivity, reinforcing the assumption that inequality will cease to be a concern once everyone is plugged in. Eszter Hargittai, a sociologist at Northwestern University, has spent over a decade showing why this is not the case: there is a "second level digital divide" that takes the form of socially stratified variations in online skills and behaviors.

Even among the highly connected college-age set, Hargittai's work reveals a stark divergence in rates of participation, dependent on socioeconomic status, race, and gender, with men considerably more likely to participate online than women. Despite the

opportunity to engage in the creation and distribution of personal projects, only a small minority of young people actually do
so—there is an "unequal uptake," as Hargittai describes the phenomenon.

Creative participation, it turns out, is neither universally nor ran-
domly distributed among a diverse population. "These findings sug-
gest that Internet access may not, in and of itself, level the playing
field when it comes to potential pay-offs of being online," Hargittai
warns. "Rather, those from more privileged backgrounds may reap
more of its benefits if they are more likely to use it in potentially
beneficial ways."

The ways in which inequality off-line carries over to our online
lives is dramatically evident if we focus on gender. Within families, women shoulder a disproportionate share of household and
child-rearing responsibilities, with substantially less leisure time to
devote to going online. Though a handful of high-powered celebrity "mommy bloggers" have managed to attract massive audiences and ad revenue by documenting their daily travails, the odds
of the Internet converting your experience into fame and fortune
don't look so good, especially if you aim to write about something
other than child-rearing, your rugged cowboy husband, or sponsored
products.[3] In the professional fields where blogging has become
popular, such as philosophy, law, and science, women are notoriously
underrepresented; by one count only around 20 percent of science
bloggers identify as women.[4]

An otherwise optimistic white paper by the UK think tank Demos
on the rise of amateur creativity, much of which takes place online,
reported that white males are far more likely to commit seriously to
"pro-am" activities—to be hobbyists with professional standards—
than other social groups, while low-income women with dependent
children lag far behind.[5] The only way to close the gap, the authors
suggested, would be to improve access to educational resources,

expand career opportunities, and equalize domestic duties between women and men—to transform, in other words, the material and social conditions in which women find themselves.

Yet there are obstacles to engagement that can't be explained by external factors alone. They are psychological, unconscious, and insidious. In a revealing study conducted twice over a span of five years—and yielding the same results both times—Hargittai tested and interviewed one hundred Internet users and found that there was no significant variation in their online competency. In terms of sheer ability, the sexes were equal. The difference was in their self-assessment. The men were certain they did well, while the women were wracked by self-doubt.[6] "Not a single woman among all our female study subjects called herself an 'expert' user," Hargittai noted, "while not a single male ranked himself as a complete novice or 'not at all skilled.'"

This misperception, Hargittai warns, likely contributes to women's reluctance to engage online. The problem, despite its technological spin, is not new. As the historian Germaine Greer said in her 1979 study of the obstacles female painters faced through the ages (almost all of whom were the talented offspring of established artists, otherwise they would not have had access to materials or training): "Daughters were ruled by love and loyalty; they were more highly praised for virtue and sweetness than for their talent, and they devalued their talent accordingly."[7]

Reading Hargittai's study, the results hardly surprised me. I've seen innumerable female friends be passed over by less talented but more assertive men. I've had countless people—older and male, always—assume that someone else must have conducted the interviews for my documentary films, as though there's no way a young woman could have managed such a thing without assistance. Research shows that people routinely underestimate women's abilities, not least women themselves.

When it comes to specialized technical know-how—whether it be science or math, cinematography or audio engineering—women are assumed to be less competent unless they prove otherwise. In tech circles, for example, new gadgets and programs are often introduced as being so easy your mother or grandmother could use them, the implication being that your father and grandfather already get it.

Curiously, these belittling attitudes are frequently displayed by members of the very subculture inclined to celebrate the freedom that comes from anonymity online, often invoking the caption of the now-classic *New Yorker* cartoon, "On the Internet, nobody knows you're a dog." Worse, the Internet has become a vehicle for hounding women and members of racial and sexual minorities. The hateful trolling—the racist, sexist, and homophobic comments that plague the Web like some untreatable rash—is only part of the problem; threats of sexual violence are depressingly routine.[8]

"The people who were posting comments about me were speculating as to how many abortions I've had, and they talked about 'hate-fucking' me," blogger Jill Filipovic told the *Guardian* after photos of her were uploaded to a vitriolic online forum. "I don't think a man would get that; the harassment of women is far more sexualized—men may be told that they're idiots, but they aren't called 'whores.'" Laurie Penny, a young political columnist who has faced similar harassment, put it this way: a "[woman's] opinion, it seems, is the short skirt of the internet. Having one and flaunting it is somehow asking an amorphous mass of almost-entirely male keyboard-bashers to tell you how they'd like to rape, kill and urinate on you."

Given the number of prominent women who have spoken out about their experiences of being bullied and intimidated online— scenarios that sometimes escalate to the release of private information, including home addresses, e-mail passwords, and social security numbers—it is clear that these are not isolated incidents.[9] Indeed, a

University of Maryland study strongly suggests as much. Posters with female usernames, researchers were shocked to discover, received twenty-five times the number of malicious messages compared with those whose designations were masculine or ambiguous. The findings were so alarming that the authors advised parents to instruct their daughters to use sex-neutral monikers online. "Kids can still exercise plenty of creativity and self-expression without divulging their gender," a well-meaning professor said, effectively accepting that young girls must hide who they really are to participate in digital life.[10]

Not all discrimination is so overt. Another study, published by the *Harvard Business Review*, analyzed social patterns on Twitter, where female users outnumbered males by 10 percent, to reveal the resistance women face while also unearthing signs of internalized misogyny. "We found that an average man is almost twice more likely to follow another man than a woman," the researchers reported, while "an average woman is 25% more likely to follow a man than a woman. These results cannot be explained by different tweeting activity—both men and women tweet at the same rate."[11] In the comment thread following an article explaining the results, a handful of women confessed that they used the service under male-sounding pseudonyms to be taken more seriously.

Research conducted by Matthew Hindman, a professor of media and public affairs at George Washington University, presents even more astonishing insights into the ways off-line disparities are reflected online or even amplified. In his 2008 book *The Myth of Digital Democracy*, Hindman reports the results of a survey he conducted of the top ten blogs. Only one belonged to a female writer. A wider census of every political blog with an average of over two thousand visitors a week, or a total of eighty-seven sites, yielded appalling results—only five were run by women. "These numbers are in stark contrast with traditional journalists," Hindman summed up, pointing out that the American Society of News Editors had put the percentage of female news reporters nearer to 37 percent.[12] Racial and ethnic minorities, he discovered, scored no better. There were no "identifiable African Americans among the top thirty bloggers," though there was "one Asian blogger, and one of mixed Latino heritage."

When accounting for audience share, it turns out the blogosphere is less diverse than the notoriously whitewashed op-ed pages of old-school newspapers.[13] The bloggers who get the most eyeballs are not "pajama-clad amateurs taking on the old media from the comfort of their sofas," contrary to the dominant stereotype. "Overwhelmingly, they are well-educated white male professionals." However, as Hindman observes, "most Americans are not white men"—a fact that any real version of cultural democracy would reflect.

Real-world diversity is nowhere to be seen on the rosters of technology conferences, where speakers regularly take the stage declaring a democratic upheaval, seemingly oblivious to the fact that their audience looks just like them. In early 2013, in reaction to the announcement of yet another all-male lineup at a prominent Web gathering, a pledge was posted on the Web site of the *Atlantic* asking men to refrain from speaking at events where women are not represented. The list of signatories was almost immediately removed "due to a flood of spam/trolls." The conference organizer, a successful developer, dismissed the uproar over Twitter. "I don't feel [a] need to defend this, but am happy with our process," he stated.[14] Instituting quotas, he insisted, would be a "discriminatory" way of creating diversity.

This sort of rationalization means new-media companies look remarkably like the old ones they aspire to replace: male, pale, and privileged. While the percentage of computer and information sciences degrees women earned rose from 14 percent to 37 percent between 1970 and 1985, that share declined to 18 percent by 2008.[15] An article in the *New York Times* about gender and tech reported on the barriers women face in Silicon Valley: Facebook's Sheryl Sandberg and Yahoo!'s Marissa Mayer excepted, the notion of the boy genius prevails.

Over 85 percent of venture capitalists are men looking to invest in other men, and women make forty-nine cents for every dollar their male counterparts rake in. Though 40 percent of private businesses are women-owned nationwide, only 8 percent of the venture-backed tech start-ups are. Established companies are equally segregated. The National Center for Women and Information Technology reports that of the top one hundred tech companies, only 6 percent of chief executives are women.[16] The numbers for Asians who ascend to the top are comparable despite the fact that they make up a third of all Silicon Valley software engineers.[17] In 2010, not even 1 percent of the founders of Silicon Valley companies were black.[18]

Data on gender within online communities, routinely held up as exemplars of a new, open culture, are especially damning. First, consider Wikipedia. One survey revealed that women write less than 15 percent of the articles on the site, despite the fact that they use the resource in equal numbers to men. Collaborative filtering sites like Reddit and Slashdot, heralded by the digerati as the cultural curating mechanisms of the future, cater to users who are up to 90 percent male and overwhelmingly young, wealthy, and white.[19]

Reddit, in particular, has achieved notoriety for its misogynist culture, with threads where rapists can recount their exploits without fear of reprisal and photos of underage girls are posted under headings like "Chokeabitch," "Niggerjailbait," and "Creepshots" ("When you are in public, you do not have a reasonable expectation of privacy," moderators posted. "We kindly ask women to respect our right to admire your bodies and stop complaining").[20]

Despite being held up as a paragon of political virtue in contrast to its propriety counterpart, open source programming employs very few women, only 1.5 percent of programmers, a number far lower than the computing profession as a whole. Analysts have cited as the cause everything from chauvinism and assumptions of inferiority to outrageous examples of real-life impropriety (including sexual harassment at conferences where programmers gather) to a lack of women mentors and role models. Yet the advocates of open source production continue to insist that this culture exemplifies a new and ethical social order ruled by principles of equality, inclusivity, freedom, and democracy.[21]

These statistics are significant not only because they give the lie to the egalitarian claims of techno-utopians but because they indicate the relatively limited experiences and assumptions of the people who design the architecture and systems through which we navigate and use the Internet. The values of programmers and the corporate officers who employ them shape the online worlds we inhabit. The choices they make can segregate us further or create new connections; the algorithms they devise can exclude voices or bring more people into the fold; the interfaces they invent can expand our sense of human possibility or limit it to the already familiar.

Online and off, the people who create social structures need to be aware of and sensitive to human difference. This difference is crucial to realizing the democratizing potential of technology. The range of voices and perspectives exposed must be expanded; cultural diversity and cultural democracy are intertwined.

In a powerful sense, programmers are the new urban planners, shaping the virtual frontier into the spaces we occupy, building the boxes into which we fit our lives, and carving out the routes we travel—which is why more of us need to learn to write code. What vision of a vibrant, thriving city informs their view? Is it a place that fosters chance encounters or somewhere that favors the predictable? Are the communities mixed or gated? Are they full of privately owned shopping malls and sponsored billboards or are there truly public squares? Is privacy respected? Is civic engagement encouraged? What kinds of people live in these places and how are they invited to express themselves? (Why, for example, is the word "like" so pervasive online as opposed to "interesting," "important," or "outrageous"?) As the writer Charles Petersen has observed, we are still waiting for the digital equivalent of Jane Jacobs to appear. Let her come quick.

In 1970 a woman named Jo Freeman published "The Tyranny of Structurelessness," a critique of the informal nature of women's consciousness-raising groups popular during that period.[22] The article spread like wildfire and remains a classic to this day, for it articulated a problem many women had felt but could not quite put into words. Though Second Wave feminism had been inspired by the civil rights movements of the 1960s, bringing the "problem that has no name" into sharp relief, it also emerged partly in reaction to the New Left, the student movement against the Vietnam War, which united around an idealistic vision of "participatory democracy."

In theory the New Left wanted to remake society, but in practice old divisions of labor went unchallenged: men got all the glory, becoming leaders and spokespeople, while women were left with the dull office work, their efforts invisible behind the scenes. Fed up, women sought to create their own spaces, free from male domination and expectation. In the feminist community, at least, there would be no leaders and no followers. Equality would be total.

Freeman said it wasn't that easy. The open nature of the new groups, she argued, hadn't gotten rid of the problem of domination but obscured it. Her point, radically simplified, was that the disavowal of power within the women's liberation community had actually concealed its covert manipulation. Informal elites, she persuasively argued, can be more pernicious than formal ones because they deny their own existence. The result is more of the same: power imbalance and a lack of diversity.

"Contrary to what we would like to believe, there is no such thing as a structureless group," Freeman wrote. Instead, "the idea becomes a smokescreen for the strong or the lucky to establish unquestioned hegemony over others."

> Thus structurelessness becomes a way of masking power, and within the women's movement is usually most strongly advocated by those who are the most powerful (whether they are conscious of their power or not). As long as the structure of the group is informal, the rules of how decisions are made are known only to a few and awareness of power is limited to those who know the rules. Those who do not know the rules and are not chosen for initiation must remain in confusion, or suffer from paranoid delusions that something is happening of which they are not quite aware.

I've felt that paranoid delusion myself. How do you explain inequalities in a system where explicit discrimination doesn't exist? How do you make sense of homogeneity when there's no sign on the door excluding different types of people? For example, what accounts for the fact that so few women direct movies—9 percent, by some counts—despite the fact that they attend film school in roughly equal number to men? Why does the celluloid ceiling persist when the field is, supposedly, open to all?

Freeman's essay provides some insight, which is why I often recommend it when I hear talk about the inherently open and egalitarian nature of the Internet, for it helps to explain the troubling persistence of inequality within online communities. Joseph M. Reagle, author of *Good Faith Collaboration: The Culture of Wikipedia*, is among those who have begun to challenge these claims. Reagle notes that the habits, dynamics, and values of open communities like Wikipedia actually aggravate the gender gap instead of closing it.

The peculiar brand of libertarianism in vogue within technology circles means a minority of members—a couple of outspoken misogynists, for example—can disproportionately affect the behavior and mood of the group under the cover of free speech. The "ideology and rhetoric of freedom and openness," Reagle explains, is too often used to "(a) suppress concerns by labeling them as draconian or 'censorship' and to (b) rationalize low female participation as simply a matter of women's personal preference and choice." Women are not supposed to complain about their treatment, but if they leave the community that's a decision they alone are responsible for.

As Freeman made clear in her essay, women's groups assumed that the absence of structure would help free them from oppression and elitism, bureaucracy and convention; few paused to reflect on the limits of this strategy or critically assess the new power dynamics that were emerging. The early adherents of openness failed to reflect on the benefits of institutions, which, as the sociologist Max Weber observed, offer some protection against arbitrary forms of charismatic authority, however problematic bureaucratic arrangements can be. In the four decades since Freeman's essay was published, structurelessness has ossified into ideology and can be seen in the current reverence for "openness."

When the democratic protests spread across Egypt in early 2011 and then again in 2013, the romantic ideal of structureless organizing appeared to fulfill its promise. Westerners watched in awe as a diffusely connected public ousted an authoritarian, top-down government and were inspired. Technological pundits credited the Web, proclaiming that the revolution was powered by social media, the peer-to-peer connections made possible by Silicon Valley. One Egyptian family even named their newborn daughter Facebook. The use of communicative tools, it was said again and again, had facilitated a "naturally" "leaderless" revolution. Social networks had over-thrown a dictatorship.

Zeynep Tufekci, a sociologist at the University of Maryland, took issue with these claims in a fascinating post called "Can 'Leaderless Revolutions' Stay Leaderless?" Even if the democratic movement in Egypt had truly lacked leaders (a debatable assertion given the role trade unions played, for example), Tufekci argued that social media and peer-to-peer networks in no way guaranteed that the situation would stay that way. Social media, Tufekci explained, do not guard against the "iron law of oligarchy," the tendency of even democratic groups to develop oligarchic characteristics—they may, in fact, facilitate it. "Networks which start out as diffuse can and likely will quickly evolve into hierarchies not in spite but because of their open and flat nature," she explained.[23] "Influence in the online world can actually spontaneously exhibit even sharper all-or-nothing dynamics compared to the off-line world, with every-thing below a certain threshold becoming increasingly weaker while those who first manage to cross the threshold becoming widely popular."

To illustrate her case, Tufekci crunched data from the social media feeds of various Egyptian activists, demonstrating that the authority and visibility of a few figures had been swiftly and dra-matically enhanced, skyrocketing in comparison to their comrades. Despite the Web's amazing potential for political mobilizing, Tufekci's experiment demonstrates a countervailing tendency, underscoring the way new technologies have the capacity to entrench advantage and amplify the sway of a small group.

"A fact little-understood but pertinent to this discussion," Tufekci continued, "is that relatively flat networks can quickly generate hier-archical structures even without any attempt at a power grab by emergent leaders or by any organizational, coordinated action." A few lucky individuals, in other words, don't necessarily have to try very hard to propel themselves to prominence. Instead, their ascension happens through a perfectly common process called preferential attachment, also known as the "bandwagon" or "Matthew" effect, the latter name inspired by a biblical quotation: "For to all those who have, more will be given, and they will have an abundance; but from those who have nothing, even what they have will be taken away."[24]

Tufekci's results are fairly counterintuitive, but a growing number of scholars and concerned experts are corroborating the complexity of power online. The problem goes well beyond the vacuums of authority Jo Freeman warned about, for the Web is not actually unstructured, despite the fact that it is open. An elaborate system organized around hubs and links, the Web has a surprising degree of inequality built into its very architecture.[25]

There are different types of networks and few are truly flat. Over the entire Web, traffic and links are distributed according to "power laws." These distributions tend to follow what's known as the 80/20 rule, exemplified by a situation in which 80 percent of a desirable resource goes to 20 percent of the population: 20 percent of a society's citizens possessing 80 percent of the wealth or land are the classic examples. They are winner-take-all, rich-get-richer scenarios, which means that power laws are less equal than the classic bell curve.

Human height, for example, follows a bell curve. If our size followed a power-law distribution, a small percentage of the population would be thousands of feet tall while the majority of people would be very short. Because power laws are so heavily weighted toward the top (the head), most elements are actually below average (the tail), however strange that sounds: a handful of large events coexist with numerous small ones.

Consequently, power laws are starkly inegalitarian. The top elements are far more popular than those in the middle, and those, in turn, are far more popular than the ones on the bottom. They are also ubiquitous online, a fact that has serious ramifications for political and cultural democracy and diversity. In his book *Linked*, physicist Albert-László Barabási investigated network phenomena by mapping online space and came to this dramatic conclusion: "The most intriguing result . . . is the complete absence of democracy, fairness, and egalitarian values on the Web."

These dynamics partly explain why, for all of its overwhelming, exciting variation, the Internet has a strange tendency toward monopoly. Aided by preferential attachment and network effects (the phenomenon of a good or service becoming more valuable the more people who use it), a handful of winners emerge, overshadowing other available options. While you can find something related to any subject online—medieval polyphonic music, lepidoptery, retroviruses, you name it—there is still one leading search engine (Google), one major bookstore (Amazon), one predominant market (eBay), one popular place to see movies (Netflix—a site that accounts for more than 40 percent of U.S. bandwidth usage most evenings), and so on.

Meanwhile, data from Compete, a Web analytics company, indicate that digital concentration may only be increasing: in 2001, ten Web sites accounted for 31 percent of U.S. page views; by 2010, that number had skyrocketed to 75 percent. "Big sucks the traffic out of small," Yuri Milner, an investor who owns a chunk of Facebook, told *Wired* magazine. "In theory you can have a few very successful individuals controlling hundreds of millions of people. You can become big fast, and that favors the domination of strong people."

Preferential attachment, network effects, and the power laws they produce matter, in part, because they intensify and epitomize the old inequities we hoped the Internet would overthrow, from the star system to the hit-driven manufacturing of movies, music, and books. Winner-take-all markets promote certain types of culture at the expense of others, can make it harder for niche cultures and late bloomers to flourish, and contribute to broader income inequality.[26]

More specifically, where cultural production is concerned, the persistence of power laws refutes the myth of independent creators competing on even ground. The most vocal proponent of this myth, Chris Anderson, has declared the end of the "water cooler era" when we "listened, watched, and read from the same relatively small pool of mostly hit content," for an age when "we're all into different things." In his book *The Long Tail*, Anderson describes the Internet as an infinite shelf at the biggest store in the universe (a depressingly reductive image, though that's another issue), where demand will inevitably move from the head to the tail, trickling down from the top of the distribution curve to the bottom. The bigger will get smaller and the smaller, bigger; the tail will not just elongate but fatten. The creative fringes will therefore flourish at the expense of the commercial center, and eventually the sales of "misses" will grow until they equal, or outpace, the sale of "hits."[27]

The evidence all around us contradicts this view. Charts are still topped, box offices smashed, sales records broken. In 2013 Hollywood had its best summer ever. The head and tail are not coming closer together but spreading apart, macro- and micro-dilating, as the stuff in between disappears. The rise of e-books, experts point out, has coincided with the polarization of the publishing industry, with mid-size companies closing shop or being swallowed up by conglomerates, the gulf between small and large companies widening. It's a phenomenon Matthew Hindman called the "missing middle" after observing that online traffic to news Web sites is even more concentrated than print circulation at both extremes, the very top and the very bottom.

Anita Elberse, a Harvard Business School professor, came to a similar conclusion based on her study of data from music streaming and movie rental services: "Although no one disputes the lengthening of the tail (clearly more obscure products are being made available for purchase every day), the tail is likely to be extremely flat and populated by titles that are mostly a diversion for consumers whose appetite for true blockbusters continues to grow."[28]

Closer examination by Elberse and others shows that the leveling power of the long tail has been overstated. Netflix sees eight-tenths of 1 percent of inventory generating 30 percent of all rentals.[29] A study of YouTube showed that the top 10 percent of most-played videos made up almost 80 percent of total plays, with the top 20 percent making up almost 90 percent. In music, too, the head still prevails: of the 76,875 new albums released in 2011 that sold at least one copy, the top 1,500 accounted for approximately 90 percent of sales. Of those, a mere 11 albums sold 1 million or more copies.[30] And even when we look beyond sales figures to other Web-based metrics, it's undeniable that big hits dominate.[31]

Spotify's most popular playlists generally mirror the Billboard charts and in 2012 Nicki Minaj, Katy Perry, and Coldplay were among the most streamed artists on the planet. Meanwhile, the circle of winners at the top is shrinking: back in 1986, there were thirty-one number one songs by twenty-nine different artists; by 2008, six artists were responsible for almost half of the sixty-six songs that had risen to number one.[32] Shockingly, the majors control a larger portion of market today than they did in the late nineties, before people started downloading music en masse.

In journalism the story is the same, with an enormous amount of attention concentrated on a handful of name-brand sites. Thus the annual State of the News Media report stated:

> Critics have tended to see technology democratizing the media and traditional journalism in decline. Audiences, they say, are fragmenting across new information sources, breaking the grip of media elites. . . . The reality, increasingly, appears more complex. . . . Even with so many new sources, more people now consume what old-media newsrooms produce, particularly from print, than before. Online, for instance, the top 10 news Web sites, drawing mostly from old brands, are more of an oligarchy, com-

manding a larger share of audience than they did in the legacy media.

According to Nielson, which looked at forty-six hundred news and information Web sites, the top 7 percent attract 80 percent of all traffic, with organizations like CNN and MSNBC luring the bulk of the audience.[33] Couple this with Matthew Hindman's research and the image of the Internet as a Robin Hood stealing from the audience rich to give to the audience poor is completely obliterated.

In an analysis of political blogs, what Hindman found was striking: "Instead of the 'inevitable' fragmentation of online media, audiences on the Web are actually more concentrated on the top ten or twenty outlets than are traditional media like newspapers and magazines." Not only was "traffic far more concentrated on top bloggers than newspaper readership is on top journalists" (thus fitting the winner-take-all pattern common on the Web), bloggers were arguably more "elite" than their old-media counterparts when looking at factors such as educational attainment, professional achievement, race, and gender.

In an interview with the consulting firm McKinsey, Google's Eric Schmidt provided a reality check. "I would like to tell you that the Internet has made such a level playing field that the Long Tail is absolutely the place to be, that there's so much differentiation, so much diversity, so many new voices. I'd love to tell you that that's in fact how it really works. Unfortunately, it's not," Schmidt said. "While you can have a long tail strategy, you better have a head, because that's where all the revenue is." Moreover, he added, the Internet will probably lead to bigger blockbusters and more concentration of brands. "It's a larger distribution medium and when you get everybody together they still want to have one superstar. It's a bigger superstar. It's no longer a U.S. superstar, it's a global superstar. Global celebrities, global scandals, global politicians."[34]

In online culture, as in off, advantage begets advantage. When we click on the top search results or watch the FrontPage videos on YouTube or read established blogs, we are jumping on invisible bandwagons, causing the Matthew effect to kick in. Most-read lists and top search results create a feedback loop perpetuating the success of the already successful. When an article becomes "most e-mailed," it garners more attention and thus its reign is extended. The more a viral meme spreads, the more likely you are to catch it. As a consequence, the same silly gags land in all our in-boxes, a small number of Web sites get read by everyone, and a handful of super-celebrities overshadow the millions who languish in obscurity.

The big difference between the real world and the virtual may simply be speed and scale. Online, popular stories are born and die at a breakneck pace, flaring up and burning out like a million miniature supernovas. And yet this fleeting moment of fame is what creators are told to aspire to. No matter that it has been shown that you have better odds of winning the lottery than seeing your video take off (meager odds that plummet even further if your offering does not contain a jokey song, a cute baby, a cat, someone being injured, someone stripping, or a pop culture hook), "going viral" is presented to emerging artists as the secret to creative success.[35]

It seems democratic enough, at least at first glance. Anyone can throw his or her hat into the ring and, who knows, they may give "Charlie Bit My Finger" or "Gangnam Style" a run for its money, or become the next Justin Bieber, or rival whatever obscurity-to-ubiquity tale is currently being peddled as the act to follow. But cultural democracy is not reducible to a contest of attention, the winner rewarded with clicks and likes and retweets and reblogs and—if they're really lucky—dollars.

It's true that the very idea of cultural democracy is a bit of an oxymoron, as if talent and motivation are evenly distributed, but the concept has value nonetheless. Cultural democracy means that a diversity of voices and viewpoints is expressed and accessible; that visibility and notoriety should not be the consequence of cumulative advantage alone; and that influence within the cultural field is achieved by a variety of factors, not simply ceded to those who can afford to pay to be seen and heard.

Democracy also implies the need to protect the minority from the tyranny of the majority. Thus, true cultural democracy is not a popularity contest at all but entails supporting work that not everyone will like and some may even despise—and ensuring that citizens will occasionally be exposed to things they don't necessarily agree with or want to see. Democracy, in both its cultural and its political incarnations, depends on the contact between conflicting perspectives.

Whatever ambiguities attend the concept of cultural democracy—and many do—a fascinating experiment led by network-theory scientist Duncan Watts involving forty-eight songs and fourteen thousand listeners shows what a strange and ultimately unsatisfactory vehicle virality is for achieving it, with implications worth examining in detail. To begin, participants were divided into two groups. One was made up of individuals who knew only the names of the songs and the bands that performed them; they were given no information about their peers' listening preferences or selections. The other group was further divided into eight subgroups, each of which was shown how many times each song had been downloaded by the other participants in their subgroup. The subgroups were called "social-influence worlds" by the researchers, and in each of those worlds songs became hits. Compared to the first group (where listeners were not influenced by the tastes of others), the most popular songs were much more popular and the less popular ones less so when social influence was introduced.

Quality, the researchers determined, wasn't totally irrelevant, it was just overwhelmed by signals from other listeners. "When people knew what other people were doing the success of the songs became more unequal and unpredictable. The song that happened to be successful with the first users in one room became more successful and that led to these kinds of popularity snowballs. Stars became megastars and flops became megaflops," Watts explained.

The Matthew effect holds true even in academia, an arena where one would expect to see more objective standards applied. Yet, as a thorough study by University of Chicago sociologist James Evans published in the esteemed journal *Science* revealed, online academic databases tend to amplify new and already popular material, reducing the number of articles researchers cited and "narrowing" scholarship compared to paper databases. As the number of sources available online broadened, fewer journals and articles were cited, those that were cited were more recent, and citations were connected to fewer sources.

"The forced browsing of print archives may have stretched scientists and scholars to anchor findings deeply into past and present scholarship," Evans explained. "Searching online is more efficient and following hyperlinks quickly puts researchers in touch with prevailing opinion, but this may accelerate consensus and narrow the range of findings and ideas built upon." The trade-off appears to be one between efficiency and diversity. While there is technically more information available than ever before, the speed at which scholars can find "prevailing opinion" online also makes them more likely to follow it. This self-reinforcing consensus about what is important means that other potentially interesting and valuable sources fall by the wayside.[36]

Whether these studies should give succor to culture makers or send them spiraling into despair, I'm unsure. On the one hand, they can take comfort in the fact that the stratospheric success of some is less a referendum on talent than the result of cumulative advantage achieved through a chain of events largely beyond their own control. Or they can bemoan the fact that luck is in far shorter supply than ability when the gulf between the haves and have-nots grows to such extravagant proportions.

Whatever one's view, the song experiment poses a profound challenge to the common misconception that the Internet provides a rational, unmediated marketplace where up-by-their-bootstraps creators meet discerning consumers and the most deserving succeed. The Internet will not effortlessly create a cultural meritocracy ("meritocracy" being a term, it's too often forgotten, with origins in a political satire, a concept invented to mock an imaginary society in which inequality is considered just). The best does not rise to the top. In the off-line world, we always knew that was the case. What is shocking is how profoundly the old wisdom still applies.

What do we lose if we let the middle go missing, if the creative sphere splits in two, a few megahits orbited by trillions of mega-flops? The topology of our cultural landscape has long been twisted by an ever-shrinking number of corporations. Powerful entertainment companies have bought up their competitors, consolidating into a handful of colossi, much the way big-box stores have decimated mom-and-pop shops, paving America over with brand-name sameness and dictating social and economic terms to our society. For years we have understood that this dynamic is detrimental and citizens have pushed back. What is the effect of the expanding corporate goliaths and super-celebrities online?

"We are losing a diversity of institutions in the move to a digital terrain, and it is worth investigating what impact that loss has," writes Tom Slee, a software engineer and author of a book on Walmart's effect on communities. He challenges the assumption that online goliaths are selfless enablers of niche culture just because they offer a bounty of goods. It's entirely possible for each of us, as individuals, to experience an increase in diversity while overall diversity decreases, however paradoxical that may seem.[37] Think of it this way. You get to read national publications like the *Globe and Mail* and the *New York Times* and the *Guardian* online even though your city's two papers have shut down; you can look at a variety of Web sites and peruse digital libraries, while small publishers, libraries, and bookstores close.

Maintaining real-world cultural institutions may be more crucial for diversity and equality than we are currently inclined to admit. For example, it turns out that those imperiled brick-and-mortar bookstores are where people discover interesting titles, even if they often eventually buy them on Amazon: physical stores outperform virtual ones three to one in introducing buyers to books, though more sales take place online.[38] Bookstores, with their limited shelf space, make literary culture more heterogeneous.

Interestingly, it turns out that those online arenas that do not obey power-law dynamics, that do not display the clear winners-take-all hierarchies so common elsewhere on the Web, are closely tied to preexisting networks or real-world establishments, such as university home pages or local newspapers.[39] The variegated nature of the off-line world—its uneven geography, the deep connections of rooted communities, and their distribution bottlenecks— yields different kinds of distribution curves. Would we want to go back to a time when all we had access to was the hometown weekly or the neighborhood cinema? Of course not. But such structures may nonetheless have something to offer us as a way to resist the inequality of online cultural markets.

There are reasons to believe that maintaining diversity will become even more of a challenge as the Internet evolves. While more people are coming online and more content is being uploaded, our experience of the Web is becoming increasingly personalized. New mechanisms have emerged that sift through the chaos of online content, shaping it into a targeted stream. As a consequence, our exposure to difference may actually decrease.

Eli Pariser, the former executive director of MoveOn.org and founder of the viral content site Upworthy, calls this problem the "filter bubble," a phenomenon that stems from the efforts of new-media companies to track the things we like and try to give us more of the same. These mechanisms are "prediction engines," Pariser says, "constantly creating and refining a theory of who you are and what you'll want next."[40]

This kind of personalization is already part of our daily experience in innumerable ways. If you and I search the same category on Google, we get different results based on our search histories. Amazon and Netflix recommend different books and movies depending on what we've previously bought or watched. And there are those ads that follow us across the Web, like the animations promoting Pariser's book that kept popping up after I read about it online.

Pariser says he became interested in the issue when he realized that his conservative contacts had disappeared from his news stream, which made him wonder about the implications for political discourse. What does it mean to be shown only items we already agree with? Before too long, Pariser says, Web sites will cater to our unique sensibilities—the headline on my version of a news site, for example, may be radically different from the one called up for you.

Concern that the Web will lead to narcissism, echo chambers, and balkanization is nothing new, but Pariser's analysis points to something more insidious than the problem of homophily. The filters he warns about are not of our own making. We are not purposefully retreating into our own distinct worlds, becoming more insular. Instead, invisible filter bubbles are imposed on us. Online, no action goes untracked. Our prior choices are compiled, feeding the ids of what we could call algorithmic superegos—systems that determine what we see and what we don't, channeling us toward certain choices while cutting others off.

And while they may make the Internet less overwhelming, these algorithms are not neutral. "The rush to build the filter bubble is absolutely driven by commercial interests," Pariser warns. "It's becoming clearer and clearer that if you want to have lots of people use your Web site, you need to provide them with personally relevant information, and if you want to make the most money on ads, you need to provide them with relevant ads."[41]

Ironically, what distinguishes this process from what Nicholas Negroponte enthusiastically described as "the Daily me"—the ability of individuals to customize their media diets thanks to digital technology—is that the personalization trend is not driven by individual demand but by the pursuit of profit via targeted advertising. And the process will only intensify as technology evolves. Google, for example, is already able to build a "three-dimensional profile" of each of us: first, "the knowledge person"—who we are based on search queries and click-stream data; second, "the social person"—who we are based on whom we communicate to and connect with through e-mail and other social tools; and third, "the embodied person"—namely, our whereabouts as revealed by the physical position of our computer or mobile device. With the Internet-of-things on the horizon, opportunities for data collection will increase as more everyday objects go online. Soon our ovens and automobiles may deliver personalized sales pitches.

In theory, Pariser argues, algorithms could be fairer than fallible humans, introducing us to wider range of material than we may otherwise seek out, expanding our exposure to diversity by being less conscious of race, gender, and class or things like political orientation. But that can happen only if those values are written into the system, a sense of civic responsibility folded purposely into the code. Failing that, the algorithms being created are likely to reflect the dominant social norms of our day and, perhaps, be even more discriminatory than the people who devised them.

We are entering a new age where every aspect of a creative artifact's life can be quantified, measured, and analyzed. The filter bubble and journalism have collided: a generation of new-media moguls targets its products to respond directly to readers' whims, scouring search engine trends, poring over most-e-mailed lists, and crafting content. Big data and entertainment have also intersected, every aspect of the Netflix series *House of Cards*—plotting, casting, directing—undertaken in consultation with the company's staggering reserve of intelligence about users' viewing patterns.

Books are not immune to this data-driven approach (it has been reported that some writers are weaving cliffhangers 10 percent of the way through their novels, right when the standard free sample of an e-book is up, shaping the plot to maximize sales[42]). Electronic readers, by design, read us; the same connection that enables the downloading of manuscripts beams back all manner of information about not just what we are reading but how (and also where and who we are). "They know how fast you read because you have to click to turn the page," Cindy Cohn, legal director at the Electronic Frontier Foundation, told NPR. "It knows if you skip to the end to read how it turns out."

One can imagine the information gathered compiled into new lists: most frequently finished, most often abandoned, or the quickest or slowest page-turners. Those who are privy to this kind of information are busy studying consumer habits. They may deduce that the plot of a certain novel lags midway through by observing that the pace of reading slows, or notice that readers of a nonfiction work skip specific sections. From there it's a step to personalized texts, each copy catered to the individual purchaser's taste—that person hates sad endings, another likes to cry; that person prefers it when the protagonist triumphs while they want the love interest to be blonde.

"If people are buying books but not reading them, or they're quitting after a relatively short period of time reading the book, that ultimately tells you that the customer in this case is dissatisfied," remarked a business consultant with ties to the publishing world.

"Better understanding when people stop reading or stop engaging with your content would help you create better products." But of course there are no objectively better products where art is concerned, only better sellers. What would have happened to *Moby-Dick*, one of the most illustrious flops in the history of literature, if Melville had deep analytics on the rejection of his work?

"It will be very hard for people to watch and consume something that has not, in some sense, been tailored for them," Google's Eric Schmidt predicts. It's a statement that makes sense if your ultimate goal is to match product to person. If my past click-stream shows that I enjoy articles written by white pop music lovers in their thirties, or videos that feature adorable pets in funny situations, why lead me to anything else? If I mainly read recipes or follow investment banking, why feature links about Libya or energy policy? If I'm a voter who cares strongly about abortion rights or gun control, why show me a wider variety of issues?

Instead of being pushed beyond our comfort zones, we'll be cosseted by things we're already accustomed to. Other places and people, other cultural forms and conversations, may slowly disappear from our private, purified corners of the Web. There may be more stuff out there than ever before, but there's a chance we'll be seeing less of it.

Back in the early seventies, fearing that a cultural "gray out" was imminent as a consequence of mass media, the eminent folklorist Alan Lomax was moved to write "An Appeal for Cultural Equity."[43] He began by lambasting those who celebrated commercial media's triumph, decrying the unfair advantage of the centralized "star system" over regional traditions, and highlighting the local musicians put out of work. While some argued that only the "weak and unfit among music and cultures" would vanish, Lomax called that view "false Darwinism applied to culture."

Something precious, he believed, was being lost. With the disappearance of each system, "the human species not only loses a way of viewing, thinking, and feeling but also a way of adjusting to some zone on the planet which fits it and makes it livable; not only that, but we throw away a system of interaction, of fantasy and symbolizing which, in the future, the human race may sorely need." The only way to halt this degradation, Lomax maintained, was to put the principle of cultural equity on par with principles of political, social, and economic justice.

Cultural equity, for Lomax, was not an isolationist creed or a philosophy aiming to freeze cultures like museum exhibits so the rest of the world can gawk. On the contrary, he recognized that cross-pollination makes culture richer and more robust. The most generative and vibrant creative centers in human history have typically occupied migration crossroads and trade routes, where different types of people intersect and infect each other with new ideas and approaches to life. Exchange is essential—the only reason modern communication systems have posed a threat to local cultures is because they have been too one-sided.

Lomax hoped multi-channeled electronic communication would remedy this imbalance. "A properly administered electronic system could carry every expressive dialect and language that we know of, so that each one might have a local system at its disposal for its own spokesmen. Thus, modern communication technology could become the prime force in man's struggle for cultural equity and against the pollution of the human environment," he enthused. All cultures could have their fair share of the airtime on an imaginary system he came to dub the "global jukebox," a vision that introduced criteria by which to gauge cultural equity. To what degree is the system a "two-way street"? Are people both listening and being listened to? Are diverse voices both speaking and being heard?

If there was ever a communication technology with the potential to encourage cultural multiplicity, the Internet is it. And yet the capacity Lomax imagined as central to a multi-channeled system—the potential for increasing exposure to difference and dialogue—is not some inherent or immutable trait of the network. For every attribute that encourages diversity and decentralization on the Web, there is a countervailing push toward homogeneity and concentration. Despite the ease and the immense potential of transcultural communication, there is evidence that we are exposed to surprisingly little of other cultures online. Americans are prone to drastically overestimating just how international they are.

Media scholar Ethan Zuckerman calls this state "imaginary cosmopolitanism."[44] We think we're seeing everything from the hilltop of our home computers, but that's not the case—we may actually be seeing less than we once were. When Lomax wrote his essay, network television devoted around 45 percent of airtime to international news, a number that has plummeted to 15 percent. In an analysis of online consumption, Zuckerman found that we read a whopping 95 percent of our news from domestic sources, despite the international options now available. Studies show that we're equally parochial on social media. Though hundreds of millions of people around the globe use Twitter, "we're far more likely to follow people who are physically close to us than to follow someone outside our home country's borders, or even a few states or provinces away."[45]

What matters is not just who speaks but who is heard. Lomax, for example, imagined some enlightened DJ, playing a representative variety of tunes for a global listenership, a sort of centralized control the Internet thankfully lacks. Given the fact that everyone can voice their opinions online, marginalized voices are often told the solution is to speak more loudly, to make their presence known. If you're feeling left out, start a blog or join Twitter.

The problem with this advice is that it shifts responsibility to populations that have historically been disenfranchised while letting the dominant groups off the hook. After all, no one has to read your latest update just because you wrote it, which means the polyphony of the Web goes unappreciated by the very people who need to hear it. True, blogs and other spaces on the Internet can serve as energizing and organizing tools for those who are disadvantaged or oppressed but, as research has established, minority groups already know more about the experiences of dominant groups than vice versa. The onus to nurture cultural diversity should be on those who are closer to the center, not those who are peripheral.

But who occupies what position, center or periphery, inside or out, included or excluded? These categories are fluctuating, unstable. Back in the pre-Internet days, there were a few obvious ways to prove that diversity was lacking in the cultural realm, even if the actions needed to remedy it were too rarely taken. Directors Guild of America numbers provided incontrovertible proof of the celluloid ceiling. A quick flip through the television channels revealed a whitewashed nation. Magazine mastheads and reporter bylines displayed heterogeneity or lack thereof. The Guerrilla Girls marched through America's museums and found women overrepresented in art—painted on canvas, carved into stone—but rarely present as artists.

It's much harder to measure diversity and discrimination on the vastness of the network with all its nooks and crannies and warped, personalized topography. And when we know bias and bigotry are present—as is often the case now—how are we to address it? Institutions made it possible to install formal mechanisms, such as the Equal Employment Opportunity Commission, to monitor discrimination. It is not clear how such oversight should operate in a fluid digital space.

What is clear is the need to find innovative ways to confront the fact that opportunity and audience remain deeply stratified along predictable lines: race, class, gender, and national origin. Despite the Web's lowered barrier to entry, not everyone has equal resources or time to devote to the creation of art and culture and its promotion. Meanwhile, like still congregates around like, and influence too often trickles up according to luck or money. Big players can ensure prominent placement on iTunes or a seemingly "objective" recommendation on Amazon, which are, like the front tables at Barnes and Noble, bought and paid for. With their ample budgets, they can get their products onto our screens whether we want them there or not, buying advertising or the endorsement of A-list stars or securing other attention-grabbing signals.

The idea, too often promoted by people who write books and command large followings, that things like LOLcats and comment sections have made culture "participatory" is hollow. Democratizing culture means choosing, as a society, to invest in work that is not obviously popular or marketable or easy to understand. It means supporting diverse populations to devote themselves to critical, creative work and then elevating their efforts so they can compete on a platform that is anything but equal.

Perhaps we'll choose to ignore these challenges, satisfied with the Internet as it is and the bounty of choice it offers us. After all, we already have at our fingertips more content than we could consume in a lifetime. Why bother working to ensure that there is even greater diversity? Or we could acknowledge the emerging stratifications and inequalities, which have few checks and balances.

Powerful hierarchies have come to define the medium, as Matthew Hindman observes: "This hierarchy is structural, woven in to the hyperlinks that make up the Web; it is economic, in the dominance of companies like Google, Yahoo!, and Microsoft; and it is social, in the small group of white, highly educated, male professionals who are vastly overrepresented in online opinion." Hierarchy may be a legitimate and unavoidable way to organize the abundance of online content, he continues, but "these hierarchies are not neutral with respect to democratic values." To think otherwise is to sell most of the world short.[46]

If equity is something we value, we have to build it into the system, developing structures that encourage fairness, serendipity, deliberation, and diversity through a process of trial and error. There are methods that could be employed to prevent the transformation of flat, relatively unhierarchical networks into hierarchical ones, just as it is possible to program search-and-discovery systems and utilize big data to encourage risk taking instead of reinforcing prior preferences. Any strategies adopted need to account for the socioeconomic inequalities that warp the real world, for the social biases and prejudices that run rampant online, and for homophily.

No doubt, some will find the idea of engineering platforms to promote diversity or adapting laws to curb online harrassment unsettling and paternalistic, but such criticism ignores the ways online spaces are already contrived with specific outcomes in mind: they are designed to serve Silicon Valley venture capitalists, who want a return on investment, and advertisers, who want to sell us things. The term "platform," which implies a smooth surface, misleads us, obscuring the ways technology companies shape our online lives, prioritizing and upraising certain purposes over others.

The question of how we encourage, or even enforce, diversity in so-called open networks is not easy to answer, and must combine engineering and public policy. Openness is a philosophy that can easily rationalize its own failure, chalking people's inability to participate up to choice and, keeping with the myth of the meritocracy, blaming any disparities in audience on a lack of aptitude or will. That's what the techno-optimists would have us believe, dismissing potential solutions as threats to Internet freedom and forceful interference in a "natural" distribution pattern.[47]

But as we've seen, the decisions we make online—the culture we consume, the pages we click, the stars we gaze upon—are not pure expressions of our inner desires; they are shaped by myriad factors including what's available and what we hear about, the lure of the bandwagon, and marketing and advertising. Online as off, people's choices are influenced by circumstances beyond their control. The word "natural" is a mystification, given that the systems being discussed—technology, markets, and culture—are not found growing in a field, nurtured by dirt and sun. They are made by human beings and so can always be made better.

5

THE DOUBLE ANCHOR

Not long after the premiere of my documentary *Examined Life*, a film made up of a series of walks with contemporary philosophers, I found the entire thing online, ninety minutes posted in full or cut into random snippets spread across the Internet. I had expected such a thing to happen and had planned my response: a pleasant note that began in a tone of gratitude, thanking the various uploaders for their enthusiasm and support of the project. Then I told them that the movie had been quite costly to produce and we were about to release it in theaters and to home viewers. I'd like a few months, I went on, to try to recover some of the film's expenses by charging people to see it, in part to encourage future investment in similarly offbeat work. After this window I was prepared for people to post the film. Would they mind, I wondered, removing the clips in the interim?

Of the four or five people I wrote to, only two bothered to reply. One remarked that since my film was about philosophy and since philosophy, in a moral and historical sense, belongs to everyone in the world, my film does, too. It also should be accessible to people in the developing world, this person added. The other respondent essentially took the same view while adding a few expletives, telling me that philosophy is free.

The movie clips remained online and I gave up on writing to strangers. I had naively dipped my toe into an angry debate about the future of media, the technical infrastructure of the Internet, computing capacity and software design, the history of intellectual property, theoretical questions about cultural value and ownership, utopian visions of open access to art and ideas, and quotidian considerations about the ability of creative types to make a living from their work. I had stumbled into the copyright wars.

My first documentary was about a Lacanian Marxist cultural theorist, so perhaps I'm more inclined to agree with the unrepentant uploaders than most filmmakers. Philosophy does indeed belong to everyone; knowledge cannot be owned and we have a responsibility to share it. Isn't that what the Enlightenment was all about? I also believe we makers of art and culture do not, in a strict sense, possess the work we make, at least not in the way I own the mug I'm drinking from or the socks I'm wearing. Like most cultural producers, I create to affect other people, which means, in a sense, that I want the audience to take ownership of the work, to incorporate it, to make it part of themselves.

As a documentarian it's particularly difficult to delude myself into thinking I'm somehow the sole proprietor of my productions; I didn't invent the reality I film or dream up my subjects or script what they say. The work is made from the world and is part of it; in a fundamental way, it is part of what people now call the cultural commons, the vast repository of art and ideas that is our collective inheritance, the fruits of human imagination and invention that all acts of creative expression build and expand upon.

My aim has been to make philosophy more accessible by using the power of cinema to convey ideas that might intimidate or bore in another context. The problem is that making movies is not cheap, even in this age of digital video, and support for unusual projects is dwindling. My film, which had the backing of an independent production company in Toronto, cost over five hundred thousand dollars to create, a whopping sum I disbelieved until I began to compose the budget line by line. I was paid a flat fee of twenty thousand dollars for more than two solid years of work, a modest income but one for which I was incredibly grateful, given the opportunity it represented and basic survival it ensured, at least when coupled with a credit card.

The rest of the funds rapidly diminished, even though my crew and I stayed in one-star hotels with shared bathrooms and sublets found on Craigslist and I served as field producer, location scout, driver, production assistant, and coffee runner. There was gear rental, wages for sound and camera, travel costs, tape conversions, an editor, a sound mix, insurance, and so on. On one occasion I drove an interviewee around in my old station wagon, hands on the wheel, while trying to hold a conversation through the rearview mirror.

Though the film was not conceived to make a profit, there was the hope that it would recoup some of the costs, or that the process of promoting and screening it might let us break even, a challenge given that many independent films lose money in theatrical release. Small companies in Toronto and New York City had invested scarce resources into the distribution, paying for film-outs and high-definition copies and DVD screeners and mailing lists and spending time and energy spreading the word. If not for such expensive efforts, I doubt anyone would have even heard of the film to upload it.

While we all know what "expensive" means, "free" has a fundamental ambiguity, an ambiguity central to the Internet. Free can mean something that no one can own, that belongs to all. It can also mean free in cost, like Socrates's teachings in the streets of

Athens for which he famously refused to take a fee. There's "free" as in speech and "free" as in beer, as the famous software programmer Richard Stallman likes to say.

In the digital world both kinds of free are heralded as the future. The Internet, as some techies point out, is nothing if not a copy-making machine, a place where replicating things and passing them along are effortless and essential, whether the file contains a short text message or a pornographic image or a movie that took me years to make. Every time you send an e-mail to a friend or refresh your Web browser, a facsimile is made. First something is copied into your computer's memory, then maybe to your computer's CPU, then it goes out into the network, and from there to the other people's computers, and the process repeats itself, replication occurring at every step. In a digital realm, unlike its analog counterpart, digital copies never degrade; each one is as perfect as the copy before it. We can share, endlessly, without diminishing our own stock.[1]

Because of this capacity, we are moving from a creative economy of scarcity to one of abundance, in which the law of supply and demand dictates that the cost of something infinitely reproducible will be driven, inevitably, down to nothing. When creative work is available without limit, freely accessible, it tends also to become free of charge. This tendency leads us straight to what's long been called the "paradox of value," or the diamond-water paradox, first pointed out by economist Adam Smith: "Diamonds are valuable for being scarce, but water, which we need to live, is comparatively worthless." Similarly, art and culture are nonetheless vital, essential even, to what it means to be human, yet digital abundance has diminished our sense of their worth.

Does it follow that culture has value only if there is a limited supply to drive up demand? And what is it that makes some bits worth paying for—food for a virtual pet, a video game app, or a song on iTunes—and others—an article, a streaming video, a photograph—not? How do we define the worth of a digital book, for example, given that it takes significantly fewer resources and effort to replicate and distribute one than the equivalent printed on paper and clothbound? Should copies be free since they are infinitely and easily replicable packets of data, or should they be priced to reflect the cost of creation?[2]

Traditional notions of cultural ownership are also being challenged. Online, creative works are decontextualized, remixed, and mashed up. We surf and skim, passing along songs instead of albums, quotes instead of essays, clips instead of films. Artists who share their work with the world (or find it leaked) see it repurposed in ways they didn't anticipate. The minute a film is released or an essay is published, it begins to race around the Internet, passed through peer-to-peer networks, posted on personal Web sites, quoted in social media streams. In one sense, therefore, any ownership claim is essentially fanciful, since, in practice, people's creations circulate in ways they cannot control.

In practice, though, the laws underpinning ownership are stronger than ever before, so strong that some experts warn we are living through a "second enclosure," a reference to the eighteenth-century privatization of collectively managed fields and forests in England. Something similar has been happening in the realm of art and ideas over the past few decades: cultural commons are being cordoned off by private interests. Virtually every cultural artifact we encounter is "owned," from the poetry of Emily Dickinson to the paintings of Georgia O'Keeffe to the songs we sing in the shower. Even single notes are licensed and paid for.[3]

The privatization of the cultural realm has made us poorer because the world is richer when art and ideas spread. Unlike many other industries, culture produces mainly positive externalities: ideas, melodies, phrases, images, and insights seep out into the wider world, infecting and inspiring others and furthering creative invention and evolution. What's more, this sharing does not deplete the original store. If I read a passage of a book to you or repost a video I found online, there is no tangible loss to the creator, and both of us get to enjoy the work. In 1813 Thomas Jefferson made this point eloquently, influencing all subsequent understanding of the issue.

> If nature has made any one thing less susceptible than all others of exclusive property, it is the action of the thinking power called an idea, which an individual may exclusively possess as long as he keeps it to himself; but the moment it is divulged, it forces itself into the possession of every one, and the receiver cannot dispossess himself of it. Its peculiar character, too, is that no one possesses the less, because every other possesses the whole of it. He who receives an idea from me, receives instruction himself without lessening mine; as he who lights his taper at mine, receives light without darkening me. That ideas should freely spread from one to another over the globe, for the moral and mutual instruction of man, and improvement of his condition, seems to have been peculiarly and benevolently designed by nature, when she made them, like fire, expansible over all space, without lessening their density in any point, and like the air in which we breathe, move, and have our physical being, incapable of confinement or exclusive appropriation.

Half a century earlier in France, Denis Diderot, the impoverished editor of the famous *Encyclopédie*, took a rather different view, making the case that authors have a natural right in the work of their making: "What property can a man own if a work of the mind— the unique fruit of his upbringing, his studies, his evenings, his age, his researches, his observations; if his finest hours, the most beautiful moments of his life; if his own thoughts, the feelings of his heart, the most precious part of himself, that which does not perish, which makes him immortal—does not belong to him?"

Eventually the Marquis de Condorcet—a man born into wealth who didn't have to worry about living by his pen—issued a rebuttal, insisting that the public's interest in the free flow of knowledge eclipses any authorial prerogative. A property right that could be invoked to limit printing and publishing was "a constraint imposed on freedom, a restriction of the rights of other citizens." Condorcet blasted the idea that a literary work was property in any conventional sense: "One feels that there can be no relation between the ownership of a work and that of a field which a man can cultivate, or a piece of furniture that can be used by only one person, the exclusive ownership of which is consequently based on the nature of the thing." Ideas, he went on, arise from the world and so belong to all. A man of science, he dismissed originality as mere "style," emphasizing universal truth over subjective revelation or creative expression.[4]

Jefferson ultimately reached a position of compromise: while "the field of knowledge" may be "the common property of mankind," he came to believe that some regulation of culture was necessary in order, paradoxically, to ensure the production of more of it. The exclusive right to an idea was not a "natural right" but a provisional privilege granted "for the benefit of society." Wrestling with the concept of cultural property, Jefferson and the framers of the Constitution looked to Great Britain's Statute of Anne, drafted a century earlier to manage the emergent book trade. Formally called "An Act for the Encouragement of Learning, by vesting the Copies of Printed Books in the Authors or purchasers of such Copies, during the Times therein mentioned," the statute gave "Authors and Proprietors" exclusive rights to their works for as long as twenty-eight years.

Copyright, from day one, was designed to be both an impediment and an incentive, a mechanism of enclosure (one that prevented the unlicensed printing of texts, thereby limiting access) and a catalyst of sorts, a structure to stimulate the production of literary goods by rewarding writers and publishers for their labor. Necessarily imperfect, the system was conceived as a sort of quid pro quo to foster new work, an acknowledgment of the fact that printing technology made it more profitable to copy existing material than create from scratch, which requires time and effort and investment.

After much debate, the framers followed the lead of the British: copyright would be a temporary legal protection, a "limited monopoly privilege," as it's called, not to be mistaken for a perpetual property right or a natural one. Art and ideas, Jefferson and his colleagues determined, cannot be owned in the same way a chair or a table can be—intellectual property, in a sense, doesn't actually exist—and they wrote this proviso into the U.S. Constitution. Article I, section 8, clause 8 gives Congress the power "to promote the Progress of Science and useful Arts, by securing for limited Times to Authors and Inventors the exclusive Right to their respective Writings and Discoveries." This passage is now known as the "progress clause," underscoring copyright's generative aim.

At first, only a limited array of goods (maps, charts, and books) received copyright protection. But by 1978, the scope was expanded to apply to any "expression" that has been "fixed" in any medium, this protection granted automatically whether the maker wants it or not, no registration required. (That doodle you just drew? Protected.) And twenty-eight years has been extended to the life of the creator plus seventy years (works of so-called corporate authorship are protected for even longer: either 120 years after creation or 95 after publication, whichever ends first).

Given that the dead cannot write new books, compose new songs, paint new pictures, or think new thoughts (not to mention the fact that it is humans, not corporations, who author things), this prolongation shows the degree to which the law has been perverted, providing profit to those who had nothing to do with actually producing the work. As a consequence of this dilation, a handful of conglomerates have an incentive not necessarily to create new things but to buy up tremendous swathes of what already exists, like Bill Gates's purchase of an archive containing more than one hundred million images, many of them historic. Such companies now dominate the cultural field, their holdings encroaching into every corner of our lives. Driven by profit, not the public interest, they have become the custodians of our collective heritage.

New technologies threaten to overturn this situation. In the virtual world of the Web, stuff can spread like Jefferson's flame, "incapable of confinement, or exclusive appropriation." Yet many of the activities indigenous to the Internet, such as sharing and remixing, are in direct conflict with the law as it is currently written, forcing almost anyone who goes online into ambiguous gray zones. Simple uses of the Internet make us chronic violators of copyright, the fences of the second enclosure crumbling bit by bit as we copy and paste, download and post. One 2011 report to the UK government noted: "The copyright regime cannot be considered fit for the digital age when millions of citizens are in daily breach of copyright, simply for shifting a piece of music or a video from one device to another."

The old equilibrium between access and control has been disturbed, leaving people like myself caught between two extremes— a world in which our work is free the minute it is finished (no matter how much it cost to produce) and one where it is regulated at every juncture (no matter how it is being used and even if the use is legal). The friction of the off-line world, which helped prevent copyright holders from overcontrolling their work and users from completely undermining that control, no longer exists.

Back when paper books and vinyl records were dominant, copyright holders had little power over what their audiences did with their products (the objects could be read or listened to anywhere, loaned to friends, sold in secondhand shops, donated to libraries, thrown away, and so on) and audiences couldn't effortlessly distribute the products to thousands of people. Now things are more complicated. The very same technologies that facilitate the free exchange of culture also empower the most determined copyright holders, who monitor their products with things like content ID systems, audio/video finger-printing technology, and Digital Rights Management software— in effect, enabling owners to register every digital blip.

Material can be suddenly rescinded from electronic readers and algorithms can scan video streaming sites for copyright violations (sometime snagging legitimate uses in their automated dragnets).[5] The devices we carry in our pockets duplicate and distribute cultural products but they can also be used to track our every action, conjuring a not-so-distant future in which all cultural encounters are classified as "copyright events" and every idle click surveilled by unaccountable automatons.

Tangled in the contradiction between freedom and restraint, access and control, copyright has become one of the most controversial topics of our time, the spark of seemingly unresolvable conflict. Two camps shout past each other: the intellectual property dogmatists on one side argue that culture can be owned outright, passed on from heir to heir without concern for the wider public; on the other, adherents of the new ideology of openness claim that any restrictions on the use of cultural artifacts is an assault on individual freedom.

The first camp—epitomized by the Recording Industry Association of America and the Motion Picture Association of America— sees art as akin to any other product, property pure and simple, painting dissenters as communists and criminals, parasites and barbarians, and even terrorists.[6] Downloading is theft. The second camp, echoing Condorcet, argues that makers have no special claims over their creations, since they have inevitably built upon the work of others, which means they have an obligation to give their work away. People are only sharing what, in some essential sense, already belongs to them. The artists and culture makers themselves, more often than not, are left out of the conversation entirely.

While the RIAA and MPAA have made their position known mainly through lobbying and lawsuits, new-media thinkers helped launch a global movement for free culture, producing a mountain of books denouncing "overzealous copyright bozos" and "enemies of creativity" who deny the public access to their holdings. The free culture movement seeks to extend the principles of free and open source software production to art and culture. No one, they insist, creates in isolation and out of nothing; we all build on prior creativity, soaking like sponges on the banks of the cultural commons. Thus all art and culture should be free to use, study, redistribute, and modify, without having to ask permission first.

Creators who resist this proposal need to find a new way to survive that doesn't involve limiting access to their work. (According to the movement's official site, "We will listen to free music, look at free art, watch free film and read free books." Free culture "is one where being a cover band doesn't lose you any street cred compared to doing your own music from scratch" and "bad old TV series and movies turn into brilliant remakes and fan fiction on a regular basis—and bad remakes and fan fiction themselves generate brilliant ones after a few years.")

The free culture argument rests on two planks. First, technology is on the side of copying and the free flow of information: the clock cannot be turned back. Second, blocking access to culture props up outdated business models and stifles innovation and expression, as countless troubling instances prove: journalists sabotaged by individuals and institutions that abuse copyright to suppress free speech; home videos yanked from YouTube because a pop song is heard emanating from far-off speakers; filmmakers forced to cut scenes where families sing "Happy Birthday" because the song is not in the public domain;[7] appropriation artists and collagists whose compositions, however transformative (and thus likely legal), trigger litigation.

Consider the case of Canadian artist Jon Rafman who, in 2011, used low-resolution renderings of a variety of iconic paintings as texture in a virtual online environment. He received cease and desist letters from rights-holding societies in the United States, France, and Canada demanding that all references to creative works by artists who had died less than seventy years ago be removed, even though many of the artists in question used similar techniques: Jasper Johns and the American flag, Andy Warhol and the Campbell's Soup can, Roy Lichtenstein and comic strip characters.

As a documentarian, I live in fear that some incidental image or sound in my films will be subject to a proprietary claim. Though my usage may technically be classified as "fair use"—the vital doctrine that defends our right to comment, quote, and transform copyrighted material without permission or payment (the doctrine that ensures you can quote from this book in a review)—I dread a lawsuit, even one without merit, since a legal defense could easily double my budget and statutory damages range up to $150,000 for each work infringed upon.[8]

Without the support of a powerful benefactor, the safest thing to do is alter the reality I am documenting. I ask store owners to turn off stereos and televisions and subjects to set their phones to silent. I avoid archival footage because the licensing fees could bankrupt me. The past and present are, in many ways, effectively off-limits. Powerful corporate entities build their businesses by impeding the creative use of the sounds, sights, and symbols that surround us, making commenting on the world a privilege that must be paid for.

Thus the line between commerce and censorship can blur, making copyright a free speech issue. NBC, for example, refused to license Sam Green, an Academy Award–nominated documentary filmmaker, essential Vietnam War footage because it deemed it too graphic (a similar thing happened to the filmmaker Robert Greenwald, who has been denied the right to purchase footage from NBC, CBS, and WGBH to use in his political documentaries). "Corporate control of our culture is like the Soviets altering history books," Green told me. "They get to decide what gets to be seen."

Creators are in a bind. At its most defiant and extreme, the anti-copyright choir denounces those who resist the free exchange of their work as Luddites who don't understand the Internet or controlling authoritarians who seek to govern how their work is received. Kenneth Goldsmith, the eccentric founder of UbuWeb, an online repository of experimental and obscure films, videos, and sound art, created a "Wall of Shame" to humiliate artists who asked him to take down their work, no matter what their reasoning. For Goldsmith, technology has transformed creative practice; digital abundance has made the mastery of disseminating information more important than its creation. "Writers don't need to write anything more," he says. "They just need to manage the language that already exists." (Lest you think Goldsmith is a fringe figure, in 2012 he was invited to the White House, where President Obama watched him read a poem consisting of excerpts from traffic reports from local radio stations.)

Free culture proponents present the copyright wars as a straight-forward story of David and Goliath. Abolishing copyright and liberating information will lead to a better, more accessible culture and a more democratic, inclusive world; it will break up cultural monopolies, end artist exploitation, and eliminate the star system. If nothing else, the free culture proponents are laudable for their idealism. But because of the fundamental ambiguity of the word "free," the free culture movement has attracted people from across the political spectrum, with varying levels of power and influence and sometimes widely diverging agendas.

Philosophers and business writers, progressive scholars and techno-utopians, artistic renegades and established entrepreneurs have united in their criticism of copyright law. (Anarchists tend to dislike copyright because it turns culture into property; libertarians don't like it because it creates government-protected monopolies.)[9]

While some sincerely believe that the new digital order will create an inclusive cultural commons, others—the Web 2.0 venture capitalists and entrepreneurs—see the abundance of accessible content as a way to get rich. One group thinks freedom, the other profit. "Just because products are free," Chris Anderson writes in *Free: The Future of a Radical Price*, doesn't mean that it is not possible to make "huge gobs of money."

In their battle against the old paradigm, new-media thinkers and free culture activists have aligned themselves with Silicon Valley (many of the most prominent organizations advocating for the free culture agenda, from Public Knowledge to Creative Commons, take funding from firms such as Google[10]). The struggle is not only between big copyright-hoarding corporations and besieged hobbyists but also between two very different ways of doing business.

"The basic divide at work here is between those capitalists that make money by selling *access to content*, and those that make money by controlling the content *distribution networks*," explains sociologist Peter Frase. "For content sellers like the music business, extremely harsh intellectual property laws are desirable because they create the artificial scarcity on which their whole business model depends. Companies like Facebook and Google, in contrast, mostly make their money by controlling the platforms on which people distribute various kinds of media, and selling access to their user base to advertisers." For the latter group, looser copyright laws don't pose a threat to their profits but actually facilitate them; the more copying and sharing happen, the faster their revenues grow.

It's no wonder that tech companies encourage their users to imagine themselves as remixers and DJs, curators and mash-up artists, frenetically passing around and repurposing bits of information (even as the same tech companies ferociously cling to their own intellectual property and jealously guard their trade secrets, snapping up patents at breakneck speed).[11] Nor is it any wonder that free culture activists tend to obscure the similarity between "author" and "remixer." The author, they argue, is a relatively recent invention, a romantic mystification that emerged during the Industrial Revolution and coincided with the development of the printing press and the rise of the art market—a social construct employed to justify an emerging economic and technological paradigm.

Yet the same basic observation could be made of the remixer, the DJ, the mash-up artist, and the curator; they, too, are "social constructs" that cannot be disconnected from the economic and technological realities of our time. Remix culture may possess a rogue, transgressive aura, but its methods of appropriation and distribution are perfectly aligned with the profit-making logic of digital capitalism: originality doesn't pay online, quick aggregation does. Curation, not creation, we are told, is the next "billion-dollar opportunity."[12]

That the battles between new and old media have come to resemble Goliath versus Goliath is nowhere more visible than the debate over piracy, the epitome of copyright violation since it involves the distribution of movies, television shows, music, and books in their entirety. On January 18, 2012, the tensions over piracy were spotlighted when the sites Google, Wikipedia, Reddit, and Tumblr, along with thousands of personal pages, participated in a massive day of protest, going dark or blackening their logos to draw attention to two controversial bills, SOPA and PIPA.

The Stop Online Piracy Act and the Protect Intellectual Property Act, both before the House for voting, were ostensibly designed to crack down on "rogue" foreign sites that traffic in pirated content for profit but, as critics noted, the bills were so vaguely worded that they would effectively trample both the First and Fourth Amendments, essentially legalizing censorship and eliminating due process. Instead of focusing on the removal of illegal material, the bills would give the Department of Justice the power to shut down entire Web sites without a trial on the grounds that they hosted infringing content or, going a step further, that they "facilitated" infringement, which meant that Internet service providers, search engines, advertising networks, and financial intermediaries were under threat.

As the law currently stands, Web sites are immune from this problem as long as they act in good faith to take infringing content down upon notification, thanks to "safe harbor provisions" included in the Digital Millennium Copyright Act (DMCA) of 1998. The proposed laws, in contrast, would have forced Web site operators to monitor everything they hosted and linked to, giving them an incentive to preemptively block or delete material to avoid legal hassle, even though the material may well classify as protected speech.

In a joint letter to Congress, published as a full-page ad in the *New York Times*, Google, Twitter, eBay, Facebook, Yahoo!, AOL, and other companies argued that the legislation would undermine innovation and pose a major threat to user privacy by mandating the "monitoring of websites." The public also rebelled. Thousands of concerned citizens spread the word about SOPA on social media, signed petitions, and telephoned their elected officials. Advocacy groups warned that entertainment companies—who invested heavily in lobbying for the bills—were trying to "break the Internet"; bloggers protested that they would not be able to link to other sites out of fear that those sites might contain violating links; librarians warned of the "potential to negatively impact fundamental library principles." By pushing for such an extreme and indefensible position, the old-media moguls sparked a tremendous outcry, which caused the legislation to be redrafted and then scuttled, at least temporarily.

But the defeat, touted as a victory of civil society, was also a sign of the tech industry's growing clout. For the first time, new and old media are spending similar sums to buy influence in Washington. While the entertainment companies have deep ties, professional and financial, to thirty-two SOPA sponsors, the tech industry is getting in on the game.[13] Google is now one of the top ten spenders in Washington. In 2012, the company's lobbying budget exceeded most traditional media organizations, including Verizon and Comcast; according to Open Secrets, Google produced more reports on "Copyright, Patent & Trademark" issues in 2011 than the Recording Industry Association of America.[14] As journalist Glenn Greenwald explained, "Citizen opposition, by itself, would never have been sufficient to overcome the pro-SOPA lobbying of the entertainment industry; it took a different powerful industry to stop it."[15]

Only a few months after SOPA's defeat, some of the same corporations who objected to the bill on privacy grounds supported CISPA (Cyber Intelligence Sharing and Protection Act), a cyber security bill that threatened constitutional rights by allowing technology companies to share user information with government intelligence agencies. "CISPA represents the first notable rift within the coalition of organizations and businesses that helped lead the charge against Stop Online Piracy Act." David Segal, one of the leaders of the SOPA fight, wrote after Facebook endorsed the legislation. "SOPA's opponents came together in a kumbaya moment, with almost anybody who cares about the Internet—as user, activist, or profiteer—lining up against the bill."

This opposition, Segal observed, was self-interested: SOPA's "passage would have hurt Facebook's bottom line—and probably forced it to alter basic business practices—by forcing it to aggressively police alleged piracy. And now the profit motive is causing Facebook to support CISPA, at the expense of its users, because it would relieve certain regulatory burdens and provide attractive immunities for the company."[16]

The piracy and the copyright wars might seem cutting edge—with all the talk of DNS (domain name system) blocking, streaming, and infinite storage—but what we are witnessing is actually the latest incarnation of a centuries-old debate, one reignited every time publishing technologies take a forward leap. The development of the printing press, the phonograph, the radio, the cassette tape, the Xerox machine, the CD, and the Internet—each innovation sparked a heated struggle in which a predictable array of positions and opinions were ardently defended.

In the eighteenth and nineteenth centuries writers including Alexander Pope, Daniel Defoe, and Charles Dickens wrestled with the nature of authorship and the ethics of piracy, producing interesting, idiosyncratic ruminations quite unlike our own shrill industry panic. ("Hometaping is killing music!," said the record labels in the 1980s; "The VCR is to the American film producer and the American public as the Boston Strangler is to the woman alone," the Motion Picture Association of America's Jack Valenti famously proclaimed.) In response, much as they do today, pirates positioned themselves as principled defenders of liberty and advocates of the public interest.

Over a hundred years ago, a self-described "king of the pirates" ran the "People's Music Publishing Company" in East London, using photolithography to reproduce sheet music, which he sold for a fraction of the going price. God, he said, intended for music to be shared (and, he told angry publishers, his cheap sheet music would lead to more sales of their legitimate versions). The king's comments may have reflected a self-serving attempt to claim the moral high ground, but there's no denying that over the years bootleggers have aided the spread of culture and learning, performing a service from which society has collectively benefited. Immanuel Kant—he of the Enlightenment maxim "Dare to Know!"—wrote an essay denouncing the injustice of counterfeited books. Yet knowledge, as historian Adrian Johns tells us, spread across Europe and overseas via affordable, unauthorized editions: "Enlightenment traveled atop a cascade of reprints. No piracy, we might say, no Enlightenment."[17]

Sweden's Peter Sunde, former spokesman for the Web site the Pirate Bay, is perhaps the most famous pirate of our time—freedom fighter or purloining pariah, depending on whom you ask. At the

2009 Open Video Conference in New York City, his image was beamed in via webcam so he could discuss the hugely popular Web site, which serves as the point of contact for peer-to-peer sharing of large files via a protocol called BitTorrent. The Pirate Bay's notoriety, and the network's enormousness (with twenty-five million users at its peak, it commanded a tenth of all Internet traffic), had raised the ire of the Motion Picture Association of America, which instigated a number of lawsuits against the site on behalf of various movie studios.

In the spring of 2009, Sunde and three codefendants were found guilty of copyright infringement and sentenced by Swedish court to one year in prison and the equivalent of $3.5 million in damages, which they appealed. Sunde didn't seem very worried. The Pirate Bay, he pointed out, doesn't actually host infringing material but makes it easily findable, similar to a search engine such as Google. The next year, the Swedish Court of Appeal seemed to agree: "If the nature of a search service is such that it primarily is a valuable tool in lawful activities, and of general benefit to society, if this legitimate use predominates, but the distribution or transmission of illegal material in spite of precautions cannot be ruled out, the operation of such a service should be considered as legitimate."[18]

There are many peer-to-peer file-sharing Web sites, but the Pirate Bay has been the most outspoken and conscientious about connecting freedom to share with freedom of speech. The site's high-profile lawsuit made it an international cause célèbre, spawning political Pirate Parties around the world. In Sweden, where piracy has also been recognized as a religion (specifically the Church of Kopimism, derived from the words "copy me"), the Piratpartiet took more than 7 percent of the vote in the 2009 European parliamentary elections. Sunde, who has severed any formal ties to the Pirate Bay, announced that he would run for a seat in the EU Parliament in 2014 in Finland, where he is eligible for office, on the Pirate ticket. Though it has struggled recently in the polls, the Pirate Party has been the most successful in Germany, with seats won at various levels of government, encroaching on the Green and Social Democrat parties' turf and threatening long-standing progressive coalitions.[19]

The Pirate Party takes pride in being politically unaligned, neither traditionally left nor right, while promoting a platform that emphasizes core issues of government transparency, online and off-line privacy, and copyright reform, including the right to download. The party stands, broadly, for what it calls Internet freedom, which has led members to fight online censorship in various ways, from providing hosting support for WikiLeaks to resisting German legislation that blocks access to sites containing child pornography.[20]

The enthusiasm for pirate politics keeps spreading, particularly through academic circles, with a number of scholars writing elegies to "pirate philosophy." Pirate "practices exceed the limit of individual production and succeed in so far as there is a collective accumulation of knowledge to be shared" and "offer an alternative way to relate to the cultural artifacts," says one media theorist. Another argues that piracy is best understood in connection to "communitarian cultures of sharing, borrowing, copying, and openness"—after all, the vast majority of people, the author points out, aren't copying things for profit but for private use.[21]

Raising the stakes of the argument, University of Virginia professor Siva Vaidhyanathan insists that "peer-to-peer systems are about more than music. . . . The battles over control of cultural distribution can be read as a prelude to more overtly political battles to come."[22] *Property Outlaws*, written by Eduardo Peñalver and Sonia Katyal, two law professors, opens by comparing purposeful violations of copyright law to the lunch counter demonstrations of the civil rights movement. They see the heroic actions of HIV-infected patients clashing with pharmaceutical companies, whose claim to exclusive patents blocks the manufacture of affordable, generic drugs, as akin to "peer-to-peer file sharers, who are challenging the record industry's failure to offer digital distribution of music, and the Norwegian hacker who landed in jail after reverse-engineering Hollywood DVDs so that they could run on a Linux-based computer."[23] In the words of Vaidhyanathan, we've gone from "liberty, equality, fraternity" to "rip, mix, burn."[24]

As a result of these connections, a growing number of people equate file-sharing with activism. A comprehensive study by the Social Science Research Council found that downloading is "widely understood in economic justice terms." At an event in Brooklyn with a founding member of the Pirate Bureau, Sara Sajjad, invitees were advised to bring their "laptop, USB stick or hard drive, and share, swap and propagate like the pirate you arrrrrr!" The "Guerrilla Music Swap" was conceived as an anticapitalist statement, an affront to the greedy policies of the RIAA and MPAA. The idea that piracy is an effective form of resistance, a direct attack on the corporate empire, is confirmed by the reaction it has provoked: the excesses of digital rights management, the egregious lawsuits against music lovers (including children and even a deceased grandmother), and the desperate attempts to shut down file sharing through bills like PIPA and SOPA.

Thus creators have found themselves at the center of a bizarre struggle waged in their name. On one side, the giants RIAA and MPAA and, on the other, file sharers ("I'll stop downloading books when publishers stop ripping off writers," one self-proclaimed pirate announced on the popular literary Web site the Millions). Established corporate giants position themselves as protectors, defending the very artists they have exploited for so long, while downloaders pose as liberators, emancipating creative expression from the clutches of the market.

Defendants of file sharing often take pains to point out the old-media industry's duplicity, highlighting stories of creators taken advantage of by big business. They mention Peter Jackson, director of the *Lord of the Rings* films, who sued New Line Cinema for revenue fraud, and the litany of complaints made by successful musicians who have been ripped off by their labels. They link to a recent story by NPR's *Planet Money*, which revealed the movie industry's questionable accounting. Walking listeners through the numbers on a recent action movie, they show how executives claim that the film lost money even though it grossed almost a quarter of a billion dollars at the box office. The trick lies in a series of maneuvers that the *Wall Street Journal* has likened to a "tranche of collateralized debt obligations," including the levy of a hefty fee, around 30 percent, by the very studio that produces the movie.[25] The result, according to the book *The Hollywood Economist*, "is that a film, after paying this enormous tariff, rarely shows a profit, even if the studio is making a profit from the distribution fee, and so the writers, directors, actors and other participants in the profit rarely see anything but red ink on their semi-annual statements."[26]

Steve Albini, the legendary music producer, exposed the similarly unsavory practices of the record industry in his blistering critique of industry misconduct, "The Problem with Music." Breaking down what happens to a hypothetical band given a $250,000 advance for an album that earns $3 million in gross retail revenue, he reveals how they still end up owing the label money: the recording company makes about $700,000 in profit; the producers, managers, agents, and lawyers get their cut; yet the band ends up "unrecouped" and $14,000 short of earning royalties.[27]

This structural greed is well documented and appalling. Under the corporate record and film studio systems, the companies that invest in a creative work also control the copyright attached to the finished product, which leaves the creators, the songwriters and performers or directors and crew, with no say over or stake in the work's afterlife. One strange outcome of this arrangement is that musicians—most famously the funk legend George Clinton—have been sued for sampling themselves. In the corporate music world, it's not uncommon for five companies to own chunks of one song, while the artist is cut out of the arrangement completely.

The fact that artists have been dispossessed of their work has long been invoked as evidence of the immorality of the culture industries, and the music business in particular. Why should the label own recordings and not the musicians who composed or performed the actual sounds? Why should an essayist have to surrender all rights to a magazine that published his piece or a filmmaker be forced to assign ownership of her creation to a corporate entity? And yet the most vocal critics of these disagreeable practices increasingly share the assumption that artists must forfeit control of their work, only with control going not to executives but to what Jaron Lanier calls the "hive mind."

The problem, though, is that it is not clear how file sharing actually addresses financial improprieties or points the way to an arrangement that's more equitable: unlike a label or studio, where a percentage of profits trickles back to creators, peer-to-peer sites and online locker services return nothing to artists, though they can be incredibly lucrative for those who run them.[28] The Pirate Bay, for example, is bedecked by advertising. The now-defunct Megaupload (parent company of Megavideo and Megaporn) made its flamboyant owner, "pirate king" Kim Dotcom, over $40 million in 2011 alone (wealth he famously flaunted all while comparing himself to Martin Luther King).[29] Meanwhile, piracy has set a new, low baseline for artists' negotiations. Where free culture enthusiasts justify their position by invoking the exploitation of artists under the old model, digital capitalists, looking to build profitable businesses by storing or streaming creative work produced by others, defend microscopic or nonexistent payments by arguing that the alternative is nothing at all.

Historian Adrian Johns calls piracy the "definitive transgression of the information age." Yet he also notes that while piracy signifies "a repudiation of information capitalism at one extreme," it marks information capitalism's "consummation" on the other.[30] If Peter Sunde represents the first pole, Matt Mason, who took the conference stage at the Open Video Conference after Sunde's image flickered out, embodies the second. Mason, author of the book *The Pirate's Dilemma: How Youth Culture Reinvented Capitalism*, acknowledged that piracy can sometimes cut into profits. But in crisis, as they say, lies opportunity.

He gave the example of drug companies distributing widely pirated copies of their patent medicines without charge. "They started winning corporate social responsibility awards," Mason rhapsodized. "And all the advertising money in the world couldn't help them do that." Or take shoes; instead of suing a Japanese bootlegger for selling altered versions of their sneakers, Nike made a fortune appropriating the redesigns. "Pirates are taking over the good ship capitalism, but they're not here to sink it. Instead they will plug the holes, keep it afloat, and propel it forward," he promised. His message was clear: you can give up control of copies and still gain market share. The speech earned a hearty cheer. According to Mason's Web site, his speaking performances have left Procter and Gamble "delighted," struck the executives of Miller Genuine Draft as "amazing." Disney, only slightly more restrained, found Mason "very stimulating!"

Mason's argument also holds true for most mainstream culture. The most downloaded files are, without fail, the biggest blockbusters and mainstream hits. While peer-to-peer networks can be used to share amateur and independent creativity, in practice they are more often used to trade Lady Gaga or *Game of Thrones*. Of course, big business is loath to lose potential sales to free distribution (the push for SOPA and PIPA in the United States and the draconian "three strikes" laws abroad, which can slow or suspend Internet access to repeat copyright infringers, prove as much), but pirate sites also increase the reach of American commercial culture, spreading it around to distant corners of the globe. Thus the pirates who run these sites are at once defenders of free expression and enablers of free consumption.

While the more politically conscious people who use these services might believe they are striking a blow against Hollywood and the major labels, they are also increasing the power of those institutions by helping people consume their products, shaping their desires and values as a result (strengthening commercial culture's hegemony, as the academically inclined might say). The best way to resist old media's dominance may be to abstain from its offerings entirely, free or not.

Free culture leaders and activists sincerely believe that violating copyright—illegally downloading films and music or remixing and recontextualizing pop culture products—is an effective way to subvert corporate culture and defy market values.[31] "There's a pretty strong case to be made that 'free' has some inherent antipathy to capitalism," the writer Cory Doctorow has said.[32] It's a view reflected in a documentary about the virtues of remix culture, *Steal This Film II*, which illustrates the rampant abuse of intellectual property by big business and the rise of file-sharing services. "This is the question that faces us today," the voice-over says. "If the battle against sharing is already lost, and media is no longer a commodity, how will society change?" The movement persists in maintaining a core, misguided assumption: if something is free, that means it has been de-commodified.

This misapprehension is applauded or at least tolerated by Silicon Valley, where the democratic impulse of liberal legal scholars and anarchist filmmakers finds a cynical echo and where open platforms have achieved massive stock market valuations. Likewise, there's no quarrel from those pirates who run file-sharing sites for private gain. Nor from television executives whose trade is offering up free shows in exchange for our attention, which they sell to advertisers.

Of course the advertisers themselves want nothing more than for all of us to encounter their offerings, to "engage" and "interact" with them. We have known for years that culture can be a commodity even when you don't have to pay for it outright. Those who would protect the cultural commons must see that the challenge is not only copyright, but those who own the platforms and channels through which culture is increasingly shared. On their watch, the cultural commons has become little more than a radically discounted shopping mall, a consumers' paradise of free entertainment propped up by advertising. What's being hoarded now are the means of delivery, the channels through which the economic value of culture is realized. The commons can be commodified without being enclosed outright.

Jem Cohen was dismayed to find his recent film about the venerable punk band The Ex on file-sharing sites before its official release. An implicit social contract had been broken, Cohen felt. "The message was, don't bother to make this movie next time," he told me. "If something that I've made is just plain not accessible, then I'm not going to hold it against somebody for making it available," he said, referring to movies that have fallen out of circulation. "But when I put out a documentary about a diehard progressive left-wing punk band that has been around for twenty-five years doing their hard work and I put it out on an independent label, that's just insane."

Cohen has stayed committed to independence despite plenty of invitations to join mainstream production companies and advertising agencies. An acclaimed filmmaker and photographer, he grew up in Washington, D.C., surrounded by people who founded the fabled punk band Fugazi and the label Dischord (the subjects of his 2003 documentary *Instrument*). Inspired by Fugazi's example,

Cohen made a conscious decision to work outside the studio system, producing uncompromising work, including narrative features, documentary meditations, and experimental collages, as well as countless collaborations with musicians such as Patti Smith, Godspeed You! Black Emperor, Vic Chesnutt, and Elliott Smith. Cohen has to improvise the financing for each project, occasionally combining grants with support from museums and cultural institutions, including in Europe, which is more friendly to his unconventional approach. But without a paying audience at screenings or through DVD sales and other royalties, his work is not viable.

In an article for *Vertigo* magazine, Cohen made the case for something he called the double anchor. "Sometimes we need to remind ourselves that the relationship between those who make creative work and those who receive it should be one of mutual support," Cohen writes. "Each end holds up the other." With the Internet, Cohen continues, came the promise that artists would be able to eliminate middlemen, get rid of costly hard copies, and cultivate massive new audiences.

Yet the revolution hasn't played out precisely that way. "I fear that an ugly dichotomy is sliding into place," Cohen says. "On one side, there's a receiver for whom, with a few clicks, everything is available, free, and exists to be shared without consideration or consequence. On the other side there are interests, usually corporate, envisioning how with more restrictive copyright and insistent branding, everything can become even more commodified than it already is."

Cohen has no interest in protecting the assets of Hollywood, major music labels, or other conglomerates, nor does he support reprisals against those who don't obey their dictates. Yet he thinks we need to be as conscientious about the culture we take in as we are about the food we eat. "When people want the option of a delicious organic tomato that actually has flavor, they don't expect it to be free," Cohen explained, mentioning those vegetable stands in the country, where a farmer places a small box next to the produce to collect payment.

"The people who pass by understand that if they want the vegetables to keep showing up on the table, they can't just grab them, even if no one is looking. The person who grows them doesn't put them out at exorbitant prices. The box solution is based neither on capitalist greed nor on some sense of entitlement to 'free,' but on mutual respect and mutual support. And that to me is the very simple kind of thinking that's getting lost. A factory farmer or a freegan are not the only two positions to take."

Cohen is highlighting a value that has long been central to any progressive movement: respect for labor. From this angle, it's clear that "copyleft," as the free culture position on copyright is sometimes called, is not "left" in the traditional sense. As Richard Stallman told me, he designed copyleft to ensure the freedom of users to redistribute and modify copies of software. Freedom to tinker is the paramount value it promotes, but a left worthy of the name has to balance that concern with the demand for equality, parity of wealth, and redistribution of power.

Copyleft, with its narrow emphasis on software freedom, even when broadened to underscore the freedom of speech implications of such a position, offers a limited political response to entrenched systems of economic privilege, and it does not advance limits on profitability or promote fair compensation. Free culture, with its emphasis on access, does not necessarily lead to a more just social order. To pay to watch an independent movie does not mean capitulating to the privatization of knowledge but rather recognizes the work that went into making it and provides some support so that the effort can continue.[33]

Jem Cohen priced the DVD of his movie modestly. It "took me seven years to make—seventeen dollars doesn't seem like too much to ask. It is about an exchange that is fair," he says. In contrast to the hyperinflation of the art world, where art stars like Jeff Koons and Damien Hirst sell their creations for millions of dollars, there's a countervailing hyper-devaluation of work online. "I think we have to return to sustainability as a key word," Cohen told me. "We have to be thinking about why we value things that are made by individuals, why we value that which is homegrown, how we can recognize the kind of labor value of things that are not made by corporations." To this end, Cohen advocates what he calls the "realizable dream" of "a new economy of fair trade for artists and audiences."

In discussions about digital culture, complex dynamics are reduced to stark, binary terms. There's the record industry ensnaring people in despotic lawsuits and ruining lives; Disney denying people the ability to reference its imagery in their creative projects; big corporations removing amateur videos from the Web for infringing copyright. And then there's a culture of free, where opposition to copyright and downloading is understood as a straightforward act of political resistance, and the remixer, mash-up artist, and pirate are portrayed as romantic rebels.

Most cultural producers, however, sympathize with both sides and wind up somewhere in between. There are artists who go to great lengths to prevent their music or films from leaking online, while others upload their own work to Torrent sites. Some individuals take different approaches, depending on the work at hand (there are large-scale projects that I want to introduce to the world with care and restraint, and others that I am happy to toss into the ether without consideration of credit or remuneration). Where copyright is concerned, there's often a kind of dual consciousness; people want to pilfer *and* protect, access *and* control.

Even those artists who have written eloquently on the fallacy of intellectual property, the ubiquity of creative influence, and the myth of originality—figures like Lewis Hyde, Jonathan Lethem, Cory Doctorow, and David Shields—reserve some, if not all, of their rights. "Who owns the words? Who owns the music and the rest of our culture?" asks Shields. "Reality cannot be copyrighted," yet the book I quote from is. Though Richard Stallman encourages copying, he releases his writing under a no-derivatives license; he believes people should be allowed to modify all software, but he is not convinced the same holds for expressive works. While there are exceptions, most people whose creativity depends on being able to incorporate outside material tend to be sensitive to conflicting perspectives, intuitively aware of the "bargain" copyright is supposed to provide in its ideal form.[34] Beyond a shadow of a doubt, we have lost sight of this equilibrium in recent decades.

We need to push back against the copyright extremists who abuse the law to guard entrenched interests from competition, lobbying for ever greater and arguably unconstitutional protections. First and foremost, we need to fortify two existing principles, fair use and de minimis—the principle that some uses are simply too trivial to regulate—by emboldening creators to stand up for rights they already have.[35] (And if copyright holders insist on outsourcing intellectual property enforcement to algorithms, they must also program them to account for these rights and exceptions.)

Second, we must shorten copyright's duration and eliminate the ability of corporations to endlessly and retroactively extend their monopolies on work made by deceased creators (related to this, we must also revamp the patent system, which is structured to encourage hoarding and litigation, too often thwarting technological progress instead of promoting it).

Third, we should require those who want to renew their copyrights beyond an initial limited period to register them, an arrangement that would likely flood the commons with new work and help solve what is known as the "orphan works" problem, where material is caught in a legal limbo because the copyright holders can't be found. Intelligent proposals worth considering include more radical approaches, such as a "reverse liability rule" for sampling, which would require copyright owners to pay the government a small fee to block remixing of their work.

A compulsory or blanket license is probably the only way to turn music into a true public utility, and some have already put forth thoughtful plans detailing how this might work, including ways to distribute funds so that they do not all accrue to those with the biggest marketing budgets or who have benefited from cumulative advantage.[36] There are many possible solutions that honor and abide by copyright's legitimate purpose, granting the possibility of a limited period of private monopoly privilege followed by mandatory public service.[37]

For all its flaws, copyright provides some incentive for people to take on the risk of creating new work by allowing for the possibility of some economic benefit. It also provides the only legal mechanism creators have to defend themselves from various forms of exploitation and misuse, granting what I believe is an important noneconomic right—the right, under certain conditions, to say no.[38] The band Minor Threat had nothing but copyright to stop Nike from using its album art in a marketing campaign it morally opposed; David Byrne forced the governor of Florida to apologize for using one of his songs in a political advertisement without his consent; the cartoonist Bill Watterson has maintained an embargo against ancillary products, preventing his beloved comic *Calvin and Hobbes* from being made into a Happy Meal toy or 3-D movie.

Perhaps no one embodies the idea of dual consciousness better than Public Enemy's Chuck D, an originator of sample-based hip-hop. "We looked at music as an assemblage of sounds, and you couldn't copyright a sound," he has said. But Chuck D has spent plenty of time on the other side, instigating numerous copyright infringement lawsuits of his own over the years, including one against Notorious B.I.G.'s estate for unlawful sampling in the song

"Ten Crack Commandments" and against the Coors Brewing Company for the same.

The crux of the issue wasn't money, Chuck D has said, but the use of his work to promote messages at odds with his values. Early on in his career, Mr. Len, a rapper and producer featured in the documentary *Copyright Criminals*, was busted by composer Philip Glass for unlicensed sampling, a move that forced Len's label to recall his record. "It all depends on what side of the fence you're sitting on," he told the film's director. "Like, if you're the one infringing someone's copyright, of course you feel like, 'Hey man, this copyright law sucks.' But if it swings back and someone samples your music for a bestiality flick, you're gonna be a little pissed about it."[39]

The problem comes down to power. Left unregulated, those companies with market dominance could make use of the world's creative output without crediting or paying the people who produced it. Nike could use any song on earth to peddle its wares, and companies like Google, Apple, Netflix, and Spotify could build their empires on top of the world's content and without kicking in even a small portion of their revenue to creators. Hollywood and the recording and publishing industries would no doubt be displeased by such a turn of events, but the cultural field would not suddenly become noncommercial.

Eliminating copyright could theoretically equalize opportunity, allowing everyone uniform access to everything ever made, but this is not necessarily the case. The commons has also historically been used as a source of raw materials for colonizers and corporations seeking to profit from traditional lands, assets, and knowledge, which well-capitalized entities are better positioned to take advantage of than comparatively poor locals. Not everyone benefits equally from openness. The ocean may be common, but a company with a large fleet of trawlers is uniquely situated to exploit its riches; Disney is better able to reach mass audiences with films based on folktales in the public domain; Google holds an almost unassailable advantage when it comes to indexing all the public data posted on the Internet, spending billions annually on infrastructure.

The commons are accessed asymmetrically, like the massive repositories of genomic data that have been made available online by scientists who hoped the repositories would become a "global resource, shared equally," but which have been overwhelmingly used by private biotech firms in a handful of wealthy countries. The romance of the commons—the idea that a resource open to all will be accessed equitably and create a more just outcome, that differences evaporate online, openness ensures fairness, and the goods can be "free" to all without negative consequence—ignores the problem of inequality. In reality, differing circumstances, abilities, assets, and power render some better able to take advantage of a commons than others.[40]

Elinor Ostrom, who won a Nobel Prize in economics for her work on the commons, provides an interesting complement to this view. Through her observations of lobster fishermen in Maine, farmers in Nepal, Swiss Alpine cheese makers, and other real-world communities, Ostrom rigorously proves that commons which actually last over the long term are not "open" or "free" by any means. Instead, they are "stinted"; true commoning always involves establishing limits of some kind.

Britain's Magna Carta and its lesser-known companion the Great Charter of the Forest promised a range of limited subsistence rights to the poor, protecting gleaning by law. People had the right to collect vestige crops, fish in streams, and graze animals or drive swine on land they did not explicitly own. Widows were permitted to gather estovers, or firewood, and freemen were allowed to take any honey they could find.

Thus it is wrong to think that the commons were a resource anyone could exploit at will. Instead, the commons were as much a thing and an activity, both a noun and a verb—a set of social relationships, a bundle of rights and restrictions, a mode of being for mutual aid. The commons were neither completely open nor completely closed, but negotiated.[41] "In one essay Ostrom and her coauthor, librarian Charlotte Hess, argue that this wisdom must be applied to Web-based "knowledge commons," which, they warn, can produce outcomes that are "good or bad, sustainable or not." New-media thinkers insist that the cultural commons, unlike their material counterpart, cannot be tragic because they cannot be depleted. Ostrom and Hess challenge this view. We are at risk, they argue, of a new kind of tragedy of the commons—a tragedy not of enclosure but of underinvestment. The issue is not simply control of culture but its creation.

To put it another way, the problem of the production of the commons is just as urgent as the problem of access. It is true that copyright maximalists pose a grim threat, gobbling up our shared cultural heritage and exploiting it for commercial gain, enclosing it into private preserve. Where the Charter of the Forest prohibited the fencing of "arable land" out of respect for one's neighbors, today's cultural commons is increasingly fenced in, the invisible barricades of copyright, trademark, and patent law locking down what should, to a significant degree, exist for the benefit of all. The more art and ideas are owned, the more people are kept out, denied access to the sights, sounds, and insights that make up the cultural environment they call home.

But there are challenges of production, too. New work involves allowing creators to build on the creativity of those who came before and they must be able to sustain their productions economically. We need new social protocols for a networked age: ethical guidelines for engagement and exchange, restrictions on both privatizing and freeloading, and fair compensation not predicated on perfect control. Instead of the defensive obsession with ownership, we should foster an ethos of stewardship: a steward preserves and protects, looking both forward and back, tending to what is not his.

On the issue of economic sustenance, we might take some inspiration from the mounting push for open access to federally financed scholarship, a cause made more visible by the programmer and progressive activist Aaron Swartz, whose prosecution by the Department of Justice for downloading copyrighted documents from the nonprofit academic database JSTOR led him to commit suicide in 2013 (Swartz never shared the documents and JSTOR tried to get the charges dropped).[42] In the wake of this tragedy, the White House Office of Science and Technology Policy issued a memorandum instructing federal agencies of a certain size to develop plans to make research they have supported freely available: "citizens deserve easy access to the results of research their tax dollars have paid for," the program's director declared.

A related, if reversed, logic could be applied to art and culture more broadly. Due to technological shifts, all manner of creative works have effectively become open access, and now we need to fund them. For the common good that's free for all to enjoy, we will have to invest in it, which means reconsidering the role of public subsidy.

We will grapple with the ownership of culture—for how long? by whom? on what grounds?—as digitization continues. Yet it is just as urgent to ask why it is acceptable for a small and elite group of entrepreneurs to position themselves to capture the wealth generated by our collective creativity. Despite their passionate critiques of intellectual property and devotion to collaboration and "social production," technology gurus never raise the possibility that the platforms through which we access and share culture should belong to people whose participation makes them valuable.

Surely if the rights of artists over their own work can be contested, there are grounds to challenge the proprietary claims of digital capitalists, particularly those who have acknowledged their dependence on the creations, contributions, and uncompensated labor of others.

With this model in mind, we should strive to cultivate the cultural commons as a vibrant and sustainable sphere, one that exists for its own sake, not to be exploited by old-media oligarchs, new-media moguls, insatiable shareholders, for-profit pirates, or data miners and advertisers. The copyright wars prove that many people are frustrated by the current arrangement, but the remaking of our media system will not happen by downloading alone.

6

DRAWING A LINE

When we talk about the cultural commons, it should be self-evident that production is a precondition of access. An article needs to be researched and written before it can be read; a canvas must be painted before it can be shown. Yet we live in a society oddly reluctant to recognize that this is the case. Dominant economic theories emphasize exchange: the value of a good has nothing to do with how it was made but, instead, the price it can command in the marketplace.

And when we try to break with the market to talk about gift economies, bestowing as opposed to buying, we still focus on the way things circulate rather than how they are created. More often than not, those who speak enthusiastically about the cultural commons stay safely inside what Karl Marx called "the noisy sphere" of consumption, "where everything takes place . . . in full view of everyone," instead of descending into "the hidden abode of production," which in fact shapes our world even if we choose to look the other way.

This means we are telling only half the story. Consider Thomas

Jefferson, whose commentary on the problem of intellectual property is often quoted by new-media thinkers ("he who lights his taper
at mine, receives light without darkening me"). Again and again, Jefferson is invoked as a model of creative citizenship for a wired age.
Committed to the principle of free exchange, he passed up potentially lucrative opportunities to privatize knowledge, releasing details
of a new method for "braking and beating" hemp to forestall those
who would patent the innovation.

Jefferson was, in Lewis Hyde's words, "a commonwealth man"
who made his invention available to all and promoted the progress
of science over personal gain. But what open culture advocates fail
to acknowledge, even in passing, is that Jefferson was able to distribute his ideas for free because others were working to feed his
belly (in his case, slaves). Their labor enabled him to live a life of
political and intellectual engagement, to devote himself to devising
ingenious inventions.

Again, Web utopians emphasize the immaterial—ideas, freely
shared—while ignoring material conditions—the hundreds of people
held as property who farmed and manufactured goods under Jefferson's command. Their work over "belching smoke and clanging
hammers" made the flame of Jefferson's metaphorical taper possible.
The point is not to belabor the hypocrisy of the founding fathers
but to remind us to consider the modes of production, the systems of
sustenance and support, that underpin our gift economies.[1]

A material reality supports the digital commons in all its facets:
hardware, infrastructure, and content. Think, for a moment, about
the free phone you got when you signed up for mobile service or
whatever electronic device you recently obtained at a rock-bottom
price. If we descend into the hidden abode, looking at what lies
below the gleaming surfaces of our technologically enhanced lives,
what we see isn't pretty, cost free, or particularly modern.

The weightless rhetoric of digital technology masks a refusal to
acknowledge the people and resources on which these systems

depend: lithium and coltan mines, energy-guzzling data centers and server farms, suicidal workers at Apple's Foxconn factories, and women and children in developing countries and incarcerated Americans up to their necks in toxic electronic waste.[2] The swelling demand for precious metals, used in everything from video-game consoles to USB cables to batteries, has increased political instability in some regions, led to unsafe, unhealthy, and inhumane working conditions, opened up new markets for child and forced labor, and encouraged environmentally destructive extraction techniques.[3] It is estimated that mining the gold necessary to produce a single cell phone—only one mineral of many required for the finished product—produces upward of 220 pounds of waste.[4]

The environmental cost doesn't stop there. After they are sold, wireless conveniences guzzle energy at a not insignificant rate. Small electronics account for carbon emissions equivalent to the vilified airline industry; the average tablet or smartphone, if used to watch an hour of video weekly, consumes more energy than two new refrigerators.[5] The International Energy Agency estimates that digital culture may suck up 30 percent of residential electricity supplied globally by 2022, and 45 percent by 2030.[6] Add to that the more than three million data centers worldwide, the cloud's home on earth. In the United States, data centers account for approximately 2 percent of the country's energy consumption and climbing, with each center guzzling as much electricity as a small town, and the power overwhelmingly provided by the burning of coal, a cheap but filthy fuel source.[7]

The demand for electricity to power and cool these centers doubled between 2000 and 2005 and increased 56 percent between 2005 and 2010, leading to talk of a "potential energy crisis" and inspiring executives from companies including Google, IBM, and Hewlett-Packard to meet with representatives from the U.S. government to discuss how it might be averted.[8] "It's just not sustainable," one former utility executive told a reporter. "They're going to hit a brick wall."[9]

To catch a glimpse of some of high tech's more earthly effects, we need look no further than Silicon Valley, where many data centers appear on the Toxic Air Contaminant Inventory, a state government list of major polluters.[10] The futurist mecca is also home to the most concentrated number of Superfund sites in the United States (sites federally recognized as hazardous to human health), nineteen of which were contaminated by firms during the manufacture of microprocessors, a process that requires approximately two thousand different materials and chemicals to complete, leaving behind tainted water and solid waste.

These sites are laced with chemicals that include Freon, trichloroethane, polychlorinated biphenyls (PCBs), and trichloroethylene (TCE), a carcinogen known to cause reproductive and developmental damage, impaired neurological function, autoimmune disease, and other ailments in human beings—and a substance recently determined to be "5 to 65 times as toxic as previously thought, with pregnant women and other sensitive populations being most at risk." It's a solvent widely used to clean electronic parts, including computer chips, and one well known to my family: my sister is disabled because a chemical cocktail including TCE was improperly disposed of by a military contractor and seeped into the public aquifer outside of Tucson, Arizona. My mother, then pregnant, drank from and bathed in it.

Today, most high-tech production has moved out of California, outsourced abroad as companies pursue lower wages and less stringent labor and environmental standards. A few years ago, while working on a film, I met a group of young women working in foreign-owned electronics factories in Tijuana, Mexico, for long hours and meager pay, living in shantytowns down in a dusty valley without basic services. Some of them spent every day dipping their bare fingers in the chemical to wipe adhesive off electronics, risking their health and that of their future children to make goods that would be shipped across the border to American shopping centers. Our southern neighbors, building things on our behalf and absorbing the toxins that result, make our lives lighter, more instant, more connected, with the human and environmental consequences all but invisible.

Still we are assured that the digital revolution is a turn for the better, toward a world that is more inclusive, more egalitarian, greener. Consider the example of electronic publishing: not only are we promised that e-books will inaugurate an era of mass enlightenment by creating portable, infinite libraries, but also that they are more environmentally sound than their printed counterparts, a boon to the world's trees. While this could be the case, if device manufacturers made waste reduction a priority, for now the ecological benefits of paperless reading are dubious at best.

The *New York Times* evaluated the environmental impact of a single e-reader versus printed books, taking the minerals, water, and fossil fuels used during the manufacturing, transportation, operation, and disposal into account: one e-reader consumes the resources equal to approximately forty or fifty books; in terms of global warming it was equivalent to one hundred books; with respect to human health, the number was somewhere in between. These numbers inspire confidence at first glance, but the complication is the life span of the device.

The average e-reader is used for less than two years, disposed of, and then replaced, much like the cell phones we throw away after an average of twelve months. According to a Pew survey, e-book owners claim to read around twenty-four books a year (non-e-book consumers say they only read fifteen), but this number does not necessarily correspond to the number of new books they purchase. There, the national average is something closer to ten. This means that if every American abandoned paper for digital and bought a dedicated e-reader, the environmental impact of reading would go up not down, doubling, using the *Times*'s low estimate of forty books and assuming the device lasts a full two years. If we use a higher figure and assume a life span more akin to that of a cell phone, the figure can climb by a factor of ten.[11]

Printed books, it turns out, are a surprisingly resilient technology. I have editions on my shelves that are a century old and are still perfectly functional; they have been owned and read by others, they have been moved, and dropped, spilled on, and written in. While I may lust after my grandmother's library, my grandchildren will not care to inherent an antique Kindle or an iPad any more than I want last decade's clunky desktop. Some may protest that this is the nature of technological innovation, but much of our consumption is driven not by advances in engineering but by planned obsolescence.

Products "designed for the dump," as people in the business call them—made to break and engineered to be difficult or impossible to fix—ensure a steady revenue stream. Thus a company such as Apple, seeking to shorten the replacement cycle of their wares, makes it easier and more affordable for consumers to buy a new gadget than change the battery in an old one. We are deceived into thinking longevity is not an option.

When Steve Jobs died, many people circulated a quote in which he compared himself to a dedicated craftsman: "When you're a carpenter making a beautiful chest of drawers, you're not going to use a piece of plywood on the back, even though it faces the wall and nobody will ever see it. You'll know it's there, so you're going to use a beautiful piece of wood on the back. For you to sleep well at night, the aesthetic, the quality, has to be carried all the way through." But Jobs's masterpieces, if they can be called that, were designed to expire—to appear, suddenly, used up and outmoded, and, more important, replaceable. He made planned obsolescence so irresistible, it has ceased to be shocking.

Marketers play their part to encourage the perception of datedness. Apple, to stick with one company, spent almost $1 billion on advertising in 2012, pushing new and improved versions of goods many people already possess. Our laptops and handheld devices may work as well as ever, but they begin to look démodé in a mat-

ter of months, so we send our barely used machines to the dump
and get something up-to-date, something second generation instead
of first—a source of fleeting satisfaction, a symbol of our allegiance
to innovation and progress. Sixteen new cell phone models are introduced into the American market every month.[12] The possibility of a
more fashionable handset or faster interface or newfangled feature
perpetually beckons.

And so our mountains of e-waste grow three times faster than
the piles of regular garbage accumulating all around us. Hundreds
of millions of still-functional gadgets—billions of pounds of hazardous waste–leaching stuff—are thrown away every year.[13] Small
devices, expensive and difficult to disassemble, are even less likely to
be disposed of properly than their larger counterparts; up to 10 percent get recycled.[14] By 2005 there were already more than half a billion outmoded mobile phones tucked away in American desk
drawers, a number that has surely risen over the intervening years.

Some scientists and researchers argue that the price of your average fast-food hamburger should actually be around two hundred
dollars, a number that accurately reflects the real cost of things such
as clear-cutting of forests, contamination of water, damage to human
health, government subsidies, and so on. What, one wonders, is the
real price of a "free" cell phone or a cheap reading device, tablet, or
computer—objects so easy to come by that we mistake them for
worthless?

A sustainable digital future means making these hidden costs
visible and tackling the problem of obsolescence—technical, planned,
and perceived—head on. Each upgrade, every enhanced version of a
previously existing product, should be matched by parallel ecological and social progress. The ultimate new and improved product is
not just one that is faster, cooler, or more useful than what came
before it, but one that does less damage to the environment, is more
durable and repairable, and is less harmful to the people who made
it and those who will live long after its screen goes forever black.

———

Culture, too—what these devices deliver—has been peddled as cheap and disposable. It's all part of the continuum of free stuff we have come to expect: free phones, free Web searches, free e-mail, free apps, free access, free content. But we know there's no such thing as free: somebody has to cover the cost. What matters is who is paying—and why.

When we descend into the hidden abode of cultural production, what system supports the creation of these gifts? More often than not, the answer online is advertising. While we hear about the demise of industrial-era dinosaurs—doomed record labels and publishers, panicking television and movie executives, and the death of the CD, the DVD, the book, and the newspaper—advertising has, if anything, increased, picking up the tab for more and more of our cultural consumption. The central pillar of the old mass media landscape shows no sign of impending collapse.

"We expect that advertising-funded search engines will be inherently biased toward the advertisers and away from the needs of consumers," Sergey Brin and Larry Page wrote in a paper when their new start-up, Google, was still part of Stanford University in 1998. "The better the search engine is, the fewer advertisements will be needed for the consumer to find what they want. . . . We believe the issue of advertising causes enough mixed incentives that it is crucial to have a competitive search engine that is transparent and in the academic realm."

This idealism did not last for long, however, and the founders soon abandoned their mission to build a search engine that was nonprofit and ad free. Today Google reigns as the most successful advertising company on earth, commanding around half of the online market, which is predicted to quadruple over the next four years and hit $200 billion in the next ten.[15] In 2012, advertising accounted for 95 percent of the company's over $50 billion in annual revenue.

Ironically, the "contempt" and "disgust" Google has for traditional advertisers continue to be widely reported, becoming a central facet of the company's mythology. It's a posture that points to a
gaping disconnect between appearance and reality, a willful denial
of what's really keeping the entire Internet economy afloat. Many
of the Silicon Valley enterprises that have been variously presented
as technologically innovative and exciting—not just Google but also
Yahoo!, AOL, Facebook, Twitter, Foursquare, Instagram, Tumblr,
Pandora, and so on—depend almost entirely on the advertising dollar, if only by commodifying and monetizing the attention of their
users and their personal information.

On the surface the algorithmically determined advertisements
that Web companies offer up seem harmless enough, especially considering the bounty of free services we get in return. Since we don't
see all the data being harvested from our Web searches, e-mail correspondence, and social networking, it looks like we get more than
we give. But we give an awful lot.

In a multipart investigation, the *Wall Street Journal* found that
after subjects visited the Web's fifty most popular Web sites, a total
of 3,180 tracking files were installed on its test computers. Using a
toolkit that includes cookies, supercookies, beacons, digital finger-
printing, and even deep packet inspection, hundreds of middlemen
(advertising networks, tracking companies, and data brokers) stalk
us as we move online, monitoring our mouse movements and
recording our keystrokes, scanning what we do in real time—often
evading or subverting our privacy settings.[16]

One leading broker, Acxiom, has an average of fifteen hundred
items of data on 96 percent of adult Americans.[17] So-called scrapers
scour the Web for the digital equivalent of pocket lint—things we've
written on message boards, comments we've posted on news sites,
product reviews, social network details, résumé and work histories—
analyzing and packaging the results. The apps we use covertly collect details about us including our age, gender, and location, as well

as the unique ID number assigned to our phones and tablets. ("We watch what apps you download, how frequently you use them, how much time you spend on them, and how deep into the app you go," a representative of an ad network told the *Journal*.) These unique identifiers, able to trail individuals across multiple mobile devices, will expedite new intrusive modes of advertising, including "proprietary emotional targeting" to reach users when they are most vulnerable and "receptive to brand messages." That would be Monday mornings, for example, when marketers claim that women feel most insecure."[18]

Companies are now able to target ads based on our current location (Amazon has a patent for Kindle that not only serves ads based on where we are but where the algorithms predict we will go) and which people we interact with (Apple has a patent that includes advertising based on what's in your friend's media library).[19] "Personal privacy is no longer an individual thing," warned an MIT computer scientist. "In today's online world, what your mother told you is true, only more so: People really can judge you by your friends."

If we don't realize the degree to which we are being tracked and targeted, that is partly because companies know that we tend not to approve of their actions when they ask for permission. Unlike in Europe, where tougher privacy standards are enforced, our information can be surreptitiously collected without our explicit consent and with little oversight. As many advocates point out, our privacy laws are pitifully out of date, written long before third parties could dream of observing everything we do online.[20]

Moreover, there is no baseline, cross-sector privacy law in the United States, which means that when new products come onto the market—facial recognition software, to name one potentially game-changing example (some stores are now using it to spot VIP shoppers)—there are rarely clear rules or legal safeguards governing them, no matter how sensitive the information collected.[21]

Though there has been some progress in recent years, including attempts to standardize Do Not Track browser features and the

Obama administration's "Consumer Privacy Bill of Rights," our personal data—the networked world's most valuable resource—remain up for sale, virtually unregulated. In part the difficulty is technological, as rules are often out of date by the time they have been formalized (new methods have been developed to circumvent Do Not Track and efforts to protect personally identifiable information are insufficient when other types of indirect data can be parsed to predict our behavior with uncanny accuracy). But if the advertising industry has been successful in its fight against consumer protection laws thus far, that is also the result of a lopsided battle: the data-mining industry has revenues of around $5 billion and employs one hundred thousand people, dwarfing the Federal Trade Commission (FTC), the government agency tasked with regulating it.[22]

At the same time, politicians are reluctant to put meaningful restrictions on Silicon Valley, a bright spot of economic growth and innovation. "The industry has gotten more powerful, the technology has gotten more pervasive, and it's getting to the point where we can't do too much about it," Michael Copps, former commissioner of the Federal Communications Commission, lamented.[23] For the foreseeable future, there is no foolproof way to "opt out" except for staying off-line altogether.

Though they pay lip service to privacy, new-media companies are resistant to any supervision or legal limits on how data are gathered or used, for the simple reason that their profit margins depend on accessing that information. The erosion of privacy online is not an inevitability but rather the result of bad public policy and business incentives that have turned the rush to gather more personal data into a veritable arms race.[24] Despite its famous maxim "Don't Be Evil"—a motto made in reference to specific advertising methods—Google has violated its own principles on more than one occasion.

The search giant that once resisted advertising now owns AdMob, AdSense, Analytics, and DoubleClick. Similarly, techniques it once found suspect, such as tracking, have been reconsidered. Egged on

by the threat of competition, Google pooled the extensive information it gathers from users to build an ambitious data exchange,
allowing advertisers to target individuals and "buy access to them
in real time as they surf the Web."[25] In early 2012 Google crossed a
new threshold when it announced a change to its privacy policy:
the company would soon begin compiling all of the information it
collects about us from multiple services to a single profile, linking
what's in our Gmail accounts with what we watch on YouTube
with what we search for and so on. ("Bastards!" an early employee
reports Google founder Larry Page exclaiming in response to those
who raised concerns about privacy.)[26]

Thus, the company has evolved beyond its big innovation—the
efficient matching of specific search terms to relevant advertising—
to enter the business of helping vendors devise new ways to ply us
with promotions based on our friends, our location, our fears, and our
desires. And soon, thanks to wearable devices, our glances. Google
has been granted a patent that conjures a future of "pay-for-gaze"
advertising, where marketers are charged according to the on- and
off-line ads users look at and how long their attention lingers.

Other new-media companies face similar pressure, but none more
than Facebook. The company's record-breaking public offering in
May 2012 was predicated on assumptions of mind-boggling growth,
all based on advertising. "Facebook, in many ways, is like a mining
company sitting on valuable deposits that are hard to dig up and
refine," the New York Times reported on the day of the company's
IPO. "At a market value of $104 billion, investors think Facebook is
sitting on gold." The immediate tumbling of the company's share
price only intensified the quest to exploit those reserves—the "unri-
valed repository of human desire" the company has built from the
personal information of well over one billion users—and meet the
revenue expectations built into that initial massive figure (which
marked Facebook as more valuable than the vast majority of American companies, including General Motors and McDonald's).

By the summer of 2013 the company had succeeded in meeting this goal by making progress in the challenging realm of mobile advertising. Facebook executives met with emissaries from various companies to figure out how to better serve them, including letting advertisers see more of what users are doing and saying. Their clients seem pleased: Ford and Coca-Cola have stated that the collaboration has had a positive impact on sales, and Facebook's stock has risen accordingly.[27] We want to make it "easier for marketers to reach their customers," Mark Zuckerberg assured investors in late 2012, right around the time it was revealed that Facebook was working with a company called Datalogix to track what users bought offline, in brick-and-mortar stores, to provide an even more granular view of user habits.[28] As the company works to match promotional messages with people, the trick, according to the *Times*, "is to avoid violating its users' perceived sense of privacy or inviting regulatory scrutiny."[29]

We are witnessing the beginning of a "revolution in the ways marketers and media intrude in—and shape—our lives," Joseph Turow, author of *The Daily You*, has written.[30] Yet despite all the democratic rhetoric about the Internet empowering consumers, it is clear that this revolution is not of the bottom-up variety. As the example of Facebook shows, it is resolutely advertiser driven: "Advertisers in the digital space expect all media firms to deliver them particular types of individuals—and, increasingly, particular individuals—by leveraging detailed knowledge about them and their behaviors that was unheard of even a few years ago."[31] Omar Tawakol, CEO of BlueKai, a data exchange that sells tens of millions of tiny bits of information about individuals' browsing habits for fractions of a penny apiece—is more blunt: "Advertisers want to buy access to people, not web pages."[32]

With remarkable precision, advertisers are now able to home in on weight-conscious teenage white girls, Midwesterners who suffer from migraines, comedy-loving fathers having midlife crises, rape victims, and more, and target them directly.[33] We are anonymous, experts warn, in "name alone"; the personal profiles these companies have on us can include zip code, income, age, race, gender, educational attainment, religious leanings, health and marital status, and preferred entertainment options such as recently viewed TV shows and films. By gathering detailed demographic information (who we are), geographic information (where we are), behavioral information (how we act), and social information (who we know), companies compile highly detailed dossiers, which they use to tailor the content we see.[34] After the advertiser-led revolution is complete, an Ivy League graduate will see completely different ads and content than someone who has completed only high school.

We are being sorted into "reputation silos" that can be surprisingly difficult to get out of, labeled as either *targets* or *waste*, segmented down into an audience of one and steered accordingly. This prejudicial system shapes what information we are exposed to and what products we are offered while reinforcing preexisting inequities.[35] For example, in 2013 a Harvard researcher showed that searches containing names associated with African American people were dramatically more likely to generate results suggesting criminal activity and arrest.[36]

Just as worrying are the ways our personal profiles have already started factoring into not just what ads we see but also the prices we are charged for specific goods and, eventually, may affect the rates we are offered on mortgages and credit cards.[37] A growing number of companies offer services that analyze social media profiles to determine whether individuals are a lending risk, a move that may enable creditors to consider information they are banned from requesting on certain loan applications (for instance, race and religion and even what we read and who we associate with online) facilitating unfair treatment and exclusion.[38] What we are witnessing is the emergence of a new form of discrimination, one led by companies you can't see, using data you didn't give them permission to access, dictating what you are exposed to and on what terms.

The first newspaper advertisement in the colonies appeared in 1704 in Boston, but America's romance with advertising began in earnest in the late 1800s when sales pitches began to fatten publications across the country, the ample profits building dynasties and underwriting journalism, muckraking and yellow alike. A couple of decades later, when radio was still a novelty and television hadn't yet colonized living rooms around the world, it became clear that there were, broadly speaking, two divergent paths for funding the production of "free" broadcast media—public money or private money, state or market. Britain blazed one trail, followed by the rest of Europe and Canada, with the establishment of the BBC, a public interest corporation designed to be independent of both the government and industry and financed through the collection of license fees from the sale of radio receivers and then television sets. The United States blazed the other, securing corporate underwriting through commercial breaks and sponsorship. Almost a century later, advertising remains the subsidy of choice for America and, increasingly, the world.

The path chosen by the United States was not a foregone conclusion, however, and, in the beginning, many rallied to keep the airwaves independent of the hustling spirit. Trumpeting goods and services would only sully a medium that could serve a higher purpose, Secretary of Commerce Herbert Hoover argued at the first national radio conference in 1922: "It is inconceivable that we should allow so great a possibility for service, for news, for entertainment, for education, and for vital commercial purposes to be drowned in advertising and chatter." Listeners overwhelmingly agreed, but a few months after his address a radio station in New York transmitted its first ad—a ten-minute spot for a new real estate development in Queens—inaugurating the era of "entertainment that sells."

Stations began their battle for audience share in order to attract advertisers, and advertiser influence grew accordingly. The company paying the bills controlled the content. On the radio you could tune in to the *Maxwell House Hour* and *General Motors Family Party*. The first proper television news broadcast was *The Camel News Caravan*, named for the cigarette manufacturer; it shared space on the dial with *The Colgate Comedy Hour* and *Texaco Star Theater*. Soap operas, of course, sold soap.

"There is something radically wrong with the fundamental national policy under which television operates. The principle of that policy is that for all practical purposes television shall be operated solely for private profit," critic and journalist Walter Lippmann complained in an influential column in 1959. "While television is supposed to be free, it has in fact become the creature, the servant, and indeed the prostitute, of merchandising." Following fast on the heels of a national scandal—it had just been revealed that popular quiz shows were rigged by sponsors—Lippmann's comments touched a nerve. America's laissez-faire approach was failing; the true price of advertising-supported content was becoming clear; commercially driven media and mass persuasion were distorting democracy. The public was hungry for reform.

The quiz show affair, barely remembered today, was a pivotal moment in American media history, bathing advertisers in ignominy and opening a space for two long-ignored but good ideas to gain traction. One was a call for public service broadcasting. The other was the principle that the line between programming and marketing, editorial and advertising, should be clearly drawn. Congress strengthened sponsorship disclosure laws, and radio and television producers seized the moment to reassert some modicum of independence from their funders. By 1968, fewer than 3 percent of all radio and television programs were created by advertisers or ad agencies, down from a high of more than half, even as advertising flourished in the mass media.

Marketers, understandably, have never wanted to underwrite an independent content industry, but in the wake of the quiz show scandal they had no choice.[39] Because newspapers, television channels, and radio stations controlled access to audiences, advertisers were strong-armed into ponying up money that funded investigative journalism and educational programming. In the analog world, publishers and broadcasters bundled people into audiences, which they sold to advertisers. But in a digital world, advertisers can "buy the audience without the publication."[40] The sorts of people who read the *New York Times*, the *Nation*, or *Cat Fancy* can be reached outside of those channels, bought and sold elsewhere on the Web at a fraction of the price, with the revenue going into other pockets.

And yet, in their quest to reach individuals online, advertisers haven't abandoned the content industry altogether. What they are able to buy in a digital space is more control. Rishad Tobaccowala, chief strategist for one of the largest marketing communication companies in the world, said that in the near future traditional media firms will no longer be able to force marketers to support the production of expensive content, be it journalism or television shows. To survive, Tobaccowala predicted, they will have to "adapt to their advertising masters' new demands." The demand, in a nutshell, is "integration." Flexing their newfound power, marketers are steadily chipping away at the barriers erected in the wake of the quiz show scandal. As a consultant at Mindshare Entertainment explained in an interview, their aim is to "break through the wall" that separates art and editorial from advertising.

Terrified by the prospect of diminishing revenue, even reputable institutions are scrambling to prove their utility to their new overlords. The double wallop of economic and technological uncertainty has made forms of advocacy and sponsorship once thought to be impolitic acceptable again. Not only are publishers tracking users and personalizing their products, but once taboo practices such as payola and sponsored journalism are proliferating. Across all types of media, product placement is on a massive upsurge, growing at a rate of 30 percent per year despite the recession, and branded content (or "brand-inspired content," as euphemists say) is all the rage. All told, the money poured into these last two markets exceeds $55 billion annually around the globe, with $25 billion spent in the United States alone. Conventional disclosure laws do not apply online or are simply impossible to enforce. This kind of "stealth marketing" has a corrosive effect on public discourse. Institutional integrity goes out the window when editorial content adapts to advertiser demands.

This tendency is troubling all around, but nowhere more so than in journalism, the field hardest hit by the exodus of traditional advertising dollars. On Gawker, Gothamist, Mashable, and other popular sites, "sponsored posts" and "content series" are composed to match the editorial voice of the publication and intermingled with the day's regular offerings. ("Our in-house writing talents handle your post from ideation to execution," Gawker explains, "infusing your brand message with our signature, conversational tone.") BuzzFeed leads the pack with what it calls "native advertising," a euphemism for advertorials. Staffers ("creative strategists") concoct posts designed to maximize audience engagement while incorporating messages from brands such as Pillsbury and Virgin Mobile, sucking up revenue from a sponsored content market estimated to be worth up to $5 billion overall by 2017. While some worry about the eroding "church-state" divide, sites such as BuzzFeed and the *Huffington Post* crow about abandoning the standards that long helped insulate journalists' work from the mandate of the people who pay the bills: instead they aim to help brands "have a conversation" with the site's readership.

Even venerable print publications seem to accept that old strictures no longer apply when they move online. Recently the popular *New York Times* financial blog *DealBook*, edited by Andrew Ross Sorkin, came under fire for accepting sponsorship from Goldman Sachs, which means one of the largest investment banking and securities firms is underwriting business reporting at the paper of record. In 2013 the *Washington Post* introduced BrandConnect to allow marketers to create content that displays on the homepage, making it the first major U.S. newspaper to go "native"; in 2014, the *Times* followed suit. In the United Kingdom the *Guardian* has signed on as global distributor of branded video content produced by *Vice* magazine, exemplified by a series called "ecomagination" about green energy sponsored by General Electric. "I think it's part of our evolution as content publishers," the global director of marketing communications at General Electric enthused about the project.

Forbes has pushed the envelope even further, selling the right to blog on its Web site to advertisers, placing organizations including Ford and Pfizer on par with magazine staffers. "At *Forbes*, we're beginning to open up our print and digital platforms so many more knowledgeable and credible content creators can provide information and perspective and connect with one another," the publication announced, sidestepping questions about potential conflicts of interest. "Today, everyone can be a creator or curator of content. What was yesterday's audience is today's cadre of potential experts who can report what they know or filter information for distribution to friends who trust their judgments. Advertisers can do the same." With plenty of unemployed journalists out there, Intel and other companies are busy building online newsrooms of their own, offering their "reporting" to any outlets that care to repost it and bypassing traditional media venues altogether. Why go through a publisher when you can become the publisher?

We are also seeing individuals—not just institutions—blurring the line between advertising and content. The digital tools that democratized creativity have also extended the chance to sell out to all. Amateur video makers can partner with brands through enterprises such as Placevine, an online automated brand integration system, Poptent, which crowdsources corporate media campaigns at a fraction of their usual cost, or YouTube-owned NextLabs, which helps video creators package themselves to better appeal to advertisers.[41] Successful online personalities, like the famed mommy blogger Heather Armstrong (a.k.a. "Dooce"), reap enormous rewards by signing up with advertising agencies. Dooce, it has been reported, brings in an estimated fifty thousand dollars a month in advertising revenue in addition to other perks, including having her office renovation sponsored by Verizon.[42]

Thanks to social media, you don't even need to make particularly creative work to cash in. Countless news sites and message board comments are actually works for hire, left by people who, under the guise of dozens of faked virtual identities, make it appear that support for their clients is widespread.[43] These Internet "astroturfers," as they've been called, are supplemented by the hundreds of thousands of people who, in return for subsidized trips, gift cards, free samples, and modest payments, have signed up to be word-of-mouth marketers under their own names, shilling wares to the people in their personal networks or writing positive reviews of products and services.[44] The money is not bad: a 2010 study found that "sponsored tweets" were priced at an average of $124 and a "sponsored blog post" at $179—which, a Columbia Journalism School report pointed out, is "around the same amount a small news organization will pay for a story and far more than an average blog post would ever get from display ads," putting such fluff at a substantial advantage.[45] These "sponsored conversations" are reported to be one of the fastest-growing divisions in advertising.[46] In a world of free content, a surprising amount of it has actually been bought and paid for.[47]

The critic Gilbert K. Chesterton once said that art and morality are alike: both involve drawing a line somewhere. But that line is fading even to those who would firmly position themselves on the side of art, not advertising. Individual creators are routinely advised to align themselves with corporations to help them cover costs, a move that is often hailed as a new business model. A discussion about creativity and compensation at a respected technology conference underscored that these "new business models" are in fact strangely regressive. The moderator was the producer of a popular online series financed by Sony. One panelist, a self-described "Internet enthusiast," Julia Allison, bragged of selling individual tweets to Armani after recounting how a clip she had posted of her navel-piercing had garnered more than a million views. Others, part of a well-known music-comedy group called the Gregory Brothers, made it seem as though doing spots for big names such as Chipotle was the ultimate triumph. "It's good to have fans in companies who will support what you do and get you involved," one of them earnestly stated. "In order to exist in this ecosystem you have to work with companies." The group confessed that they had a new tactic to guarantee the popularity of their videos and ongoing financial success—remixing already viral memes, thereby riding the coattails of preexisting hits while also substantially speeding up their creative process, since a basic concept was already in place.

Well-intentioned critiques of copyright have inadvertently encouraged this trend. Instead of de-commodifying culture, weakening copyright has had the opposite effect, increasing "the prevalence of marketing in media products as cultural producers try to attract more advertising to compensate for declining royalties and other income," according to legal scholar Ellen Goodman. Moreover, since corporations want nothing more than their message to spread, brand-sponsored content, Goodman observed, is "resilient to unauthorized copying." In other words, advertisers are not undermined economically when people share their content without paying for it, since their aim is to maximize exposure to the goods or services they are trying to sell.[48]

In this way, ironically, the free culture movement's agenda unintentionally benefits the public relations industry. Since the advent of

Napster, as traditional record labels struggle to survive, companies like Mountain Dew, Toyota, and Converse have stepped in, providing recording studio space, video production services, tour support, and marketing assistance to musicians, while encouraging them to give away their music.[49] As Adam Farrell of Matador Records pointed out in an interview with journalist Chris Ruen, companies get to "look really cool . . . for cheap," since they typically pay far less to partner with a band and release a single than they would to license the same song for a traditional commercial.[50]

Artists, meanwhile, explain their involvement with these sponsors as a rational response to economic uncertainty. "In 1995, it was rare for musicians to partner with corporations; in most corners of the music industry it was seen as the ultimate sell-out," OK Go's Damian Kulash explained in the *Wall Street Journal*. "But with investments from labels harder to come by, attitudes toward outside corporate deals have changed." With their elaborate music videos underwritten by companies including Range Rover, Samsung, and State Farm Insurance, OK Go exemplifies this shift. The band is less focused on selling recordings, Kulash has said, than selling brands access to their fans.[51]

Similar funding methods are creeping into the documentary film community as DVD sales dry up and screening venues struggle to stay open. A growing number of film festivals and professional events now feature sessions on working with brand partners. A prime example is Morgan Spurlock, the award-winning director of *Super Size Me*, the takedown of McDonald's. Soon after the premiere of his feature *POM Wonderful Presents: The Greatest Movie Ever Sold*—an exposé of product placement funded entirely by product placement ("He's not selling out, he's buying in," the film's tagline declares)—Spurlock started a program to help other documentarians attract precisely the kind of support he appeared to be criticizing. Companies "have something to gain from an association with reality-oriented filmmakers who often pride themselves on speaking truth to power," a journalist writing about the program explained. In early 2012 Spurlock released *Mansome*, a movie about male grooming peppered with celebrity cameos. It was reviewed as an independent documentary, although Spurlock conceded the film was underwritten by a corporate sponsor, which *Forbes* speculates might have been Gillette, the razor manufacturer.[52]

Matt Wolf, a young filmmaker who made *Wild Combination*, a documentary about musician Arthur Russell, and *Teenage*, about the invention of the youth demographic, is skeptical of these kinds of partnerships after inadvertently taking part in one. He got a call asking him to make a series of ten short artists' portraits in conjunction with an event held in Los Angeles and New York, a rather "name droppy" affair, according to Wolf, featuring Spike Jonze and other vaguely hip luminaries. Absolut Vodka was the sponsor, but Wolf was assured the company was working only behind the scenes. His creative contribution would not be branded in any way. Broke and grateful for the opportunity, Wolf signed up for the job.

Slowly but surely, however, "the story started changing." He saw mock-ups of an "Absolut Collaboration" Web site where his films were going to be streamed. He got a memo saying his work couldn't be political, show nudity, or have any driving or sports in it. Wolf was troubled by what he felt was censorship—"Everything," he told me, "is political"—but by that point he had already shot portraits of people he knew and admired. Eventually the films were posted on a Web site that was obviously the property of Absolut; viewers had to click a button saying they were eighteen to enter, and the finished portraits conspicuously featured the alcohol company's logo. Wolf called his subjects and apologized, telling them that they were the stars of branded content though they had never consented to such a thing.

"It became this thing that I felt was disgusting, that I picked out my friends to participate in something that is really an under-resourced, under-budgeted form of advertising," Wolf said. "What they wanted was the trust of my peers—this ephemeral quality of credibility they will never possess, fishing it out of you surreptitiously and dishonestly." It was the surreptitious aspect, the fact that what the company really wanted was a way into his world, the trust of his colleagues and his audience, that was so unsettling—and they didn't bother paying him for four months.

"It was really a wake-up call. I'm not going to sell out my friends to things for money—that's wrong. Of course, I never would have stepped into the opportunity if that was how it was framed." That said, Wolf believes his distaste for advertising puts him in a minority, and a shrinking one. A good number of creators aspire to do commercial work, and he doesn't blame them since it's a way to make ends meets. Instead of "selling out," they see themselves as "getting over," taking advantage of corporate largesse to advance their careers. Wolf disagrees, seeing the game as fixed in the companies' favor. Artistic independence loses out.

New technologies have multiplied the opportunities for advertisers to exploit the integrity and social connections of regular folks, not just established artists. Millions of people follow their favorite brands on Twitter, responding to their solicitations and retweeting their offers. On Facebook you can interact with companies and products as you do your friends, liking them and leaving comments on their walls. In 2009 there was a significant redesign so that brand pages would look more like user profile pages in order to make brands seem more like peers. Products were given the virtual status of people, and within two years many of the pages with the most friends were familiar companies such as Starbucks and Coca-Cola.

Meanwhile, the personal and the commercial further merged through the arrival of "social ads," which allow marketers to turn our actions into advertisements, transforming everything we do into a form of promotion. If you "like" a product, your picture will appear, endorsing it on a friend's page. "This is in many ways the Holy Grail of marketing: making your customers your marketers," said Facebook's chief operating officer, Sheryl Sandberg, and so far it seems to work.[53]

An analysis by Nielsen "found that people who viewed ads displaying a friend's endorsement were 68 percent more likely to remember the ad than were people who saw a plain display ad" and that "they were more than four times as likely to say they intended to purchase the advertised product." With a simple click, our personal credibility rubs off on corporate behemoths, creating what Sandberg called a "marketing tunnel"—a social vortex that generates consumer demand.

It's striking, when one pauses to think about it, how essential art and culture remain to the digital economy even as most of the money floating around goes to multibillion-dollar businesses that don't invest much in either. Art and culture are the stuff that ads are sold around, the bait that causes users to divulge their preferences by clicking so their data can be mined. The profits made by many online ventures, from social networks to search engines to news sites, are "tied directly to the velocity of people's information intake," as Nicholas Carr explained in *The Shallows* in an analysis of Google's business model, though his insights can be broadly applied.

> The faster we surf across the surface of the Web—the more links we click and pages we view—the more opportunities Google gains to collect information about us and to feed us advertisements. Its advertising system . . . is explicitly designed to figure out which messages are most likely to grab our attention and then to place those messages in our field of view. Every click we make on the Web makes a break in our concentration, a bottom-up disruption of our attention—and it's in Google's economic

interest to make sure we click as often as possible. The last thing the company wants is to encourage leisurely reading or slow concentrated thought.[54]

The dominant economic model compels the quest for hits and clicks, encouraging content farm logic—search engine–optimized headlines, page-view-baiting slide shows, irresistibly shareable top-ten lists, image-heavy posts, bite-size webisodes, TV-style video promotions, and so on. As Jeff Hammerbacher, a software coder and one of Facebook's early hires, succinctly said, "The best minds of my generation are thinking about how to make people click ads. That sucks."

Whenever artists sign on with brands, their creativity and credibility are grafted on to the goods or service being plugged. The aim is to bypass or short-circuit viewer defenses by intimately associating with creative elements that people find appealing—to "engage target consumers in captive locations for extended periods of time through the power of emotional connections," as the CEO of a leading media research firm put it. Given our populist sensibilities, advertisements, as writers Thomas Frank and Naomi Klein have observed, can no longer just tell us what to buy. Instead they need to offer us what appear to be gifts—like Wolf's artist profiles—while slyly taking something, our attention or "mindshare," in return.

In this context it's common for companies to fancy themselves patrons—modern-day Medicis, they've been called—giving needy creators a boost. But there are limits to what they're willing to support. *Advertising Age*, for example, reports that blogs geared toward mothers are favored by marketers because they "steer clear of politics, sex and other controversial subject matter."[55] Music is popular for the same reason, as are comedy, cooking, and crafting videos.

The constraints of network television are exacerbated online: risk taking is underinvested. On TV there's reality programming galore, but something like PBS's investigative news program *Front-line* is unique even on public channels for its lack of corporate underwriting. The show is simply too threatening to entrenched interests to attract their backing.

The implications for book publishing could be profound. Amazon introduced a reduced-price e-reader euphemistically called the "Kindle with Special Offers," which features ads on the main menu and as screensavers. "People can vote, either online or on a Kindle app called AdMash, for their favorite of two ads, like a close-up of a model's face versus a photo of a jar of cream for Olay," the *New York Times* reported.[56] And Seth Godin formed a temporary, investigatory publishing partnership with the online colossus, releasing one of his first titles for free under the sponsorship of General Electric.

Can you imagine books like *Silent Spring* or *The Satanic Verses* coming courtesy of Aerosoles or AutoZone? One optimistic start-up, hoping to capitalize on the shift to electronic reading, aims to help authors cultivate identities as "tastemakers," partnering them with brands in order to sell things like grills and barbecue sauce to readers. This kind of corporate saturation has long been the dream of free market acolytes, including tech commentator George Gilder, whose 1994 book *Life After Television* featured full-color ads from FedEx every few pages. At the time Gilder's book seemed like a crass gimmick by a highly ideological eccentric; today it looks prophetic.

The challenge of supporting uncompromising work is growing greater, for the unbundling of digital media means the era of cross-subsidies, whereby profits from popular wares are used to support more daring endeavors, is coming to an end. The classic example is newspapers, which people bought for the classifieds or comics—these readers translated into higher advertising revenue, which helped finance foreign desks. The days for those kinds of arrangements are numbered, as Yahoo!'s Marissa Mayer made clear at a Senate hearing on the future of journalism. Individual articles are the new "atomic unit of consumption for news," she observed, a shift that requires a different approach to monetization: "each individual article should be self-sustaining."

Upon hearing her testimony, advertisers rejoiced the world over. Never again would they have to inadvertently fund accountability journalism to get their message out. Should they decide to invest in content, they can insist, as Absolut did, that political material be studiously avoided, that the potentially divisive or upsetting be left unsaid.

Predictably, recipients of corporate munificence rarely challenge their benefactors due to the strings they find themselves tied up in. There have been rare exceptions. In 2011, a tiny Seattle-based nonprofit that teaches documentary video production to young women issued two short tweets condemning the cable giant Comcast's merger with NBC. Soon after, Comcast cut its funding to the organization.

A less serious example of speech stifling happened around the same time when the comic Neil Hamburger used his inaugural *Vice* magazine column to express his disdain for one of the publication's sponsors, AXE body spray, which he tarred as "the preferred deodorant of date-rapists." A product sold by "pied pipers of shit" who "hope to convert innocents through flashy free entertainment, lending their name and money to dubious 'viral' comedy videos— recruiting third-string (one step up from me) comedians to disgrace themselves in vaguely obscene short films," Hamburger groused, "AXE recklessly attaches their brand to movie premieres, snowboarding events, comedy tours, and musical concerts, trying to latch on to any pre-existing cachet created by the artists themselves." The *Vice* editors, usually more than happy to offend, quickly folded under pressure from the company, removing the column when they were told the sponsorship would end, though Hamburger's provocation spread online through other channels.

In such cases the provisos attached to funding dollars are obvious, clear for all to see. The problem, though, is that the exercise
of power is rarely so overt. Instead of directly squelching artistic
expression when it's too brazen—a tactic that can backfire to the
artist's advantage—advertisers and sponsors protect themselves by
favoring docile voices in the first place.

Thus they alter the cultural ecology, fostering work that is apo-
litical and unchallenging, making the innocuously entertaining
more plentiful than it would be otherwise. While many hoped that
the Internet would help create a more varied cultural landscape,
advertising dollars continue to distort the market by creating perverse incentives, encouraging the production of irresistibly clickable
content. The social vista is duller as a result of their influence, our
culture more cloying and compliant. When advertisers call the shots,
they encourage only that which will help them sell.

We are now living in an "attention economy," new-media thinkers
like to say. Whether that is true or not, it is attention that corporate
patrons are interested in. Marketers want to know that their messages are having an impact; only after you have attracted a sizable
audience can you earn their sponsorship. In order to survive under
such a paradigm, creative types are advised to constantly remind
the world of their accomplishments, honing their personas and trumpeting their own horns through social media, angling around the
clock for clicks and comments, for links and likes. Celebrity has
become ever more essential to creative survival, and the cultivation
of friends, fans, and followers a full-time job.

When you're working for "reputational currency," to use one of
Chris Anderson's stock phrases, you are your most valuable commodity. You must become a desirable product whom audiences want
to "connect" with; once notoriety is achieved, Internet gurus promise, the money will pour in. ("Those $20k speaker fees soon add up,"

Anderson once boasted. And it's certainly true, if you are saying things Fortune 500 companies are eager to hear. The same organizations that write those big checks are far less likely to support thinkers who don't advance their interests, be they critics, investigative journalists, novelists, or poets—all types who are more likely to speak at schools or community centers for free than reap a fortune on the road.) Now we must advertise ourselves to survive.

The phenomenon is most visible in the mounting pressure to create a "personal brand," an idea first articulated by *Fast Company* magazine in 1997 during the early days of the dot-com boom. Management guru Tom Peters informed his readers that the lifelong, stable employment of the industrial era was over; in the information age, we would all be free agents. "Regardless of age, regardless of position, regardless of the business we happen to be in, all of us need to understand the importance of branding. We are CEOs of our own companies: Me Inc. To be in business today, our most important job is to be head marketer for the brand called You."

Becoming a brand was "inescapable," Peters argued, because the path to success had become unclear. Where there was once an obvious career ladder to climb, life had become a checkerboard, a game of constant competition and jockeying for position. "I know this may sound like selfishness. But being CEO of Me Inc. requires you to act selfishly—to grow yourself, to promote yourself, to get the market to reward yourself."

Peters's basic concept seemed a bit extreme at the time, but it is now entrenched. "Self-promotion is no longer solely the domain of egotists and professional aspirants. Anyone can be a personal branding machine," one *Wired* cover recently proclaimed. A slew of Web-savvy characters—the kind who appear on panels at South by Southwest (SXSW) and present at TED conferences—are peddling the same idea, their rhetoric spreading out from the tech world to infect other communities.

As the online marketing pioneer Tamara Hunt put it, we are all "social capitalists"; the self must be packaged and publicized and invested in so you can cash out. "Personal branding is about managing your name—even if you don't own a business—in a world of misinformation, disinformation, and semi-permanent Google records," said Timothy Ferriss, who has made a name for himself advising people on how to make names for themselves using social media.[57] The self-branding ideal puts full responsibility on the individual, who must live or die on his or her own in the open market.

The corporate ethos that drives discussions of personal branding is fundamental to the architecture of social media. Alice Marwick, an anthropologist who did her fieldwork studying the tech scene in Silicon Valley and San Francisco, argues that new communication technologies reflect the individualist and status-conscious values of the competitive, commercial milieu in which they were developed. The ideology of Web 2.0 "trumpets the radical principles of counter-cultural movements, but dampens them through the emphasis on profit and business context."[58]

Where networks could conceivably be used to further more democratic and egalitarian connections, Web 2.0 applications too often "further a view of the self and relationships that is entirely in line with current corporate business models," Marwick says. "Young professionals adopt self-consciously constructed personae which are marketed, like brands or celebrities, to an audience or fan base. These personas are highly edited, controlled, and monitored, conforming to ideals of a work-safe, commercial self presentation."

Combining the logics of engineering and capitalism, the self has become measurable and maximizable, tallied through metrics such as the number of contacts and Web hits, retweets and reblogs, five-stars, ratings, likes, notes, and comments. As a consequence, an array of programs are now available that seek to calculate once ineffable qualities of "influence" and "reputation." Twitter Counter and Peer-Index "track your impact," "graph your authority," and gauge "online social capital."

Klout provides the "standard for influence" while Twitalyzer offers "serious analytics for social business." The Viral Loop purports to tell you just how much your friends are worth, down to the penny (mine came in at $130.19). Status, if quantifiable, becomes optimizable. The goal, always, is to get more—more friends, more fans, more followers, which is why a market has opened up to buy such things (you can buy two hundred thousand Twitter followers for under five hundred dollars).

The shift to Web 2.0 has extended the logic of the box office and the best seller into our daily lives, allowing us to keep track of our public selves the way executives tally Nielsen numbers. Whereas twenty years ago it was financially prohibitive to take out newspaper or television ads about oneself, and handing out flyers featuring a list of one's achievements and assorted flattering photos would have appeared unhinged, social media have altered our sense of propriety by ensuring access to tools that package and present what Marwick calls the "edited self."

Strategically constructing an identity requires a kind of feigned authenticity that involves the continual management and monitoring of audience feedback. Self-censorship is inevitable; one must be "liked" above all. Thus the attention economy favors the attractive and obvious, the pandering and unthreatening. It puts a premium on quickness and sensation, on the emotions of anger and awe proven to trigger virality.[59] If slow-moving and sometimes solitary work was always at a disadvantage, now it is even more so.

Lauding the new, connective technologies, technology commentators often like to invoke the Protestant Reformation. As Gutenberg's printing press challenged the power structures of its day, they argue, the Internet has disrupted the established order. Old-media corporations are the Catholic Church, ossified monoliths challenged by a newly empowered laity, the persecuted networked dissidents answering Luther's call. (The state makes an occasional appearance as the monarchy, tainted by association with the papacy.) Here the Reformation is a stunning example of Schumpeterian creative destruction, an epic tale of innovation in which a new invention (the printing press) and a new idea (Protestantism) shattered old hierarchies, redistributing power and proliferating spiritual options for everyday people. By analogy, the Web is equally revolutionary.

Yet the Reformation did more than transform politics and religion. As sociologist Max Weber explained, the Reformation precipitated the removal of social barriers that had long inhibited the accumulation of capital for its own sake.[60] The systematic pursuit of profit, the focus on productivity and efficiency, the valorization of competition and struggle, and the concern with reinvestment, returns, profit, and loss were values that took hold with the rise of Protestantism. Puritanism, in particular, prized the attendant habits of self-discipline and self-assessment, encouraging a psychology of striving.

The so-called Information Reformation and the rise of the "attention economy" do indeed display similarities to the Reformation, although perhaps not in the revolutionary sense that new-media thinkers claim. They have also prompted a psychic shift, the tendency toward personal branding being one extreme example. Where the first Reformation transformed our relationship to commodities, this one has commodified our relationships and ourselves.

As institutions crumble and social safety nets fray, individuals increasingly stand alone, responsible for themselves and their well-being, just as the Puritans, no longer shielded by the church against God's unfailing judgment, struggled to prove their piety. We hoard "social capital" and try to discern evidence of our own significance. The Puritans relentlessly toiled, rewards for their work a kind of benediction; we invest in ourselves, stockpiling attention, seeking success.

Increasingly that success is tied to the scale of our social capital. It's not uncommon for employers to demand that employees cultivate and exploit their personal networks for work. If our numbers are high enough, we have a shot at making it, just like the television stations of yore. The result is that we all live in public, but not, as is regularly claimed, because digital natives have different standards and expectations than their predecessors. Silicon Valley executives argue that the tendency of young people to expose and promote themselves online proves that privacy concerns are a thing of the past. "People have really gotten comfortable not only sharing more information and different kinds, but more openly with more people," Mark Zuckerberg assured an interviewer, justifying Facebook's policies.

Yet the facts don't quite support this view. Numerous studies demonstrate that young people's attitudes about privacy are not that different from their elders. Contrary to popular opinion, there is evidence that young adults are actually *more* concerned about online privacy, about who sees their personal profile and what happens with it, and more inclined to use a variety of strategies to be less visible online than older segments of the population (this is especially true for girls, who are far more likely than boys to disable location tracking).[61]

Polls have found that the majority of Americans are deeply concerned about online firms selling or sharing their personal data without permission and that they overwhelmingly value privacy and civil liberties over cybersecurity. The outcry over news of NSA surveillance and companies exploiting user information in new ways—as in the case of Google Buzz, Facebook's Beacon, and Instagram's change to its terms of service related to advertising policy—prove that we have not unquestioningly embraced openness in all aspects of our lives: people rightly understand that using social media doesn't have to entail granting permission for blanket surveillance. More fundamentally, the reality is that young and old alike are often compelled to exhibit themselves online. To compete, we are told we have no choice but to participate in the culture of disclosure.

"How terrible is it to cast an actor based on this formula?," a film producer acquaintance recently asked, only half joking: "IMDB STARmeter + # of Twitter followers + # of Google search results?" While few of us actually believe followers and hits directly indicate talent or ability, these metrics are becoming the ones by which we are measured. We live in public in part because we believe we have to. New-media moguls and the advertisers they serve benefit from the uncertainty that drives us to do so.

Creativity and commerce have a complex relationship and, in many ways, a necessary one. Nonetheless, a market in creative goods is different from creative marketing, and the latter is growing at the expense of the former. The mercantile climate has moved to the center; what was once an attribute has become a dominant feature.

This shift has been slow, from ads on public transportation and at gas pumps to where we are today, where they can even be found on library toilet paper and in prisons—"captive ads," they're officially called. In the 1970s, for example, the average city dweller saw only a fraction of the three thousand to five thousand ad messages we are exposed to today, and the younger a person is, the more marinated he or she has been in this reality since birth.

"Comparing the advertising of two or three decades ago to the commercialism that permeates our children's world today," wrote Susan Linn, a Harvard Medical School psychiatrist, in *Consuming Kids*, "is like comparing a BB gun to a smart bomb."[62] Between 1980 and 2004, the amount of money devoted to children's advertising skyrocketed from $100 million to $15 billion a year.[63]

On broadcast television, advertising to children is restricted: twelve minutes on weekdays and approximately ten minutes on weekends for every hour of children's programming.[64] On the Internet it's a free-for-all with Web sites and apps available around the clock, and with more tracking software installed on services aimed at children than those aimed at adults.[65] The distinction between entertainment and advertising is purposefully blurred by savvy marketers, with kids spending hours playing games that hype junk food and toys, "liking" and "friending" products and brands, and taking quizzes that provide free focus grouping.[66]

The technology is still in its infancy, but we should pause to reflect on the profound nature of this transformation. Right now there are artists who agonize over whether to license their work for commercial purposes, and yet we have a situation where our very likeness is used to hawk doughnuts or shoes or whatever it may be without explicit permission being granted first.[67] There are people going deeply into debt so they can work as journalists and truth tellers, but "sponsored content" is what they are told will pay the bills.

Surely our social standards will begin to shift in response to these trends. Why worry about selling out when you are already an ad and have been your whole life? Why fret over the ethics of promoting yourself when you are already being used to promote something else? Under the "open" model, where the distinction between commercial and noncommercial has melted away, everything is for sale. When there is no distinction between inner and outer, our bonds with family and friends, our private desires and curiosities, all become commodities. We are sold out in advance, branded whether we want to be or not.

For now, we continue to prefer not to pay the true price of the things we consume. We purchase cheap products and we let advertising determine the cultural menu, even if it means passing up more satisfying fare, just because it is free. Both types of discounted goods produce negative consequences, from the bloody externalities of electronics manufacturing to the rising obesity rates and eating disorders associated with exposure to commercials to the shrinking of necessary journalism for want of support.

Ad-funded sites or creators are not cutting edge but depressingly retrograde. Indeed, the only distinction from the past is the extent of our reliance. All the problems associated with advertising have metastasized in digital space, where marketers have more power and face fewer regulations than under the old paradigm.

While it may look like we are getting something for nothing, advertising-financed culture is not free. We pay environmentally, we pay with our self-esteem, and we pay with our attention, privacy, and knowledge. But we also pay with our pocketbooks, and this is key. Advertising is, in essence, a private tax. Because promotional budgets are factored into the price we pay for goods, customers end up footing the bill. That means that, all together, we spend more than $700 billion a year on advertising, a tremendous waste of money on something that has virtually no social value and that most of us despise.[68]

Advertising, after all, doesn't feed or house us, or educate us, or enlighten us, or make our lives better or more beautiful. Instead, advertising makes our culture less spirited and fearless, more servile and uninspired. Surely all that money could be better spent producing something we actually care about.

CONCLUSION

IN DEFENSE OF THE COMMONS:
A MANIFESTO FOR SUSTAINABLE CULTURE

It may seem counterintuitive at a time of information overload, viral media, aggregation, and instant commenting to worry about our cultural supply. But we are at risk of starving in the midst of plenty. A decade ago few would have thought a book with a title like *In Defense of Food* was necessary. Food, after all, had never been cheaper or more abundant; what could be wrong with the picture? A similar shift of perception needs to happen in the cultural realm. Culture, even if it is immaterial, has material conditions, and free culture, like cheap food, incurs hidden costs.

One positive step may be something deceptively simple: an effort to raise consciousness about something we could call sustainable culture. "Culture" and "cultivate" share the same root, after all: "Coulter," a cognate of "culture," means the blade of a plowshare. It is not a reach to align the production and consumption of culture with the growing appreciation of skilled workmanship and artisanal goods, of community food systems and ethical economies. The aims of this movement may be extended and adapted to describe cultural production and exchange, online and off.

The concept of sustainable culture begins with envisioning a cultural ecology. New and old media are not separate provinces but part of a hybrid cultural ecosystem that includes the traditional and digital and composites of the two. Our virtual and physical lives are intertwined, inseparable, equally "real." Whether their work is distributed by paper or pixels, creators never emerge fully formed from the ether. Individuals are buttressed by an array of plinths and braces, by families and friends, patrons and publics, and institutions that include universities, foundations, community centers, publishers, distributors, libraries, bookstores, rock venues, and cinemas, as well as the ad hoc networks that comprise scenes and subcultures, digital and analog.

We are embedded beings who create work in a social context, toiling shared soil in the hopes that our labor bears fruit. It is up to all of us whether this soil is enriched or depleted, whether it nurtures diverse and vital produce or allows predictable crops to take root and run rampant. The notion of sustainable culture forces us to recognize that the digital has not rendered all previously existing institutions obsolete. It also challenges us to figure out how to improve them.

Many structures of the old-media system, however flawed, relieved some of the burdens now borne solely by individuals. Institutions provide capital, legal protection, leverage, and also continuity, facilitating the transmission of knowledge and skills from one generation to the next. At their best, institutions can help support challenging efforts through a process the musician Damian Kulash calls "risk aggregation." Though his band OK Go left their record label and found a following online, Kulash still believes labels—though "greedy

and shortsighted"—played a crucial function in the cultural landscape, one we have not figured out how to replicate or improve upon
within the digital realm: like publishing houses, newspapers, and
film studios, they funnel revenues from more successful acts to less
successful ones.

Scale allows institutions to fight the kinds of legal battles investigative journalism requires or weather a string of losses until the
odds finally deliver that blockbuster hit, an arrangement that looks
grossly inefficient from one angle, or almost socialist from another.
Labels "invest in however many young bands a year and most of
them fail," Kulash told an interviewer. "Those bands go back to their
jobs at the local coffee houses without having to be in tens or hundreds of thousands of dollars of personal debt for having gone for
it." He credits this process with making his career possible. "If we
don't want to be just a domain of the independently wealthy and
people who can take time off from their jobs for a couple of years to
see what happens, or finance their own world tour while they figure out exactly how to make the number at the end of the column
black, then somebody has to be doing this risk aggregation."[1]

The frame of sustainable culture has other benefits as well. In
stark contrast to the emphasis on newness and nowness of most
online platforms, it encourages us to think long term. Inherent in
the concept of sustainability, after all, is the element of duration, of
time and also depth of attention, for both creators and consumers.
To escape the cycle of churnalism and expendable content in favor
of sustainable culture, we need to develop supports that allow for
the prolonged immersion and engagement artistic and journalistic
endeavors often require, nurturing projects that are timeless rather
than timely.

We also need to provide reliable means of preservation. Too often
people assume that digital content will last forever, immateriality
and reproducibility encouraging the false impression that anything
uploaded to the cloud is safely stored for posterity. In reality, we

lose an estimated quarter of all working links every seven years and digital files can quickly become incomprehensible due to the swift churn of technological obsolescence. Sustainable culture includes building archives that will allow people to explore their cultural heritage for years to come.[2]

Additionally, the concept of sustainability poses a direct challenge to both the fixation on rapid growth and quick profits and the fantasy of sidestepping the issue of finance altogether. Material factors cannot be ignored or wished away.[3] Free culture advocates have it right that excessive copyright regulation can inhibit creativity, and the current copyright regime is in urgent need of reform. But "free" is not the answer: too many creative endeavors fail due to lack of investment; countless creative experiments go untried; important investigations never get off the ground; voices that refuse to peddle or pander go unacknowledged; truth seeking and beauty making are undervalued, all while mediocre ideas prosper, aided by the fertilizers of advertising dollars and manufactured desire.

A vision of sustainability acknowledges the damage incurred by the sole pursuit of wealth while trying to build an equitable system that can enable the production of socially valuable goods. The proliferation of crowdfunding Web sites, which allow people to back creative projects without expectation of financial return, are an encouraging development and a critical source of support to artists and tinkerers—yet they are no panacea. There are limits to individual, one-off fund-raising campaigns, which cannot substitute for broader, more stable support structures.

Finally, a sustainability movement would harness new communications tools to shift the current conversation from free culture to fair culture. Established fair trade principles, known to anyone who has purchased coffee with the telltale label, include transparency and accountability, payment of just prices, nondiscrimination and gender and racial equity, and respect for the environment.

These principles speak to many of the problems raised in this

book: the secretive methods of many Internet companies, the feudal business model of Web 2.0, the increasingly common expectation that people work without compensation, the persistence of
inequality and intolerance online, and the disastrous consequences
of high-tech manufacturing techniques and the constant upgrading
and disposal of still functional, but no longer fashionable, gadgets
on our natural world.

The shift to sustainable culture is possible, but implementing the
necessary changes cannot fall to individuals and the marketplace
alone. The solutions we need require collective, political action. Not
unlike American agriculture businesses, which receive billions in
federal aid while flooding the market with processed food, heedless
of the effect on small farmers, today's corporate media and technology firms depend on substantial and unacknowledged public subsidy, putting them at an unfair advantage at all of our expense.

Strengthening our cultural commons requires profound changes
in policy, animated by the same spirit as the 1965 congressional resolution that established the National Endowment for the Arts: "While
no government can call a great artist or scholar into existence, it is
necessary and appropriate for the federal government to help create
and sustain not only a climate encouraging freedom of thought,
imagination, and inquiry, but also the material conditions facilitating the release of this creative talent."

The dominant idea today is that the Internet, by lowering barriers
to entry, will do this work for us, creating a free market in art and
ideas and ushering in a "utopia of openness." A free and open web
will spark innovation and competition and a cultural revolution will
result. This assumption channels political activism to the fight for
network neutrality and against regulation like SOPA (where the
interests of the public and of large technology firms are generally
compatible), while explicitly progressive causes that push back against
business interests—battles against consolidation, commercialization,
unfair labor practices, and the lack of diversity—take a backseat.

Yet, as we know, open systems can be starkly inegalitarian and open markets cannot be counted on to provide everything people want or need, which is why there are many areas we strive to at least partly shield from capitalism's excesses, such as scientific research, health, and education. A laissez-faire system will inevitably underinvest in less profitable cultural works, no matter how worthy, enriching, or utterly vital they are. No matter how technically "disruptive" or "revolutionary," a communications system left to the free market will not produce the independent, democratic culture we need.

In the language of economists, culture is a public good. Like a sunset we can all enjoy without its being diminished, a song isn't used up when people sing it. Moving beyond the academic definition, culture is also a public good in the sense that it benefits all: our lives are improved by the positive externalities art and ideas produce, our world more beautiful, more interesting, more ambitious. The word has other meanings as well. On the one hand, something can be public in the sense of being open to all, like a public meeting. But the word also means "shared": something that is public belongs to everyone, like a local library; it is funded by the public purse. It is this last meaning—public in the sense of ownership and funding— that technology commentators too often sideline. We envision a cultural commons accessible to all but shy away from discussing how to make this aspiration a reality.

The truth is that the public good is increasingly financed by private money. Google Books, despite the legal troubles that dogged the endeavor, is a prime example of this phenomenon. While often described as a "universal library" the project is anything but. More accurately, it was devised with the aim of transforming the library from an institution that collects and distributes information to the public into one that collects and distributes the public's information in service of Google's core advertising business.[4]

Google Books is a perfect example of what media scholar Siva Vaidhyanathan calls "public failure," a situation where private actors perform services for gain that would be better left to the public sector.[5] Vaidhyanathan has proposed something called the Human Knowledge Project, a government-led effort to create a truly global online library aimed at "satiating curiosity," not "facilitating consumption."

Other countries have instigated modest alternatives: in Norway, citizens can check out newly released books from the national digital archive; France pledged 750 million euros for the digitization of the nation's "cultural patrimony"; the Netherlands has a ten-year plan to digitize every Dutch book, newspaper, and periodical produced since 1470. There is also the European Union–sponsored Europeana, a meta aggregator that links the collections of almost thirty countries.

In the United States, however, the idea of a publicly funded digital repository for our shared heritage is a pipe dream, a circumstance that has led an intrepid group of librarians, academics, archivists, and activists to begin the process of slowly trying to build a noncommercial alternative to Google Books, the Digital Public Library of America, which went online in 2013. This freely accessible network of resources from libraries, archives, museums, and universities is looking to foundations for support.[6]

"Clearly, we should not trust Google to be the custodian of our most precious cultural and scientific resources," cautions Vaidhyanathan. "Without firm regulations, a truly competitive market, or a competing project, we have no recourse in the event of sub-standard performance or malfeasance by the company."

This warning applies well beyond books to the majority of online platforms where we spend our time. They are "public" in a limited sense of the word: they are open spaces, but they are also private ones, where the rights Americans claim to hold dear—namely, protections for free speech and privacy—do not apply. When the CEO of Twitter tells users to "think of Twitter as a global town square," he elides the fact that we don't have to click "agree" on a Terms of Service, a binding contract, before entering an urban plaza. Similarly, Lawrence Lessig, when expounding on the value of social media sites for the cultural commons, does a disservice when he quotes one of the founders of the Yahoo!-owned photo-sharing site Flickr likening the operation to a "land trust" and his colleagues to "custodians." Flickr is no such thing, just as Google is not operating a library. They are commercial enterprises designed to maximize revenue, not defend political expression, preserve our collective heritage, or facilitate creativity, and the people who work there are private employees, not public servants.[7]

The not-for-profit, donor-supported, volunteer-produced Wikipedia is often held up as the archetypal organization of an information age. Yet Wikipedia is utterly unique among the world's most popular Web sites. Average Internet users spend most of their time visiting sites operated by for-profit companies. Web sites maintained to serve the interests of civil society, not shareholders, are losing ground.[8]

While there might be many exciting, small experiments online, there are no large spaces dedicated to the public good. And while the Internet could have offered an alternative to the sphere of commodity exchange, private and often monopolistic markets now dominate; contrary to expectations, digital concentration set in more rapidly than with previous mediums. The revolutionary nature of technology was simply no match for the underlying economic imperatives, which have driven new-media companies to amass power and capital and struggle for market dominance. Consider Twitter. The service has been a powerful tool for activists around the world but this may change. "It is not difficult to imagine a scenario in which Twitter will have to sacrifice its values, at least somewhat, on the high altar of the quarterly earnings report," as Elias Grol warns in *Foreign Policy*.[9] In theory, Twitter's founders could have considered alternative business models. Instead of rushing to debut on the Stock Exchange they could have chosen to operate as a nonprofit, low-profit, or, following the example of the popular online crafts marketplace Etsy, a certified B Corporation, a relatively new designation that takes social and environment impacts into account.

Why not resurrect the vision of an advertising-independent search engine that initially inspired Google's founders, or launch a cooperatively owned version of iTunes or Netflix (perhaps modeled on successful institutions such as New Day Films, a documentary distribution collective that has survived for four decades), or start online associations based on Community Supported Agriculture (known as CSAs) that allow readers to purchase advance shares to fund local news gathering? There are plenty of inventive financial arrangements that could put sustainability and civic responsibility front and center, yet so far they mostly go untried.

In the digital realm, who stands for the public interest? The state remains the most powerful entity that can be employed to advance the cause of sustainable culture. Americans, however, are deeply skeptical of the government's involvement in culture and the arts. The exceptions have been few and far between, including the Works Progress Administration (WPA) of the New Deal and the establishment of the National Endowment for the Arts, the National Endowment for the Humanities, and Public Broadcasting in the 1960s.

With the founding of these institutions, the United States joined the rest of the developed world in providing state subsidy to creative endeavors. Direct government support of the arts petered out after the Cold War, during which fear of a Soviet planet prompted a variety of cultural outreach programs at the behest of the State Department, a concerted effort to contrast American dynamism to the drab Eastern Bloc. Since the fall of the Berlin Wall, the venture capital model has ruled supreme.[10]

Just as emphatically, technology is regarded as an arena that the government must not touch, the state said to be too ossified and slow to keep up with Silicon Valley's rapid pace. The Internet, in particular, is presented as territory upon which regulation should not encroach.[11] The weaknesses and hypocrisies of this libertarian fallacy aside, it is a philosophical orientation that, by holding up private enterprise and free markets as the primary drivers of innovation and progress, obscures a profound truth: the computer industry and the Internet would not exist without massive and ongoing funding from the federal government of the United States, which invested hundreds of billions of dollars over the course of many years to create it.

Early on, the government funded the invention of the microprocessor and was its first major consumer, jump-starting the modern technology industry. Later, the Internet and the World Wide Web came into being as a consequence of state financing that included military and scientific funding in the United States and Europe, combining countercultural, academic, and public service values such as decentralization, openness, and interactivity. From Apple products to Google's search engine, from GPS to voice recognition to touchscreens to the anonymity-enabling software TOR, we have public investment to thank for many of the tools we use every day, yet the private sector reaps all of the rewards and credit.[12]

In the standard narrative of techno-triumphalism, all of this history is repressed, as is the increasingly pro-active role the government played throughout our nation's communications history: designing the free-expression-enabling network known as the post office, promoting newspapers through postal subsidies, instituting a decentralized public broadcasting system, and, of course, creating the Internet. Nonetheless, pundits insist we are entering a new, "open" world that has transcended markets and states and made regulation obsolete.

Technology companies, cable providers, and Hollywood are

happy to agree, insisting that the means smaller governments employ to maintain their cultural distinctiveness—production subsidies, broadcast quotas, spending rules, selective taxes and levies, and national ownership—are no longer needed because "spectrum scarcity," long the leading justification for investment in public media and protectionist cultural policies, does not exist online.[13] On the Internet the "dial is infinite," to quote Jacob Glick, Google Canada's policy counsel.[14] Yet the infinite dial means that countries at a disadvantage in terms of population and GDP will find themselves using Web sites promoted by a handful of big Silicon Valley players and swamped by ready-made American culture.[15]

What technology boosters ignore is the fact that the steady erosion of regulation and checks on corporate power was a major factor in the development of the "old model" they so vociferously decry. For example, it was the 1996 Telecommunications Act (the "coup de grace of media deregulation") that reduced the number of telephone service providers, unleashed a torrent of mergers and acquisitions that culminated in the ill-fated marriage of AOL and Time Warner, and opened the way for Clear Channel's dramatic takeover of commercial radio. Without intervention, we will find our options similarly diminished in the digital realm.

There is no such thing as a public Internet: everything flows through private pipes. However, using the Internet for the consumption of culture or to search for information is nearly as essential to participating in modern life as having electricity or plumbing in your home (try going to school or applying for a job without it). Thus a growing chorus of progressive technologists and critics argues that both the service providers and the most popular platforms should be regulated as public utilities (indeed, Mark Zuckerberg refers to Facebook as a "social utility").

This is one example of the kind of media policy we need. There are other possibilities worth considering. To prevent what may be the next wave of consolidation, Tim Wu, coiner of the term "Net neutrality," argues that a "Separations Principle" is necessary, erecting a firewall between firms that transport and create information. Wu is worried about the potential vertical integration of companies like Verizon and Google or AT&T and Facebook into "information empires," but his principle would also have more immediate effects. Apple, for example, would not be able to sell or stream music or movies at a loss to buoy the sale of hardware; Amazon would be prevented from pursuing its ambition of controlling the book market (a scenario in which most volumes are either published by or self-published through the company and tethered to the Kindle platform); and Google would be forbidden to promote its own products above competitors' in search results.

Given the reality of digital convergence—the fact that once distinct channels of telephony, television, radio, film, and print media have merged—a movement for sustainable culture must concern itself with every layer of our communications infrastructure, from the creative works distributed online to the Web sites we visit to the mud and wires that make our connections possible. Reform might begin with the phone, cable, and Internet providers who hook up our homes and mobile devices and have carved the United States into noncompetitive fiefdoms, enabling them to extract enormous rewards from what are essentially natural monopolies. As a result, cable incumbents enjoy up to 95 percent profit margins on broadband service.

A proposal to nationalize these service providers would be a hard sell, but at minimum such powerful private actors should be subject to strong common carriage obligations. Network infrastructure expert Andrew Blum has pointed to the local food movement as a potential model. "We're all consuming the Internet equivalent of iceberg lettuce," he says. In a handful of successful cases municipalities have begun to offer fast and affordable fiber broadband to residents. But these alternatives won't be won without a fight. Cable and telecom companies have fought tooth and nail against these community broadband initiatives, spending over $300,000 to derail a referendum on the issue in a single town. Millions more have been spent lobbying to effectively block cities from providing high-speed access, with legislation passed in nineteen states.[16]

At present, the United States occupies the worst of both media worlds, lacking either a competitive market or meaningful government investment or oversight.[17] Contrary to conventional wisdom, government intervention is sometimes the only way to ensure competition. When left to their own devices, wired and wireless Internet service providers stifle innovation.

One might assume such profitable companies would eagerly upgrade their facilities and replace cable wires with optical fiber to satisfy customers' appetite for high-speed data transmission, but this is not the case. Wall Street would punish them for the substantial capital expenditures required, and with no pressure from rivals, stock prices and dividends take precedent over people's needs. (This dynamic explains why the digital divide has not been bridged; private investment markets would rather cherry-pick districts packed with well-to-do customers than invest in broadband infrastructure to serve poor and sparsely populated regions.)

Something similar holds true in the field of journalism, where government occasionally plays a positive role, for example through Federal Communications Commission requirements that broadcasters serve the public interest in return for using the public spectrum. These rules have been eroded since the Reagan era, but the bottom line is that educational programming and costly news departments, which often scrutinize the actions of the state, were established and maintained only at government behest, not because of market ingenuity.

More robust public support for the fourth estate would produce even greater freedom and diversity. In direct contradiction of stereotypes about the chilling effects of "state-controlled media," countries enjoying such support are home to an unimpeded and vibrant press. Norway's generous government subsidies have yielded the highest number of newspaper readers per capita and the country has repeatedly ranked as the number one democracy by the *Economist*, hardly a bastion of left-wing thinking.

There's evidence that Americans would appreciate a similar approach, for they display surprising devotion to the limited public broadcasting options available: public radio's audience has more than doubled since the late 1990s, and viewers have deemed PBS the "most trusted source of news and public affairs" among broadcast and cable sources. Polls show that money spent on public broadcasting is believed to be well spent, which sets it apart from most other expenditures.[18] The irony is that public broadcasting in the United States decreasingly qualifies as such. Regular fund-raising drives are designed to compensate for the minimal direct federal funding granted to PBS and NPR for operations (indirectly, federal funds make up about 15 percent of PBS's annual budget and a mere 2 percent of NPR's).

Our per capita spending for public media currently stands at about $1.63 a citizen a year, while Finland and Denmark spend seventy and eighty times that amount. This lack of direct government sponsorship opens a widening space for corporate underwriting, despite the compromising and sometimes overtly censoring effects of this strategy.[19] (Canada, unfortunately, may be following in its southern neighbor's footsteps, with CBC's Radio Two carrying advertising after a four-decade ban in response to budget cuts instituted by the conservative administration.) The obvious solution of building on the success of these enterprises and expanding government subsidy for a more expansive public media goes unconsidered because of widespread and deeply held misconceptions.

We must find ways to adapt and extend tried and true policies while taking the unique architecture of twenty-first-century communications technologies into account. The historic conception of public broadcasting is insufficient for twenty-first-century communications technology. Public media policy will need to address infrastructure and information, conduit and content, thus spanning a broad array of issues including Net neutrality, anti-trust, user privacy, copyright reform, software production, the development of new platforms for engagement and discovery, and subsidy and promotion of cultural products, whether they are classically crafted novels or avant-garde apps.

While some have suggested that crowdfunding sites like Kickstarter can replace government agencies to do much of this work, such a view is shortsighted. Crowdfunding allows individual creators to raise money from their contacts, which gives well-known and often well-resourced individuals a significant advantage. In contrast, a government agency must concern itself with the larger public good, paying special attention to underserved geographic regions and communities (taxation, in a sense, is a form of crowdfunding, but with far wider obligations).[20]

Public agencies, in other words, have to consider the whole cultural ecology. Thus other countries not only fund individual creators but assist independent institutions including community centers, cinemas, and booksellers. France's *loi Lang*, for example, prevents the discounting of books in order to protect small shops from being forced out of business by supermarkets, chains, and Amazon, acknowledging their proven role in encouraging diverse reading habits and nurturing literary culture. Most discussions about the Internet's effect on art and culture do not account for the heterogeneity that brick-and-mortar institutions foster.[21]

Nonetheless, a skeptic may still insist that these proposals for supporting sustainable culture are too costly to seriously consider.[22] But the money for such an undertaking exists, indeed it is already being spent, but with great inefficiency. We pay a small fortune for the devices and connections required to use the Internet (global spending on consumer electronics surpassed $1 trillion in 2012, despite the recession).[23] We also pay dearly for the services and culture we con-

sume online through the opaque, private tax referred to as advertising (and we also pay with our privacy).

The over $700 billion spent annually on advertising could be
subject to a transparent public tax and put to good use. Additional
funding streams exist to be tapped. In 2009 the Associated Press
revealed that the U.S. Army spent $4.7 billion and employed nearly
thirty thousand people to do public relations, an unaccountable
form of taxpayer-financed media. A small fraction of these assets
could be appropriated and applied to beef up our paltry public
broadcasting budget.

Other options would be to demand that radio and television
broadcasters pay the market rate for spectrum licenses or make
technology companies help foot the bill for the content they depend
on for survival. The most straightforward method may be to force
leading technology firms to pay their taxes, which they have been
diligently dodging through cunning accounting schemes, loopholes, and shelters. These machinations have allowed Google to
effectively pay an overseas tax rate of as little as 2.4 percent, Apple to
shield approximately $74 billion from the Internal Revenue Service
between 2009 and 2012, and Amazon to spend years refusing to collect sales tax, starving states of revenue (Jeff Bezos is said to have
considered establishing Amazon on an Indian reservation to avoid
paying taxes).[24]

A portion of these funds could be earmarked to underwrite and
promote art, culture, and journalism. The fruits of such investment
could be made widely available, free of copyright restrictions, much
the way a dedicated community of academics working under the
banner of "open access" is making publicly funded research readily
available to anyone who wants to learn regardless of income or institutional affiliation.

The fact is that, as with the research and development of technology, the state is already present. The industries discussed in this
book hardly operate in a free market. Our public airwaves, worth

hundreds of billions of dollars, are handed over without charge to radio and television broadcasters, or auctioned off to the highest bidding phone companies, all for private profit. Much of the infrastructure cable and telecommunications providers depend on was subsidized by taxpayers, who are stuck with patchier, inferior, and more expensive service than citizens of other countries (meanwhile Comcast has increased its lobbying budget from $570,000 in 2001 to $19.6 million in 2011 in order to maintain this cushy arrangement).

Media conglomerates receive tax write-offs for the costs of marketing their wares. Lucrative copyrights are indefinitely extended and dubious patents protected to appease entertainment and technology executives, these government-granted monopolies funneling massive fortunes into corporate coffers.[25] Public subsidies abound, though one would be hard pressed to say they are in the public's interest.

In the cultural realm we are told that the Internet and a medley of ever-evolving devices and services will automatically and effortlessly improve our media system. That sounds wonderful, but we need to identify what, precisely, was broken about the old arrangement so those problems don't carry over. We also need to reflect on where we are heading. What does it mean to "democratize culture"?

Too often technology gurus talk about democratizing culture as though the meaning of the phrase was self-evident. Everyone has a chance of making it online, they insist, pointing to individuals who use social media to pull away from the pack or dropouts who founded billion-dollar businesses in their basements. While it sounds empowering, the presence of a small number of superstars is actually detrimental to democracy, not emblematic of it. Instead of facilitating the fame and fabulous wealth of a lucky few, democratizing culture involves mitigating against the winner-take-all effects of digital networks and finding ways to bolster the missing middle.

A more democratic culture means supporting creative work not because it is viral but because it is important, focusing on serving needs as well as desires, and making sure marginalized people are given not just a chance to speak but to be heard. A more democratic culture is one where previously excluded populations are given the material means to fully engage. To create a culture that is more diverse and inclusive, we have to pioneer ways of addressing discrimination and bias head-on, despite the difficulties of applying traditional methods of mitigating prejudice to digital networks. We have to shape our tools of discovery, the recommendation engines and personalization filters, so they do more than reinforce our prior choices and private bubbles. Finally, if we want a culture that is more resistant to the short-term expectations of corporate shareholders and the whims of marketers, we have to invest in noncommercial enterprises.

There is no shortage of good ideas. By not experimenting, we court disillusionment. The Internet was supposed to be free and ubiquitous, but a cable cartel would rather rake in profits than provide universal service. It was supposed to enable small producers, but instead it has given rise to some of the most mammoth corporations of all time. It was supposed to create a decentralized media system, but the shift to cloud computing has recentralized communications in unprecedented ways. It was supposed to make our culture more open, but the companies that dominate the technology industry are shockingly opaque. It was supposed to liberate users but instead facilitated all-invasive corporate and government surveillance.

Instead of eliminating middlemen and enabling peer-to-peer relationships, it has empowered an influential and practically omnipresent crop of mediators. Instead of making our relationships horizontal and bringing prosperity to all, the gap between the most popular and the practically invisible, the haves and have-nots, has grown. Instead of unshackling individuals from the grip of high-priced spectacles, it has helped entertainment firms dominate global audiences. Instead of decommodifying art and culture, every communication has become an advertising opportunity.

The utopian undercurrents that suffused these erroneous predictions are not the problem. The problem is that we have not confronted the obstacles that have impeded them, particularly the economic ones. A more open, egalitarian, participatory, and sustainable culture is profoundly worth championing, but technology alone cannot bring it into being. Left to race along its current course, the new order will come increasingly to resemble the old, and may end up worse in many ways. But the future has not been decided.

Our communications system is at a crossroads, one way leading to an increasingly corporatized and commercialized world where we are treated as targeted consumers, the other to a true cultural commons where we are nurtured as citizens and creators. To create a media environment where democracy can thrive, we need to devise progressive policy that takes into account the entire context in which art, journalism, and information are created, distributed, discovered, and preserved, online and off. We need strategies and policies for an age of abundance, not scarcity, and to invent new ways of sustaining and managing the Internet to put people before profit. Only then will a revolution worth cheering be upon us.

NOTES

PREFACE

1. Nathan Jurgenson, "The IRL Fetish," *New Inquiry*, June 28, 2012.
2. Tough questions include asking what we mean by "the Internet." Are we referring to physical infrastructure, software, particular sites, content, or functions, or an amalgamation of these things? Evgeny Morozov has raised important issues about whether the phrase "the Internet" obscures more than it reveals, implying a unified, fixed, and permanent entity when we should instead be talking about the specificities of a range of interconnected technologies and capabilities. I'm sympathetic to his argument, but worry that Morozov's insistence on adding scare quotes to "the Internet" ultimately reinforces the Internet-centrism he aims to critique, for "the Internet" is far from the only complex, socially constructed, and contradictory concept that deserves nuanced treatment. Still, as historian Leo Marx has observed, technology is a "hazardous concept," prone to reification and distortion. In my view, the way to mitigate these hazards is to expose them while emphasizing the socioeconomic, political, and ethical aspects that often go unremarked in tech discourse.
3. Since I began working on this book, a number of interesting books critical of techno-utopianism were published, including but not limited to Douglas Rushkoff's *Program or Be Programmed: Ten Commands for a Digital Age* (New York: Or Books, 2011); Nicholas Carr's *The Shallows: What the Internet Is Doing to Our Brains* (New York: W. W. Norton, 2010); Jaron

Lanier's *You Are Not a Gadget: A Manifesto* (New York: Knopf, 2010) and *Who Owns the Future?* (New York: Simon & Schuster, 2013); Kate Losse's *The Boy Kings: A Journey into the Heart of the Social Network* (New York: Free Press, 2012); Evgeny Morozov's *The Net Delusion: The Dark Side of Internet Freedom* (New York: PublicAffairs, 2011) and *To Save Everything Click Here: The Folly of Technological Solutionism* (New York: PublicAffairs, 2013); Eli Pariser's *The Filter Bubble: What the Internet Is Hiding from You* (New York: Penguin Press, 2011); Robert McChesney's *Digital Disconnect: How Capitalism Is Turning the Internet Against Democracy* (New York: The New Press, 2013); and Siva Vaidhyanathan's *The Googlization of Everything: (And Why We Should Worry)* (Berkeley: University of California Press, 2011).

4. On the existence of a sprawling international surveillance infrastructure, see the reporting of Glenn Greenwald on Edward Snowden's leaks pertaining to the National Security Administration for the *Guardian* and Barton Gellman for the *Washington Post*. For more information about uncompetitive business practices, read about the antitrust investigation into Google, which critics say unfairly blocks or demotes its rivals. For example, Brent Kendall, Amir Efrati, Thomas Catan, and Shira Ovide, "Behind Google's Antitrust Escape," *Wall Street Journal*, January 5, 2013. On exploitative labor practices, there have been numerous exposés of labor conditions at Apple factories in China, where distraught workers committed suicide, and Amazon's American warehouses, where "associates" are paid low wages while working in extremely hot conditions—so hot that the retailer paid an ambulance service to park outside the building (the ambulance chief said approximately fifteen people were taken to hospitals, while twenty or thirty more were treated on the premises). See Charles Duhigg and David Barboza, "In China, Human Costs Are Built into an iPad," *New York Times*, January 25, 2012; and Spencer Soper, "Inside Amazon's Warehouse," *Morning Call*, September 18, 2011. All the tech giants are getting in on the lobbying game, but for one particularly controversial initiative, consider the Facebook-led lobbying group FWD.us. In 2013, Google, Facebook, and Yelp all joined ALEC, the American Legislative Exchange Council—a lobbying organization notorious for supporting climate change denial, undermining gun control, and busting unions—even as companies including Kraft Foods and Pepsi left due to consumer pressure.

1: A PEASANT'S KINGDOM

1. For the 450,000 jobs figure, see Sarah Lacy, *Once You're Lucky, Twice You're Good: The Rebirth of Silicon Valley and the Rise of Web 2.0* (New York: Gotham, 2008), 13. Rebecca Solnit wrote movingly of the negative

consequences of the first dot-com boom on San Francisco in her book *Hollow City: Gentrification and the Eviction of Urban Culture* (New York: Verso, 2001) and has written similarly astute observations on the effects of the latest boom on the community. Rebecca Solnit, "Google Invades," *London Review of Books* 35, no. 3 (February 7, 2013).

2. Doug Henwood, *After the New Economy* (New York: The New Press, 2003), 1.

3. Alan Greenspan, "The American Economy in a World Context," 35th Annual Conference on Bank Structure and Competition of the Federal Reserve Bank of Chicago, Chicago, May 16, 1999; Henwood, *After the New Economy*, 79 and 86.

4. Henwood, *After the New Economy*, 201, 217.

5. Tom Rosenstiel, "Five Myths About the Future of Journalism," *Washington Post*, April 7, 2011.

6. Eli Pariser, *The Filter Bubble: What the Internet Is Hiding from You* (New York: Penguin Press, 2011), 49.

7. Lacy, *Once You're Lucky, Twice You're Good*, 92–93.

8. The term "digital sharecropping" was coined by Nicholas Carr. Nicholas Carr, "Sharecropping the Long Tail," *Rough Type* (blog), December 19, 2006, http://www.roughtype.com/?p=634.

9. Nick Bilton, "Disruptions: Facebook Users Ask, 'Where's Our Cut?'" NYTimes.com, February 5, 2012, http://bits.blogs.nytimes.com/2012/02/05/disruptions-facebook-users-ask-wheres-our-cut/.

10. Trebor Scholz, digitallabor.org.

11. This issue is the subject of interesting, if slightly esoteric, academic debate that is beyond the scope of these pages. Suffice it to say, there is an argument about whether our activities online should be considered labor at all, or "microlabor" or "playbor," and whether these activities are actually what create value or profit for technology companies like Google and Facebook. After all, both Google's and Facebook's revenues do not directly flow from the participation of users but from advertisers who, in turn, make their profits from companies creating goods and offering services. Advertisers, ultimately, depend on a surplus created by workers who produce things. According to this view, it is misleading to think of the digital economy as heralding a new type of labor, "microlabor," or "playbor" that is harnessed by technology companies; ultimately technology companies, via advertisers, depend on fairly traditional systems of labor and commodity production.

12. To give just one example, the Tumblr terms of service include the following: "When you transfer Subscriber Content to Tumblr through the Services, you give Tumblr a non-exclusive, worldwide, royalty-free, sublicensable, transferable right and license to use, host, store, cache, reproduce, publish, display (publicly or otherwise), perform (publicly

or otherwise), distribute, transmit, modify, adapt (including, without limitation, in order to conform it to the requirements of any networks, devices, services, or media through which the Services are available), and create derivative works of (including, without limitation, by Reblogging, as defined below), such Subscriber Content." This policy was accessed October 1, 2013, at http://www.tumblr.com/policy/en/terms_of_service. The fact that the company has the right to alter these terms at any time is one of the many issues investigated in detail in the 2013 documentary *Terms and Conditions May Apply*, directed by Cullen Hoback.

13. Marina Gorbis, "Ain't Gonna Work on Arianna's Farm No More," Institute for the Future, *Future Now* (blog), September 1, 2010, http://www.iftf.org/future-now/article-detail/aint-gonna-work-on-ariannas-farm-no-more/.

14. For example, both Clay Shirky (in *Cognitive Surplus: Creativity and Generosity in a Connected Age* [New York: Penguin Press, 2010]) and Lawrence Lessig (in *Remix: Making Art and Commerce Thrive in the Hybrid Economy* [New York: Penguin Press, 2008]) take time to dispute the digital sharecropping argument.

15. Fred Turner, *From Counterculture to Cyberculture: Stewart Brand, the Whole Earth Network, and the Rise of Digital Utopianism* (Chicago: University of Chicago Press, 2006), 238, 247.

16. For a good discussion of this history, see Evgeny Morozov's profile of Tim O'Reilly, supporter of the open source movement and founder of O'Reilly Media. Evgeny Morozov, "The Meme Hustler," *Baffler*, no. 22 (2013).

17. Openness is the "key to success," says Jeff Jarvis in *What Would Google Do?* (New York: HarperBusiness, 2009), 4.

18. Rob Horning, "Social Graph vs. Social Class," *New Inquiry*, March 23, 2012.

19. Lawrence Lessig, "The Architecture of Innovation," *Duke Law Journal* 51, no. 1783 (2002). Related arguments about the limitations of the framework of left versus right and state versus market are made by Steven Johnson in *Future Perfect: The Case for Progress in a Networked Age* (New York: Riverhead Books, 2012) and his op-ed "Peer Power, from Potholes to Patents," *Wall Street Journal*, September 21, 2012, as well as by Yochai Benkler in *The Penguin and the Leviathan: The Triumph of Cooperation over Self-Interest* (New York: Crown Business, 2011).

20. Tim Wu makes a compelling case for open systems in *The Master Switch: The Rise and Fall of Information Empires* (New York: Knopf, 2010).

21. Tim Berners-Lee, "Long Live the Web: A Call for Continued Open Standards and Neutrality," *Scientific American*, November 22, 2012. Though I use the terms interchangeably, as most people do, the World Wide Web is technically an application that runs on the Internet. The Internet was invented before Web pages were. According to Berners-Lee, "An analogy is that the Web is like a household appliance that runs

on the electricity network. A refrigerator or printer can function as long as it uses a few standard protocols—in the U.S., things like operating at 120 volts and 60 hertz. Similarly, any application—among them the Web, e-mail or instant messaging—can run on the Internet as long as it uses a few standard Internet protocols, such as TCP and IP."

22. Bill Law, "Goldcorp Mining Company Accused over Human Rights," BBC News, May 21, 2010, http://news.bbc.co.uk/2/hi/8696647.stm.

23. After writing this I discovered that Tom Slee made essentially the same point in his review of *Remix*, along with some other excellent ones. Tom Slee, "Lawrence Lessig's Remix: A Rambling Review," January 2009, http://whimsley.typepad.com/whimsley/2009/01/lawrence-lessigs-remix-a-rambling-review.html.

24. Henry Jenkins, "Interactive Audiences? The 'Collective Intelligence' of Media Fans," Society for Cinema Studies Conference, 2002.

25. Damon Krukowski, "Making Cents," Pitchfork, November 14, 2012, http://pitchfork.com/features/articles/8993-the-cloud/. The Talking Head's David Byrne spelled out the equity issue in an essay for the *Guardian*: "The labels also got equity; so they are now partners and shareholders in Spotify, which is valued at around $3bn. That income from equity, when and if the service goes public, does not have to be shared with the artists. It seems obvious that some people are making a lot of money on this deal, while the artists have been left with meagre scraps." David Byrne, "The Internet Will Suck All Creative Content Out of the World," October 11, 2013, http://www.theguardian.com/music/2013/oct/11/david-byrne-internet-content-world/.

26. Quoted in Siva Vaidhyanathan, *The Googlization of Everything: (And Why We Should Worry)* (Berkeley: University of California Press, 2011), 120.

27. David Carr, "Old Media Stalwarts Persevered in 2012," *New York Times*, January 7, 2013, B1.

28. Anne Elizabeth Moore, "Can Capitalism Tolerate a Democratic Internet? An Interview with Media Expert Robert McChesney," TruthOut, April 3, 2013, http://www.truth-out.org/progressivepicks/item/15516-can-capitalism-tolerate-a-democratic-internet-an-interview-with-media-expert-robert-mcchesney.

29. On Google traffic figures, see Robert McMillan, "Google Serves 25 Percent of North American Internet Traffic," Wired.com, July 22, 2013, http://www.wired.com/wiredenterprise/2013/07/google-internet-traffic/. Amazon's centrality in the cloud computing space is hard to exaggerate: in 2012, an outage of one of Amazon's data centers in northern Virginia temporarily took down a wide array of dependent sites including Pinterest, Instagram, and Netflix. Related to this, the fact that WikiLeaks never recovered after being booted off of Amazon's servers is another

indication of the company's dominance of the cloud computing space. Amazon also has a cloud computing contract with the CIA worth a reported $600 million. For the one-in-three-Internet-users figure, see Patrick Thibodeau, "Amazon Cloud Accessed Daily by a Third of All 'Net Users," Computerworld.com, April 18, 2012, http://www.computerworld.com/s/article/9226349/Amazon_cloud_accessed_daily_by_a_third_of_all_Net_users. On Apple's valuation see Susanna Kim, "Apple Is World's Most Valuable Company Again," ABCNews.com, January 25, 2012, http://abcnews.go.com/blogs/business/2012/01/apple-is-worlds-most-valuable-company-again/.

30. David Brooks, "The Creative Monopoly," *New York Times*, April 24, 2012, A23; and Ryan Mac, "Ten Lessons from Peter Thiel's Class on Startups," Forbes.com, June 7, 2012, http://www.forbes.com/sites/ryanmac/2012/06/07/ten-lessons-from-peter-thiels-class-on-startups/.

31. Slavoj Zizek describes this issue succinctly in his essay "Corporate Rule of Cyberspace," InsideHigherEd.com, May 2, 2011, http://www.insidehighered.com/views/2011/05/02/slavoj_zizek_essay_on_cloud_computing_and_privacy.

32. One predictable consequence of Amazon's rapid expansion has been the further consolidation of the book business. Amazon, it is widely agreed, has provoked and will continue to provoke publishers to pursue defensive mergers and acquisitions, such as the union of Penguin and Random House into a colossus that will publish a quarter of all English-language books, including the Canadian version of this one. For more information see André Schiffrin, "How Mergermania Is Destroying Book Publishing," *Nation*, November 28, 2012.

33. Christopher S. Stewart and Shalini Ramachandran, "Google Joins Race for a Web TV Service," *Wall Street Journal*, July 16, 2013, B1.

34. Amir Efrati, "Google Takes 7% Stake in Vevo," WSJ.com, July 3, 2013, http://blogs.wsj.com/digits/2013/07/03/google-takes-7-stake-in-vevo/.

35. Marco R. della Cava, "YouTube Gives Video Creators Space to Grow," *USA Today*, January 1, 2013.

36. Michael Learmonth, "YouTube's New Sell: Want to Buy a Web Series for $3.5 Million?," AdAge.com, July 14, 2011, http://adage.com/article/digital/youtube-s-sell-buy-a-web-series/228712/. Also see Michael Learmonth, "YouTube Preps Big New Round of Content Investments," AdAge.com, November 11, 2012, http://adage.com/article/digital/youtube-preps-big-round-content-investments/238248/.

37. John Seabrook, "Streaming Dreams," *New Yorker*, January 16, 2012.

38. House of Lords, "Communications, First Report," The Select Committee on Communications, June 11, 2008, http://www.publications.parliament.uk/pa/ld200708/ldselect/ldcomuni/122/12202.htm.

39. Michael K. Powell, "Should Limits on Broadcast Ownership Change?," *USA Today*, January 21, 2003, http://usatoday30.usatoday.com/news /opinion/editorials/2003-01-21-powell_x.htm.

40. Despite public promises of "a different kind of Internet," the terms of service were as restrictive as traditional ISPs. Particularly offensive to observers is the fact that Google reserves the right to ban servers on its networks, which could be interpreted to mean that customers are not allowed to use peer-to-peer software or attach "Freedom Boxes" that keep data private. Craig Aaron, "Google Reserves the Right to Be Evil," *Huffington Post*, July 31, 2013, http://www.huffingtonpost.com/craig -aaron/google-reserves-the-right_b_3685306.html.

41. Marvin Ammori, "The Next Big Battle in Internet Policy," Slate.com, October 2, 2012, http://www.slate.com/articles/technology/future_tense/2012 /10/network_neutrality_the_fcc_and_the_internet_of_things_.html.

2: FOR LOVE OR MONEY

1. Quotes from an interview with the author except for this one, which is from Justin Cox, "Documenting a Bin Laden Ex-Confidante: Q&A with Filmmaker Laura Poitras," TheHill.com, July 13, 2010, http://thehill. com/capital-living/cover-stories/108553-documenting-a-bin-laden-ex -confidante-qaa-with-filmmaker-laura-poitras#ixzz2YfhpMdXu.

2. The other person Snowden contacted was the journalist Glenn Greenwald of the *Guardian*, with whom Poitras collaborated.

3. That start-up is Narrative Science, a computer program that generates sports stories. Janet Paskin, "The Future of Journalism?," *Columbia Journalism Review* (November/December 2010): 10.

4. John Markoff, "Armies of Expensive Lawyers, Replaced by Cheaper Software," *New York Times*, March 5, 2011, A1.

5. See Janice Gross Stein's book based on her Massey Lecture: Janice Gross Stein, *The Cult of Efficiency* (Toronto: House of Anansi Press, 2002).

6. Christopher Steiner, *Automate This: How Algorithms Came to Rule Our World* (New York: Portfolio, 2012), 88.

7. I owe this observation to an exchange with Richard Nash, who went on to make the point eloquently here: Richard Nash, "What Is the Business of Literature?," *Virginia Quarterly Review* 89, no. 2 (Spring 2013): 14–27.

8. James Surowiecki, "What Ails Us," *New Yorker*, July 7, 2003.

9. William Baumol and William Bowen, *Performing Arts: The Economic Dilemma* (Cambridge, Mass.: MIT Press, 1967), 407.

10. Populism has always been a double-edged sword, sometimes devolving into anti-intellectualism, witch hunts, and worse. For two fascinating takes on this history see Richard Hofstadter's classic *Anti-Intellectualism*

in American Life (New York: Vintage, 1966) and Catherine Liu's *American Idyll: Academic Antielitism as Cultural Critique* (Iowa City: University of Iowa Press, 2011).

11. David Weinberger, *Too Big to Know: Rethinking Knowledge Now That the Facts Aren't the Facts, Experts Are Everywhere, and the Smartest Person in the Room Is the Room* (New York: Basic Books, 2012), 67 and 10.

12. Yochai Benkler, *The Wealth of Networks: How Social Production Transforms Markets and Freedom* (New Haven, Conn.: Yale University Press, 2006), 93.

13. The talk is called "The New Open-Source Economics," http://www.ted .com/talks/yochai_benkler_on_the_new_open_source_economics .html.

14. Felix Oberholzer-Gee and Koleman Strumpf, "File-Sharing and Copyright" (working paper, Harvard Business School, May 15, 2009), http:// www.hbs.edu/faculty/Publication%20Files/09-132.pdf. Dan Hunter and John Quiggin, "Money Ruins Everything," *Hastings Communications and Entertainment Law Journal* 30 (2008).

15. Clay Shirky says it is not labor if people enjoy it. Jeffrey R. Young, "The Souls of the Machine," *Chronicle of Higher Education*, June 13, 2010.

16. C. Wright Mills, *White Collar* (New York: Oxford University Press, 1956), 224.

17. Ibid., 237.

18. Kevin Kelly, "Better Than Human: Why Robots Will—and Must—Take Our Jobs," *Wired*, December 24, 2012.

19. Shirky fails to mention that many of these hours are inevitably spent filling out forms, looking at porn, watching TV online, etc.

20. Clay Shirky, *Cognitive Surplus: Creativity and Generosity in a Connected Age* (New York: Penguin Press, 2010), 209. Also see "Cognitive Surplus: The Great Spare-Time Revolution," *Wired*, May 24, 2010.

21. Clay Shirky has a blog post called "The Collapse of Complex Business Models" predicting as much, posted April 1, 2010, http://www.shirky .com/weblog/2010/04/the-collapse-of-complex-business-models/. The post looks at the failure of trying to translate and adapt the popular Web video comedy "In the Motherhood" for ABC, the television network. The Web series, Shirky writes, "started online as a series of short videos, with viewers contributing funny stories from their own lives and voting on their favorites." According to Shirky, the television version failed because of excessive bureaucracy and meddling from the Writers Guild: "The critical fact about this negotiation wasn't about the mothers, or their stories, or how those stories might be used. The critical fact was that the negotiation took place in the grid of the television industry, between entities incorporated around a 20th-century business logic, and entirely within invented constraints. At no point did the

negotiation about audience involvement hinge on the question 'Would this be an interesting thing to try?'" Shirky paints the original "In the Motherhood" as a grassroots phenomenon when it was anything but. The series was actually designed and executed by MindShare, the "branded content powerhouse." According to *Advertising Age*, it was "a joint U.S. project by Unilever and Sprint that used an integration with 'The Ellen DeGeneres Show' to drive women to inthemotherhood.com." Laurel Wentz, "Global Media Agency of the Year: Mindshare," AdAge .com, March 2, 2009, http://adage.com/article/special-report-media -agency-of-the-year-2009/media-agency-year-report-mindshare/134903/.

22. Brian Stelter, "Nielsen Reports a Decline in Television Viewing," NYTimes.com, May 3, 2012, http://mediadecoder.blogs.nytimes.com /2012/05/03/nielsen-reports-a-decline-in-television-viewing/.

23. Sociologist Juliet Schor, author of *The Overworked American: The Unexpected Decline of Leisure* (New York: Basic Books, 1993) and *Plenitude: The New Economics of True Wealth* (New York: Penguin Press, 2010), has written some of the best material on this issue. In particular, see pages 104–6 of *Plenitude*. In *Cognitive Surplus* Shirky claims to be referring specifically to the cumulative free time of the world's educated population but, according to Schor, that is just the population that has less free time compared to decades past: "Employees with low educational attainment have suffered more under- and unemployment, and those with high education are more overworked," she writes. Another good take on this topic is Peter Frase's "Post-Work: A Guide for the Perplexed," posted on the *Jacobin* magazine Web site, February 25, 2013, http://jacobinmag.com/2013/02/post-work-a-guide-for-the-perplexed/.

24. Edward C. Prescott, "Why Do Americans Work So Much More Than Europeans," *Federal Reserve Bank of Minneapolis Quarterly Review* 28, no. 1 (July 2004): 2–13, www.minneapolisfed.org/research/QR/QR2811.pdf; and Rebecca Ray, Milla Sanes, and John Schmitt, "No-Vacation Nation Revisited," Center for Economic and Policy Research, May 2013 .

25. Robert Reich, "Unjust Spoils," *Nation*, July 19, 2010.

26. Richard Florida, *The Rise of the Creative Class: And How It's Transforming Work, Leisure, Community and Everyday Life* (New York: Basic Books, 2002), 37, 77.

27. Ibid., 191.

28. Richard Florida, "The Future of the American Workforce in the Global Creative Economy," Cato Unbound, June 4, 2006, www.cato-unbound .org/2006/06/04/richard-florida/future-american-workforce-global -creative-economy.

29. Ross Perlin, *Intern Nation: How to Earn Nothing and Learn Little in the Brave New Economy* (New York: Verso Books, 2012), 125.

30. James Mulholland, "Neither a Trap Nor a Lie," *Chronicle of Higher Education*, March 12, 2010.

31. Linton Weeks, "A Temporary Solution for a New American Worker," NPR.org, December 14, 2010, http://www.npr.org/2010/12/14/131942175/a-temporary-solution-for-a-new-american-worker?ps=rs.

32. Josh Eidelson, "Apple Store Workers Share Why They Want to 'Work Different,'" InTheseTimes.com, June 24, 2011, http://inthesetimes.com/working/entry/11557/.

33. For a discussion of a Linux Foundation report that is one source of this figure, see Tom Slee's blog post, "Linux Grows Up and Gets a Job," April 19, 2008, http://whimsley.typepad.com/whimsley/2008/04/linux-grows-up.html.

34. Quotes from page 3 of the introduction to Don Tapscott and Andrew D. Williams's *Wikinomics* (New York: Portfolio, 2006). The use of social production for less-than-revolutionary ends is also on display in Lawrence Lessig's often commendable work. In an essay about the benefits of what he calls the "sharing economy," he describes the tens of thousands of volunteers who "make Microsoft richer by solving its customers' problems" through a variety of online newsgroups. The riches accrued to Microsoft, though "great," shouldn't be shared with the volunteers, Lessig says, because money would be "harmful" to the community by confusing incentives. Lawrence Lessig, "Do You Floss?," *London Review of Books* 27, no. 16 (August 18, 2005): 24–25.

35. The author corresponded with the directors, whose film is sponsored by Ericsson, a telecom/technology company: http://www.ericsson.com/campaign/presspauseplay/.

36. Much has been written on this topic but for this statistic and a quick overview see Steven Greenhouse, "Our Economic Pickle," *New York Times*, January 13, 2013, SR5; and Felix Salmon, "Chart of the Day: The Long Decline of Labor," Reuters.com, September 26, 2012, http://blogs.reuters.com/felix-salmon/2012/09/26/chart-of-the-day-the-long-decline-of-labor/.

37. Richard Fry, D'Vera Cohn, Gretchen Livingston, and Paul Taylor, "The Old Prosper Relative to the Young: The Rising Age Gap in Economic Well-Being," Pew Social and Demographic Trends, November 7, 2011.

38. This is Ross Perlin's estimate, Perlin, *Inter Nation*, 124.

3: WHAT WE WANT

1. Zadie Smith, "Generation Why?," *New York Review of Books*, November 25, 2010.

2. Sven Birkerts, "You Are What You Click," *American Interest* 6, no. 1 (September/October 2010).

3. Nick Bilton, *I Live in the Future & Here's How It Works* (New York: Crown Business, 2010), 14.

4. Ibid., 130.

5. Harvard University Institute of Politics, Spring 2011 survey.

6. Francesca Borri, "Woman's Work," cjr.com, July 1, 2013, http://www.cjr.org/feature/womans_work.php.

7. The Pew Research Center for the People and the Press, "Press Accuracy Rating Hits Two Decade Low," September 12, 2009. A more recent Pew survey (July 11, 2013) from the Religion and Public Life Project is even more dire: "Compared with the ratings four years ago, journalists have dropped the most in public esteem. The share of the public saying that journalists contribute a lot to society is down 10 percentage points, from 38% in 2009 to 28% in 2013. The drop is particularly pronounced among women (down 17 points). About as many U.S. adults now say journalists contribute 'not very much' or 'nothing at all' to society (27%) as say they contribute a lot (28%)."

8. Rick Edmonds, "Newspapers Get $1 in New Digital Ad Revenue for Every $25 in Print Ad Revenue Lost," Poynter.org, September 12, 2012.

9. This deficit was down 30 percent from the year prior, in part because the Guardian Media Group sold assets and took money out of joint ventures. For more information, see Mark Sweney, "Guardian Publisher Cuts Annual Losses as Digital Revenues Grow by Nearly 30%," *Guardian*, July 16, 2013.

10. Tom Rosenstiel, "Five Myths About the Future of Journalism," *Washington Post*, April 7, 2011. A more in-depth account can be found in the annual reports *The State of the News Media News 2012* and *The State of the News Media News 2013* from the Pew Research Center's Project for Excellence in Journalism.

11. See Alan Mutter's blog post "Online Sales Are Flat-Lining at Newspapers," November 26, 2012, http://newsosaur.blogspot.com/2012/11/online-sales-are-flat-lining-at.html.

12. Michael Wolff, "Mobile and the News Media's Imploding Business Model," *Guardian*, March 27, 2012.

13. The Web site newspaperdeathwatch.com is one place to keep tabs on these developments.

14. Tom Stites, "Layoffs and Cutbacks Lead to a New World of News Deserts," Nieman Journalism Lab, December 8, 2011, http://www.niemanlab.org/2011/12/tom-stites-layoffs-and-cutbacks-lead-to-a-new-world-of-news-deserts/.

15. Pew Research Center, Project for Excellence in Journalism, *The State of the News Media 2013*.

16. Roy Greenslade, "Fewer Journalists 'on the Beat,'" *Guardian*, April

13, 2011, http://www.guardian.co.uk/media/greenslade/2011/apr/13/us-press-publishing-newspapers.

17. Paul Starr, "Goodbye to the Age of Newspapers (Hello to a New Era of Corruption)," *New Republic*, March 4, 2009.

18. Priya Kumar, "Foreign Correspondents: Who Covers What," *American Journalism Review* (December/January 2011).

19. The once robust broadcast media barely help the cause. A giant like CBS, which had two dozen foreign bureaus in 1970, now has a staff of eight covering the world, four of those based in London. "In the 1980s, American TV networks each maintained about 15 foreign bureaus; today they have six or fewer," Pamela Constable reported in the *Washington Post* in 2007. "ABC has shut down its offices in Moscow, Paris and Tokyo; NBC closed bureaus in Beijing, Cairo and Johannesburg. Aside from a one-person ABC bureau in Nairobi, there are no network bureaus left at all in Africa, India or South America—regions that are home to more than 2 billion people." Pamela Constable, "Demise of the Foreign Correspondent," *Washington Post*, February 18, 2007.

20. Natalie Fenton, *New Media, Old News: Journalism and Democracy in the Digital Age* (New York: Sage Publications, 2009), 191. The Paul Starr article is also relevant on this issue, in addition to Nat Ives, "It's Not Newspapers in Peril; It's Their Owners," *Advertising Age*, February 23, 2009; and Mark Edge, "Not Dead Yet: Newspaper Company Annual Reports Show Chains Still Profitable," paper presented to the Association for Education in Journalism and Mass Communication Annual Convention, Chicago, Illinois, August 9–12, 2012, http://www.marcedge.com/Notdeadyet.pdf.

21. Pew Research Center, Project for Excellence in Journalism, *The State of the News Media 2012* and *The State of the News Media 2013*.

22. Brian Stelter, "Campaign Ad Cash Lures Buyers to Swing-State TV Stations," *New York Times*, July 8, 2013, A1.

23. John Nichols and Robert W. McChesney, "The Money & Media Election Complex," *Nation*, November 29, 2010.

24. Federal Trade Commission Staff, "Potential Policy Recommendations to Support the Reinvention of Journalism," Federal Trade Commission, June 15, 2010, 2, http://www.ftc.gov/opp/workshops/news/jun15/docs/new-staff-discussion.pdf.

25. Monika Bauerlein and Clara Jeffery, "The Price of Truth," *Mother Jones*, September/October 2009.

26. Quoted in Michele McLellan, "Emerging Economics of Community News," in *State of the News Media 2011*, Pew Research Center Project for Excellence in Journalism. Rick Edmunds of the Poynter Institute came up with these figures. "The New Investigators," Jill Drew CJR, *Columbia Journalism Review*, May 11, 2010.

27. Michael Remez, "How Community News Is Faring," in *State of the News Media 2012*, Pew Research Center Project for Excellence in Journalism.

28. Nick Davies, *Flat Earth News: An Award-Winning Reporter Exposes Falsehood, Distortion and Propaganda in the Global Media* (London: Random House, 2009).

29. John Bellamy Foster and Robert W. McChesney, "The Internet's Unholy Marriage to Capitalism," *Monthly Review* 62, no. 10 (March 2011).

30. Davies, *Flat Earth News*, 53.

31. Clara Jeffrey, "Cost of the NYT Magazine NOLA Story Broken Down," MotherJones.com, August 28, 2009, http://motherjones.com/mojo/2009 /08/cost-nyt-magazine-nola-story-broken-down.

32. Organisation for Economic Co-operation and Development, "The Evolution of News and the Internet," June 11, 2010, http://www.oecd.org /dataoecd/30/24/45559596.pdf.

33. Christine Haughney, "Times-Picayune Plans a New Print Tabloid," NYTimes.com, April 30, 2013, http://www.nytimes.com/2013/05/01 /business/media/times-picayune-plans-a-new-print-tabloid.html; and Jason Berry, "Rolling the Dice at the 'Times-Picayune,' " TheNation. com, June 11, 2012, http://www.thenation.com/article/168330/rolling -dice-times-picayune#axzz2dxOrgV2y.

34. Jeff Bercovici, "Huffington Post vs. New York Times: A Productivity Comparison," Forbes.com, December 15, 2010, http://blogs.forbes .com/jeffbercovici/2010/12/15/huffington-post-vs-new-york-times-a -productivity-comparison/.

35. Jeff Bercovici, "Huffpo Isn't Huffpo Without the People. Does AOL Know That?," Forbes.com, February 9, 2011, http://blogs.forbes.com /jeffbercovici/2011/02/09/huffpo-isnt-huffpo-without-the-people-does -aol-know-that/.

36. The leaked document is available at http://www.businessinsider.com/ the-aol-way. Content quality claim is from Jessica E. Vascellaro, "Remaking AOL in Huffington's Image," *Wall Street Journal*, April 7, 2011.

37. James Fallows, "Learning to Love the (Shallow, Divisive, Unreliable) New Media," *Atlantic*, April 2011.

38. Traffic estimate is from the *New Yorker* profile of Denton. Ben McGrath, "Search and Destroy," *New Yorker*, October 18, 2010.

39. There are many firsthand accounts of writing for Demand Studios, including this one: http://www.nojobformom.com/2012/12/08/tip-toeing-into -demand-studios-again/. Demand Studios also outlines some of the basic aspects of its system on the official Web site: http://create.demandstudios .com/writer/ (last accessed by the author on September 4, 2013).

40. Jennifer Saba, "Demand Media Reports Record Revenue and Profit," Reuters, November 5, 2012.

41. Upworthy, a company founded by *Filter Bubble* author Eli Pariser, is an interesting case study here and counterpoint to the BuzzFeed model. It has achieved astounding viral growth while promoting socially conscious content, an approach Pariser describes as putting chocolate sauce on broccoli. While Upworthy has demonstrated that serious topics can achieve popularity online (at least when coupled with click-enticing headlines), it does not produce original work. It aggregates content from around the Web and also sticks exclusively to visual material, namely infographics and videos. While Upworthy is interesting, I did not include it in this chapter because it is not a news media organization producing the kind of journalism that is currently at risk.

42. Editors, "Are We Becoming Cyborgs?," NYTimes.com, November 30, 2012, http://www.nytimes.com/2012/11/30/opinion/global/maria-popova -evgeny-morozov-susan-greenfield-are-we-becoming-cyborgs.html ?pagewanted=all.

43. Joe Coscarelli, "Gabriel Snyder to The Atlantic Wire: On Growing Up an Aggregator," VillageVoice.com, January 31, 2011, http://blogs.village voice.com/runninscared/2011/01/gabriel_snyder.php.

4: UNEQUAL UPTAKE

1. Kevin Kelly says the "atom is the past" and George Gilder talks of overthrowing material tyranny. Kevin Kelly, *Out of Control: The New Biology of Machines, Social Systems, and the Economic World* (New York: Basic Books, 1994), 25. George Gilder, "Happy Birthday Wired," *Wired*, June 2001.

2. Susan P. Crawford, "The New Digital Divide," *New York Times*, December 4, 2011, SR1.

3. Those are examples taken from real life. For more, read these two profiles of leading figures in this field: Lisa Belkin, "Queen of the Mommy Bloggers," *New York Times Magazine*, February 23, 2011; and Amanda Fortini, "O Pioneer Woman!," *New Yorker*, May 9, 2011.

4. On the lack of women science bloggers, see Ivan Oransky, "Do Women Blog About Science?," *Scientist*, January 19, 2008, http://www.the -scientist.com/blog/display/54185/; and on lawyers, Bennett Capers, "Do Women Blog?," July 16, 2008, http://prawfsblawg.blogs.com /prawfsblawg/2008/07/do-women-blog.html.

5. Charles Leadbeater and Paul Miller, *The Pro-Am Revolution: How Enthusiasts Are Changing Our Economy and Society*, Demos, November 2004, www.demos.co.uk/files/proamrevolutionfinal.pdf?1240939425.

6. Eszter Hargittai and Steven Shafer, "Differences in Actual and Perceived Online Skills: The Role of Gender," *Social Science Quarterly* 87, no. 2 (June 2006): 432–48.

7. Germaine Greer, *The Obstacle Race: The Fortunes of Women Painters and Their Work* (New York: Farrar Straus & Giroux, 1979), 14.

8. Vanessa Thorpe and Richard Rogers, "Women Bloggers Call for a Stop to 'Hateful' Trolling by Misogynist Men," *Observer*, November 5, 2011.

9. See videogamer Anita Sarkeesian's discussion of online harassment (http://www.feministfrequency.com/2012/12/tedxwomen-talk-on-sexist-harassment-cyber-mobs/), the story of activist Caroline Criado-Perez (Elizabeth Day, "Caroline Criado-Perez: 'I Don't Know If I Had a Kind of Breakdown,'" *Observer*, December 7, 2013), and remarks by theologian Sarah Sentilles ("The Pen Is Mightier," *Harvard Divinity Bulletin* 40, nos. 3–4 [Summer/Autumn 2012]). Laurie Penny went on to release an important e-book on the topic called *Cybersexism: Sex, Gender and Power on the Internet* (New York: Bloomsbury Publishing, 2013).

10. Alex Dominguez, "Female Chat Names Generate More Threats," Associated Press, May 10, 2006.

11. Bill Heil and Mikolaj Piskorski, "New Twitter Research: Men Follow Men and Nobody Tweets," *Harvard Business Review* (June 1, 2009), http://blogs.hbr.org/cs/2009/06/new_twitter_research_men_follo.html.

12. Matthew Hindman, *The Myth of Digital Democracy* (Princeton, N.J.: Princeton University Press, 2008), 124.

13. Ibid., 127.

14. Rebecca J. Rosen, "A Simple Suggestion to Help Phase Out All-Male Panels at Tech Conferences," TheAtlantic.com, January 4, 2013, http://www.theatlantic.com/technology/archive/2013/01/a-simple-suggestion-to-help-phase-out-all-male-panels-at-tech-conferences/266837/#.

15. Stephanie Coontz, "The Myth of Male Decline," *New York Times*, September 30, 2012, SR1.

16. Claire Cain Miller, "Out of the Loop in Silicon Valley," *New York Times*, April 18, 2010, BU1.

17. Wesley Yang, "Paper Tigers," *New York*, May 8, 2011.

18. This figure and the one for forty-nine cents come from a talk given by Catherine Bracy at the 2013 Personal Democracy Forum.

19. "Social network demographics in 2012," Pingdom blog, August 21, 2012, http://royal.pingdom.com/2012/08/21/report-social-network-demographics-in-2012/.

20. Adrian Chen, "Unmasking Reddit's Violentacrez, the Biggest Troll on the Web," Gawker, October 12, 2012, http://gawker.com/5950981/unmasking-reddits-violentacrez-the-biggest-troll-on-the-web; http://www.reddit.com/r/AskReddit/comments/x6yef/reddits_had_a_few_threads_about_sexual_assault/c5jtt3p.

21. Joseph Reagle, "'Free as in Sexist?': Free Culture and the Gender Gap," *First Monday* 18, nos. 1–7 (January 2013).

22. The essay is available on Jo Freeman's Web site, jofreeman.com.

23. The original blog post, "Can 'Leaderless Revolutions' Stay Leaderless: Preferential Attachment, Iron Laws and Networks," is available at http://technosociology.org/?p=366.

24. Lada A. Adamic and Bernardo A. Huberman, "Power-Law Distribution of the World Wide Web," *Science* 287, no. 5461 (March 24, 2000): 2115.

25. As the media theorist Alexander Galloway puts it, there's generally an "internal inconsistency or inequity of the network form."

26. Sadly "winner-take-all" describes more and more areas of our economy. Robert H. Frank and Philip J. Cook, *The Winner-Take-All Society: Why the Few at the Top Get So Much More Than the Rest of Us* (New York: Penguin Books, 1996).

27. Chris Anderson, *The Long Tail: Why the Future of Business Is Selling Less of More* (New York: Hyperion, 2006), 8.

28. Anita Elberse, "Should You Invest in the Long Tail?," *Harvard Business Review* 86, nos. 7–8 (July/August 2008).

29. Lee Gomes, "Many Companies Still Cling to Big Hits to Drive Earnings," *Wall Street Journal*, August 2, 2006. Also see Hindman, *The Myth of Digital Democracy*, 93.

30. This source is thanks to Rob Reid: *The Nielsen Company & Billboard's 2011 Music Industry Report*, January 5, 2012, http://www.businesswire .com/news/home/20120105005547/en/Nielsen-Company-Billboard <#213>s-2011-Music-Industry-Report.

31. Big Champagne is one source of such metrics: www.bigchampagne .com and www.ultimatechart.com.

32. Ben Sisario, "Digital Notes: 'Call Me Maybe' Is an East Coast Hit, Spotify Says, but Gotye Is Tops," *New York Times*, June 15, 2012; and "Music's New Math: Pop's Old Metrics Don't Matter," *New York*, September 30, 2012.

33. This has been widely noted but one source is the *State of the News Media 2010* report.

34. Quoted in Chris Anderson, "Does the Long Tail Create Bigger Hits or Smaller Ones?," *Wired*, blog post, November 15, 2008, http://www .longtail.com/the_long_tail/2008/11/does-the-long-t.html.

35. Fang Wu and Bernardo A. Huberman, "The Persistence Paradox," *First Monday* 15, nos. 1–4 (January 2010).

36. James Evans, "Electronic Publication and the Narrowing of Science and Scholarship," *Science* 321, no. 5887 (July 18, 2008): 395–99.

37. Daniel M. Fleder and Kartik Hosanagar, "Blockbuster Culture's Next Rise or Fall: The Impact of Recommender Systems on Sales Diversity," *Management Science* 55, no. 5 (May 2009): 697–712.

38. Evan Hughes, "Here's How Amazon Self-Destructs," *Salon*, July 19, 2013.

39. Gary Flake et al., "Winners Don't Take All: Characterizing the Competi-

tion for Links on the Web," *Proceedings of the National Academy of Sciences* 99, no. 8 (April 16, 2002).

40. Eli Pariser, *The Filter Bubble: What the Internet Is Hiding from You* (New York: Penguin Press, 2011), 128.

41. Ibid., 132.

42. Jojo Moyes, "How e-Books Made Reading Sexy Again," *Telegraph*, March 13, 2012.

43. The essay is available at http://www.culturalequity.org/ace/ce_ace _appeal.php.

44. Ethan Zuckerman, *Rewire: Digital Cosmopolitans in the Age of Connection* (New York: W. W. Norton, 2013). Also see David Shaw, "Foreign News Shrinks in Era of Globalization," *Los Angeles Times*, September 27, 2001.

45. Ethan Zuckerman, "A Small World After All?," *Wilson Quarterly* (Spring 2012).

46. Hindman, *The Myth of Digital Democracy*, 19.

47. Amanda Hess writes about the need for updated public policy solutions and the problems and challenges of such an undertaking in "Women Aren't Welcome Here," *Pacific Standard* (January/February 2014). As Hess and others argue, anti-harassment laws could be extended to apply to new media or online abuse could be interpreted as a form of workplace discrimination, since it can inhibit women from pursuing career opportunities. For a contrasting view that doesn't specifically address sexual harrassment but looks at the persistence of inequality online see Yochai Benkler, *The Wealth of Networks: How Social Production Transforms Markets and Freedom* (New Haven, Conn.: Yale University Press, 2006), 242, on the conflict between possible policy interventions and liberal democratic theory in this arena. In a post about power laws and inequality, Clay Shirky makes a related point: "Because it arises naturally, changing this distribution would mean forcing hundreds of thousands of bloggers to link to certain blogs and to de-link others, which would require both global oversight and the application of force. Reversing the star system would mean destroying the village in order to save it."

5: THE DOUBLE ANCHOR

1. They are what economists call "non-rivalrous."

2. Most modern economists would reply that value is simply the price something can command on an open market, and if something is free, then it's simply not very valuable. A perspective to which others would reply that the value of art and culture is intrinsic, transcending the material and economic altogether; price is irrelevant. Or as the writer

Lawrence Weschler has put it: "Any work of art is somewhere between priceless and worthless. To call it anything else is comedy."

3. Donald Trump has trademarked the phrase "you're fired" and the hand gesture that accompanies it; McDonald's polices use of the Scottish prefix "Mc"; the ticking of the *60 Minutes* clock and the roar of the MGM lion are protected; Amazon has patented "one-click shopping" and a system for annotating digital books; Apple has applied for patents on turning pages and embedding author autographs in electronic titles; Google has patented its search and ranking algorithms; banks and mortgage providers stake private claim to processes associated with financial products and services; Monsanto sues farmers when the errant seeds of genetically modified crops are blown into their fields; pharmaceutical companies block the manufacture of affordable generic drugs in impoverished countries. Twenty percent of the human genome—literally the stuff of our selves—has already been patented.

4. For a more in-depth treatment of this debate, see Arthur Goldhammer, "On Diderot & Condorcet," *Daedulus* (Spring 2002).

5. Brad Stone, "Amazon Erases Orwell Books from Kindle," *New York Times*, July 18, 2009, B1; and Geeta Dayal, "The Algorithmic Copyright Cops: Streaming Video's Robotic Overlords," Wired.com, September 6, 2012, http://www.wired.com/threatlevel/2012/09/streaming-videos-robotic-overlords-algorithmic-copyright-cops/.

6. On the terrorism charge, see http://www.nakedcapitalism.com/2013/08/copyright-infringement-is-being-treated-as-terrorism.html.

7. As of 2013 Warner Music Group's ownership of the song is being challenged. Emma Woollacott, "Class Action Suit Aims to Strip Warner of 'Happy Birthday' Copyright," Forbes.com, June 14, 2013.

8. The average copyright infringement lawsuit costs over $300,000 for cases where under $1 million is at stake, which means it is more affordable for the accused to settle out of court, even when their projects are likely permissible.

9. Reading through the literature, it can be hard to distinguish the two positions. "Increasingly today, private ownership that limits access to ideas and information thwarts creativity and innovation. The privatization of the electronic 'commons' has become an obstacle to further innovation," write Michael Hardt and Antonio Negri, popular philosophers of the radical left, in *Commonwealth*. Renowned management consultants Don Tapscott and Anthony D. Williams make a similar point in *Macrowikinomics* (New York: Portfolio, 2010). Successful enterprises "need to selectively put intellectual property and other assets in the commons, thus allowing large numbers of contributors to interact freely with larger amounts of information in search of new projects and opportu-

nities for collaboration. This sounds like a potential threat to business. But, in fact, it's an opportunity for organizations to discover new pools of creativity, both inside and outside the walls of their organization."

10. Journalists Robert Levine and Chris Ruen have both provided evidence of this.

11. It has been reported that Apple and Google spend more money on patent purchases and lawsuits than on research and development. Thankfully, there has been increasing attention to the rampant abuse of the patent system. For a good overview, see Charles Duhigg, "The Patent, Used as a Sword," *New York Times*, October 8, 2012, A1.

12. So says tech evangelist Robert Scoble.

13. Jeffrey Ernst Friedman, "Sponsors of SOPA Act Pulled in 4 Times as Much in Contributions from Hollywood as from Silicon Valley," MapLight.org, December 19, 2011, http://maplight.org/content/72896.

14. Matt Brian, "Google's Lobbying Budget Is Eighth Largest in US, Surpassing Even Lockheed Martin," The Verge, June 4, 2013, http://www.theverge.com/2013/6/4/4394234/google-eight-biggest-record-lobbying-washington. According to the same outlet, Google employees gave more to Obama's 2008 campaign than any other company except Microsoft and Goldman Sachs. T. C. Sottek, "Google Joins the Lobbying Elite with Record Spending on Lawmakers in 2012," The Verge, April 23, 2012, http://www.theverge.com/2012/4/23/2968686/google-joins-lobbying-elite. For "Copyright, Patent & Trademark" reports, see http://www.opensecrets.org/lobby/issuesum.php?id=CPT&year=2011.

15. Glenn Greenwald, "Surveillance State Democracy," *Salon*, May 6, 2012, http://www.salon.com/2012/05/06/surveillance_state_democracy/singleton/. Also note a similar comment by Julian Assange, who said Google joining the SOPA fight "scared the hell out of me," because the company was beginning to see itself as a " 'political player' with enormous power over Congress." Quoted in Julian Assange, *Cypherpunks: Freedom and the Future of the Internet* (New York: OR Books, 2012), 83.

16. David Segal, "CISPA Is the New SOPA: Help Kill It This Week," *Huffington Post*, April 16, 2012. Segal also discusses this issue at length in the book he coedited with David Moon and Patrick Ruffini, *Hacking Politics: How Geeks, Progressives, the Tea Party, Gamers, Anarchists and Suits Teamed Up to Defeat SOPA and Save the Internet* (New York: OR Books, 2013).

17. Adrian Johns, *Piracy: The Intellectual Property Wars from Gutenberg to Gates* (Chicago: University of Chicago Press, 2009), 50.

18. The second trial, in November 2010, upheld the previous guilty verdict, reducing the prison terms while increasing the damages owed to the movie and recording company plaintiffs to more than $7 million. In February 2012, the Swedish High Court declined to hear an appeal.

None of the defendants has been jailed nor paid any fines. The Pirate Bay celebrated its ten-year anniversary in 2013 and remains up and running as of this writing, with traffic rising in recent years. Sunde moved on to cofound Flattr, a micro-donation start-up that allows Internet users to compensate creators by clicking buttons such as "Favorite," "Like," or "Star," in addition to other projects.

19. Nicholas Kulish, "Pirates' Strong Showing in Berlin Elections Surprises Even Them," *New York Times*, September 20, 2011, A5. Some of the setbacks and challenges since this early success have been reported in *Der Spiegel* and other sources. While still active in other countries, Pirate Party momentum has flagged a bit in Germany, with candidates winning only 2 percent of the popular federal vote in the 2013 elections and failing to win seats in the national Parliament. Kevin Collier, "Despite Anger at NSA, German Pirate Party Loses Federal Election," *Daily Dot*, September 23, 2013.

20. Merlind Theile, "Fighting for Internet Freedom: Pirate Party Makes Bid for German Parliament," *Der Spiegel*, June 26, 2009.

21. Alexander Galloway in an interview for re-public.gr.

22. Siva Vaidhyanathan, *The Anarchist in the Library: How the Clash Between Freedom and Control Is Hacking the Real World and Crashing the System* (New York: Basic Books: 2005), xvi. Picking up this theme, Marcus Boon, in his book *In Praise of Copying* (Cambridge, Mass.: Harvard University Press, 2010), wonders if "the affirmation of copia, a particular attitude towards mimesis," unites the "downloader of films sitting in a dorm room at a North American college and a vendor of shopping bags made out of used sacking in a market in a suburb of a city of the global south."

23. Eduardo M. Peñalver and Sonia K. Katyal, *Property Outlaws: How Squatters, Pirates, and Protesters Improve the Law of Ownership* (New Haven, Conn.: Yale University Press, 2010). The quote is from a review of the book by David Bollier on the Web site onthecommons.org.

24. Vaidhyanathan, *The Anarchist in the Library*, 15.

25. Sonny Bunch, "The Rules of the Game," *Wall Street Journal*, February 22, 2010.

26. Quoted in ibid.

27. Steve Albini, "The Problem with Music," *Baffler*, no. 5 (1993).

28. The original Napster was a commercial venture, the Pirate Bay takes advertising, and some storage locker sites have tried incentivizing copyright infringement by paying people who upload popular files.

29. Sean Gallagher, "The Fast, Fabulous, Allegedly Fraudulent Life of Megaupload's Kim Dotcom," *Wired*, January 26, 2012.

30. Johns, *Piracy*, 5.

31. Elizabeth Stark, "Free Culture and the Internet: A New Semiotic Democracy," *Open Democracy*, June 19, 2006.

32. Cory Doctorow, "Chris Anderson's Free Adds Much to The Long Tail, but Falls Short," *Guardian*, July 28, 2009.

33. A friend recently attended an event where a group of artists was selling a book it had produced and printed, a project that included photographs of historical sites and assorted commentaries, for five dollars. Her acquaintance wondered aloud if the book was available as a free PDF. My friend pointed out that the book was for sale right in front of them, and at a bargain price considering it was handmade. The acquaintance demurred on principle. To pay for a book would be tantamount to supporting the privatization of culture, an endorsement of the misguided idea that knowledge is property and can be bought and sold as such.

    The idea that knowledge can be stolen is also one that has long been challenged. In the premodern Islamic world, for example, book thieves were not subject to the standard punishment for theft—amputation of the hand. "Islamic law held that he had not intended to steal the book as paper and ink, but the ideas in the book—and unlike the paper and ink, these ideas were not tangible property," writes historian Carla Hesse. These debates are timeless. Copyleft, it should be noted, is a less grandiose and more complex topic, its politics deftly analyzed by academics including Christopher Kelty (*Two Bits: The Cultural Significance of Free Software* [Durham, N.C.: Duke University Press, 2008]) and Gabriella Coleman (*Coding Freedom: The Ethics and Aesthetics of Hacking* [Princeton, N.J.: Princeton University Press, 2012]). Coleman, in particular, makes a compelling case that hacking culture, and by association copyleft, though "politically agnostic," simultaneously upholds values including equalizing access to information, sharing, and unalienated labor that could be interpreted as progressive: "Hackers' insistence on never losing access to the fruits of their labor—and indeed actively seeking to share these fruits with others—calls into being Karl Marx's famous critique of estranged labor."

34. Some exceptions are celebrity artists Jeff Koons and Shepard Fairey, who have built their careers defiantly appropriating the work of others, while jealously guarding their own recontextualizations. Koons has had numerous high-profile lawsuits brought against him for copyright violation: he filed one against the producers of bookends he says resemble his *Balloon Dog* sculpture (that his *Balloon Dog* sculpture resembles a balloon dog seems to give him no pause); in 2008 Fairey, before becoming a copyright-reform poster boy because of the AP's lawsuit over his Obama "Hope" print, sent a cease and desist order to a Texas resident who altered his famous *Andre the Giant Has a Posse* stencil by adding a respiratory mask and the word "Protect" (a particularly ironic move given the legal trouble Fairey was threatened with when he first began using the Andre image many years ago). Fairey is a particularly controversial

figure among more activist artists for his habit of taking social movement imagery, decontextualizing it, and copyrighting the results. Josh
MacPhee of the artist collective Justseeds has written about Fairey and
these issues at length on his Web site www.justseeds.org.

35. Fair use is an American phenomenon. The UK and Canada have fair
dealing; France has statutory exceptions to copyright.

36. One example is the Blur-Banff proposal, but there are others.

37. Another idea worth considering is Dean Baker's Artistic Freedom
Voucher. Dean Baker, "The Artistic Freedom Voucher: An Internet Age
Alternative to Copyrights," Center for Economic and Policy Research,
November 5, 2003.

38. This is why, though I support extensive copyright reform, I am not
convinced that the public domain should be the default for creative
works. People should have the right not to allow the family photos
they have posted to be used in commercial projects or advertising, for
example. Two interesting essays touch on these concerns: Peter Frase,
"Property and Theft," *Jacobin*, nos. 11–12 (Fall 2013); and Anne Elizabeth
Moore, "Degendering Value," in the same issue.

39. Len quoted in Kembrew McLeod and Peter DiCola, *Creative License: The
Law and Culture of Digital Sampling* (Durham, N.C.: Duke University
Press, 2011), 120. The idea that there are some uses that are offensive to
the artist or violate the integrity of a creative work is, in a nutshell, the
idea of "moral rights." It's a concept many people intuitively subscribe to,
though as a principle it has no legal standing in the United States, unlike
Europe, where the moral rights persist even after the sale or licensing of
a work. Atavistic though it may be, we tend to think of creative works as
an extension of the maker, which is why many of us implicitly accept that
creators should have some say about how their creations are used.

40. I've taken the phrase "romance of the commons" from legal scholars
Anupam Chander and Madhavi Sunder. Anupam Chander and Madhavi
Sunder, "The Romance of the Public Domain," *California Law Review*
92, no. 5 (October 2004). Sunder also has an excellent book that tries to
expand the focus of the current intellectual property debate beyond
innovation and efficiency to consider social justice and well-being.
Madhavi Sunder, *From Goods to a Good Life: Intellectual Property and
Global Justice* (New Haven, Conn.: Yale University Press, 2012).

41. For more on the history of the commons see Peter Linebaugh, *The
Magna Carta Manifesto: Liberties and Commons for All* (Berkeley: University of California Press, 2009).

42. Aaron was one of the first people I spoke to when I began working on
this book, and he became a friend and source of valuable insight and
advice as I became more involved in political organizing in the fall of

2011. While there were points in the copyright debate where we dis-
agreed, our social ideals generally overlapped, for Aaron believed that
open access and the open Internet needed to coexist with sustained left-
leaning political activism and attention to issues like power, inequality,
and privilege. For a summary of Aaron's travails with JSTOR and MIT and
harassment by government authorities, see Wesley Yang, "The Life and
Afterlife of Aaron Swartz," *New York*, February 8, 2013. For insight into
Aaron's complicated perspective, read his critique of the open data
movement, "A Database of Folly," CrookedTimber.org, July 3, 2012,
http://crookedtimber.org/2012/07/03/a-database-of-folly/.

6: DRAWING A LINE

1. Quoted in John F. Kasson, *Civilizing the Machine: Technology and Republican Values in America, 1776–1900* (New York: Hill and Wang, 1999), 24.
2. Annie Leonard, *The Story of Stuff: The Impact of Overconsumption on the Planet, Our Communities, and Our Health—And How We Can Make It Better* (New York: Free Press, 2011), 205.
3. For excellent reporting on these issues, see the Fall 2010 issue of *Virginia Quarterly Review*.
4. Jon Mooallem, "The Afterlife of Cellphones," *New York Times*, January 13, 2008.
5. Mark P. Mills, "The Cloud Begins with Coal: Big Data, Big Networks, Big Infrastructure, and Big Power," National Mining Association, August 2013, 3.
6. Richard Maxwell and Toby Miller, "Greening Starts with Us," NYTimes.com, September 24, 2012, http://www.nytimes.com/roomfordebate/2012/09/23/informations-environmental-cost/greening-starts-with-ourselves.
7. James Glanz, "Power, Pollution, and the Internet," *New York Times*, September 23, 2012, A1; and also Gary Cook and Jodie Van Horn, "How Dirty Is Your Data?," Greenpeace International, 2011.
8. Nicholas Carr, *The Big Switch: Rewiring the World, from Edison to Google* (New York: W. W. Norton, 2008), 178.
9. Glanz, "Power, Pollution, and the Internet"; and Maxwell and Miller, "Greening Starts with Us."
10. Glanz, "Power, Pollution, and the Internet."
11. Daniel Goleman and Gregory Norris, "How Green Is My iPad?," NYTimes.com, April 4, 2012, http://www.nytimes.com/interactive/2010/04/04/opinion/04opchart.html. "The Rise of e-Reading," Pew Internet and Public Life, April 4, 2012, http://libraries.pewinternet.org/2012/04/04/the-rise-of-e-reading/; publishers sold 2.57 billion books in all formats in 2010

(Julie Bosman, "Publishing Gives Hints of Revival, Data Show," *New York Times*, August 9, 2011). For the sake of simplicity, I have estimated 250 million Americans buying books, which comes to approximately ten per person per year. In reality, however, book-buying patterns are much more lopsided, as many Americans report they don't read any books at all. At the same time, according to Pew, over one hundred million people own tablets or e-readers. It's still an open question whether e-books will really replace print books sales. Similar concerns have been raised about shifts in music consumption. While it is clear that CDs are becoming obsolete in a way paper books do not seem to be, it is unclear whether there will be a substantial environmental benefit as a result. For example, *Mother Jones* reported that streaming an album multiple times can quickly have more of an energy impact than producing and shipping a CD.

12. Mooallem, "The Afterlife of Cellphones."
13. Leonard, *The Story of Stuff*, 202–3.
14. Mooallem, "The Afterlife of Cellphones."
15. Chip Bayers, "Why Silicon Valley Can't Sell," *Ad Week*, July 11, 2011.
16. Julia Angwin, "Sites Feed Personal Details to New Tracking Industry," *Wall Street Journal*, July 30, 2010. Documents released by Edward Snowden reveal that corporate tracking enables government snooping: "The National Security Agency is secretly piggybacking on the tools that enable Internet advertisers to track consumers, using 'cookies' and location data to pinpoint targets for government hacking and to bolster surveillance." Ashkan Soltani, Andrea Peterson, and Barton Gellman, *Washington Post*, "NSA Uses Google Cookies to Pinpoint Targets for Hacking," December 10, 2013.
17. Eli Pariser, *The Filter Bubble: What the Internet Is Hiding from You* (New York: Penguin Press, 2011), 14.
18. Julia Angwin and Steve Stecklow, "'Scrapers' Dig Deep for Data on the Web," *Wall Street Journal*, October 22, 2010; Elizabeth Dwoskin, "Web Giants Threaten End to Cookie Tracking," *Wall Street Journal*, October 26, 2013; Lucia Moses, "Marketers Should Take Note of When Women Feel Least Attractive," *Ad Week*, October 2, 2013.
19. Scott Thurm and Yukari Iwatani Kane, "Your Apps Are Watching You," *Wall Street Journal*, December 17, 2010; Elizabeth Dwoskin, "Web Giants Threaten to End Cookie Tracking," *Wall Street Journal*, October 26, 2013.
20. One vivid indicator of how outmoded these laws are is the fact that handwritten, mailed letters enjoy more federal protections than electronic correspondence stored in the cloud.
21. Brenda Salinas, "High-End Stores Use Facial Recognition Tools to Spot VIPs," NPR, *All Tech Considered*, July 21, 2013.
22. Peter Maass, "How a Lone Grad Student Scooped the Government and

What It Means for Your Online Privacy," ProPublica, July 28, 2012; Christopher S. Stewart and Vranica, Suzanne, "Advertisers Worry About Changes to 'Cookies,'" *Wall Street Journal*, September 19, 2013; Kate Crawford and Jason Schultz, "Big Data and Due Process: Toward a Framework to Redress Predictive Privacy Harms," New York University School of Law, October 2013.

23. David Streitfield and Kevin J. O'Brien, "Google Privacy Inquiries Get Little Cooperation," *New York Times*, May 23, 2012, B1.

24. Erica Newland, "Disappearing Phone Booths: Privacy in the Digital Age," Center for Democracy and Technology, May 2012; and Jessica E. Vascarello, "Google Agonizes on Privacy as Ad World Vaults Ahead," *Wall Street Journal*, August 9, 2010.

25. Vascarello, "Google Agonizes on Privacy as Ad World Vaults Ahead"; and Michael Learmonth, "Google Readies Ambitious Plan for Web-Data Exchange," *Advertising Age*, July 11, 2011.

26. Douglas Edwards, *I'm Feeling Lucky: The Confessions of Google Employee Number 59* (New York: Mariner Books, 2012), 107.

27. Shayndi Rice, "Inside Facebook's Push to Woo Big Advertisers," *Wall Street Journal*, April 15, 2012; and Avie Schneider, "Why Are Investors in Like with Facebook Again?," NPR, *All Tech Considered*, January 11, 2013.

28. Some other potentially profitable avenues include selling user data to third parties seeking to forecast the popularity of future products and also providing "ads that are hypertargeted both socially and geographically, a moving billboard that knows exactly who you are, and where, always." Farhad Manjoo, "The Morning After," *Fast Company*, March 19, 2012.

29. Somini Sengupta, "Facebook's Prospects May Rest on Trove of Data," *New York Times*, May 15, 2012, A1.

30. Joseph Turow, *The Daily You: How the New Advertising Industry Is Defining Your Identity and Your Worth* (New Haven, Conn.: Yale University Press, 2011), 2.

31. Ibid., 4.

32. Julia Angwin, "The Web's New Gold Mine: Your Secrets," *Wall Street Journal*, July 30, 2010.

33. Ibid.; Tara Culp-Ressler, "Big Data Companies Are Selling Lists of Rape Victims to Marketing Firms," thinkprogress.org, December 19, 2013, http://thinkprogress.org/health/2013/12/19/3089591/big-data-health-data-mining/.

34. Julia Angwin and Jennifer Valentino-Devries, "Race Is On to 'Fingerprint' Phones, PCs," *Wall Street Journal*, November 30, 2010.

35. Turow, *The Daily You*, 7.

36. Latanya Sweeney, "Discrimination in Online Ad Delivery" (January 28, 2013), SSRN: http://ssrn.com/abstract-2208240.

37. Jennifer Valentino-Devries, Jeremy Singer-Vine, and Ashkan Soltani, "Websites Vary Prices, Deals Based on Users' Information," *Wall Street Journal*, December 24, 2012.

38. Martha C. White, "Could That Facebook 'Like' Hurt Your Credit Score?," *Time*, July 14, 2012; and Natasha Singer, "Senator Opens Investigation of Data Brokers," *New York Times*, October 11, 2012, B3.

39. Rishad Tobaccowala, chief strategist of one of the largest marketing communications companies in the world, said exactly that in 2010.

40. Alexis Madrigal, "I'm Being Followed: How Google—and 104 Other Companies—Are Tracking Me on the Web," TheAtlantic.com, February 29, 2012.

41. Jon Healey, "Web-based approach to product placement," LATimes .com, October 20, 2008, http://latimesblogs.latimes.com/technology /2008/10/a-web-based-app.html. Poptent offers its overview at www .poptentmedia.com/resources/poptent-overview.pdf.

42. Lisa Belkin, "Queen of the Mommy Bloggers," *New York Times Magazine*, February 23, 2011.

43. George Monbiot, "The Need to Protect the Internet from 'Astroturfing' Grows Ever More Urgent," *Guardian*, February 23, 2011.

44. Brian Morrissey, "General Mills Recruits Blog Backers," *Ad Week*, April 28, 2009.

45. Bill Grueskin, Ava Seave, and Lucas Graves, "The Business of Digital Journalism," *Columbia Journalism Review* (May 10, 2011): 116.

46. Eliot Van Buskirk, "Gaming the System: How Marketers Rig the Social Media Machine," *Wired*, July 7, 2010.

47. Caitlyn Coverly, "The Even Darker Side?," *Ryerson Review of Journalism* (May 6, 2011).

48. Ellen P. Goodman, "Stealth Marketing and Editorial Integrity," *Texas Law Review* 85, no. 83 (2006): 143.

49. Ben Sisario, "Backing Indie Bands to Sell Cars," *New York Times*, September 28, 2011, B1.

50. Chris Ruen, *Freeloading: How Our Insatiable Hunger for Free Content Starves Creativity* (New York: OR Books, 2012), 132.

51. Damian Kulash, "The New Rock-Star Paradigm," *Wall Street Journal*, December 17, 2010. The last bit of information about brands is from an interview Kulash gave with Sponsorship.com, available at www .sponsorship.com/IEGSR/2010/12/06/Marketing-Partnership-Insights -From-OK-Go-Lead-Sin.aspx.

52. Jeff Bercovici, "Morgan Spurlock Is Making Another Sponsored Documentary," Forbes.com, April 21, 2011, www.forbes.com/sites/jeffber covici/2011/04/21/morgan-spurlock-is-making-another-sponsored -documentary/.

53. Quoted in Robert D. Hof, "You Are the Ad," *MIT Technology Review*, http://www.technologyreview.com/featuredstory/423721/you-are-the-ad/. In late 2013, Google revealed plans to get in on the game as well, announcing a change to its Terms of Service that grants it the right to display users' names, photos, comments, and ratings in "Endorsement Ads." Claire Cain Miller and Vindu Goel, "Google to Sell Users' Endorsements,"*New York Times*, October 12, 2013, B1.

54. Nicholas Carr, *The Shallows: What the Internet Is Doing to Our Brains* (New York: W. W. Norton, 2010), 155.

55. Jack Neff, "At Blogher Confab, Marketers Show Moms Some Love," *Ad Age*, July 27, 2009.

56. Claire Cain Miller, "Amazon to Sell the Kindle Reader at a Lower Price, but with Advertising," *New York Times*, April 11, 2011, B1.

57. Ferriss made this point in a blog post on his Web site available at http://www.fourhourworkweek.com/blog/2008/01/28/tips-for-personal-branding-in-the-digital-age-google-insurance-cache-flow-and-more/.

58. These quotes are taken from page 55 of Marwick's dissertation; Alice E. Marwick, *Status Update: Celebrity, Publicity, and Self-Branding in Web 2.0*, New York University, 2010. It has since been expanded into a book; Alice E. Marwick, *Status Update: Celebrity, Publicity, and Self-Branding in Web 2.0* (New Haven, Conn.: Yale University Press, 2013).

59. John Tierney, "Will You Be E-Mailing This Column? It's Awesome," *New York Times*, February 9, 2010, D2.

60. Max Weber, *Protestant Ethic and the Spirit of Capitalism* (New York: Penguin Classics, 2002).

61. Lee Rainie, Sara Kiesler, Ruogu Kang, and Mary Madden, "Anonymity, Privacy, and Security Online," Pew Internet and American Life Project, September 5, 2013.

62. Susan Linn, *Consuming Kids: The Hostile Takeover of Childhood* (New York: The New Press, 2004), 5.

63. John de Graaf, David Wann, and Thomas H. Naylor, *Affluenza: The All-Consuming Epidemic* (New York: Berrett-Koehler Publishers, 2002), 55. During the same time period, the number of ads they are exposed to on television doubled to forty thousand a year. For more information on the negative consequences of advertising on children, see the briefing "The Role of Media in Childhood Obesity," Henry J. Kasier Family Foundation, February 2004.

64. Matt Richtel, "Children Fail to Recognize Online Ads, Study Says," NYTimes.com, April 21, 2011, http://bits.blogs.nytimes.com/2011/04/21/children-fail-to-recognize-online-ads-study-says/.

65. Steve Stecklow, "On the Web, Children Face Intensive Tracking," *Wall Street Journal*, September 17, 2010.

66. Matt Richtel, "In Online Games, a Path to Young Consumers," *New York Times*, April 21, 2011, A1.

67. Some parents have actually sued Facebook, upset that images of their underage children were used to endorse products without explicit permission.

68. The $700 billion figure is from the World Federation of Advertisers.

CONCLUSION

1. Damian Kulash quotes are from an interview with Andrew McMillen posted online April 26, 2010, http://andrewmcmillen.com/2010/04/26/a-conversation-with-damian-kulash-ok-go-singerguitarist/.

2. All data are encoded in files, which make up one element of a complex system that also involves hardware, software, protocols, plugins, and so on. As preservationists have noted, an archaeologist does not need to know about baking clay tables to decipher cuneiform nor does a literary critic need a vintage typewriter to study an original draft of an influential novel, but we all need software to interpret a digital artifact. This is why texts printed on papyrus and parchment are still legible thousands of years after the fact, while the same won't necessarily be said for the documents stored on our computers today. Between 1956 and 2000 there were sixty tape video formats, already a formidable number; today over three hundred video file formats exist, many of them proprietary. For files in these formats to be successfully archived, the software for playing them and machines that can run that software must be in working order. Faced with this rapid pace of change and growing stacks of outdated hard drives, Brewster Kahle, founder of the Internet Archive and leader of the open access movement, announced in 2011 that he would refocus his efforts on preserving paper books. "We're discovering what librarians have known for centuries in this new digital world," Kahle told NPR, confessing that he felt he had been naive. "The opportunity to live in an Orwellian or a Fahrenheit 451 type world, where things are changed out from underneath us, is very much present. . . . Let's make sure we put in place the long-term archives to make it so that we can check up on those that are presenting things in the future."

3. It should go without saying that plenty of people subsidize their own creative efforts; most of us have played the role of self-patron by funding our projects through money earned at a second job. Overwhelmingly, it's makers themselves—not private enterprise or government—who deserve credit for financing the production of culture.

4. On March 22, 2011, a ruling by Judge Dennis Chin rejected a complex settlement between Google Books, commercial publishers, and the

Authors Guild, putting temporary brakes on the company's momen-
tous project. Chin's forty-eight-page opinion enumerated the endeav-
or's many drawbacks, including Google's land grab of so-called orphan
works, the fact that copyright reform should be taken up by Congress,
not the courts, the lack of any competitive projects, the objections of
foreign authors and publishers, and potential privacy violations. Then,
on November 14, 2013, in a stunning victory for Google, Judge Chin
ruled that the company's scanning classified as "fair use." The Author's
Guild vowed to appeal. Where advertising is concerned, it is worth not-
ing that any kind of surveillance is anathema to traditional librarians,
who were among the most visible and vocal groups to stand up against
the Patriot Act, which granted law enforcement the ability to access
patrons' library records. Amy Goodman, "America's Most Dangerous
Librarians," *Mother Jones*, September/October 2008.

5. Siva Vaidhyanathan, *The Googlization of Everything: (And Why We Should
   Worry)* (Berkeley: University of California Press, 2011), 41.

6. Richard Darnton has been chronicling the birth of the DPLA in a series
   of articles for the *New York Review of Books*.

7. The demise of countless services, from Geocities to Google Reader,
   and the regular speculation that Yahoo! has plans to shut down Flickr
   because of slumping growth, only underscores the fact that these sites
   are not gifts aimed at facilitating creativity and securing access to our
   shared inheritance for future generations, but commercial enterprises
   designed to yield return on investment.

8. For worthwhile commentary on this issue, see Wikimedia Foundation's Sue Gardner's Web site, suegardner.org/2013/06/26/the-war-for
   -the-free-and-open-internet-and-how-we-are-losing-it/.

9. Elias Grol, "Can Twitter Go Public and Still Be a Champion of Free
   Speech?," *Foreign Policy*, September 13, 2013.

10. See Frances Saunders, *The Cultural Cold War* (New York: The New
    Press, 2001), and the afterword to the Canongate edition of Lewis
    Hyde's *The Gift*.

11. For the classic take on libertarianism and Silicon Valley see Richard
    Barbrook and Andy Cameron, "The Californian Ideology," *Alamut*,
    August 1999. More recently George Packer, David Golumbia, and others
    have written on the topic.

12. For more on the history and funding of the Internet, see parts 1 and 4
    of James Curran, Natalie Fenton, and Des Freedman, *Misunderstanding
    the Internet* (London: Routledge, 2012). For an enlightening and detailed
    discussion of public funding and the technology sector, see Mariana
    Mazzucato, *The Entrepreneurial State: Debunking Public vs. Private Sector
    Myths* (New York: Anthem Press, 2013). In a different way, the libertar-

ian fallacy has been exposed by whistle-blower Edward Snowden with his revelations of the cooperation of Google, Facebook, Microsoft, and Yahoo! with American intelligence agencies.

13. It is true that quotas may not be the best method moving forward, but I do think quotas have a role to play in some circumstances. Without them many foreign broadcasters would fill prime time with imported shows, which are cheaper than making something locally and allow for bigger profit margins. One important book that has influenced my thinking about cultural economics is Peter S. Grant and Chris Wood, *Blockbusters and Trade Wars: Popular Culture in a Globalized World* (Vancouver: Douglas & McIntyre, 2004).

14. Kate Taylor, "Digital Freedom Comes with a High Cost," *Toronto Star*, September 29, 2010.

15. The international popularity of American Web sites diminishes revenue for regional endeavors by diverting funds to Silicon Valley.

16. Susan P. Crawford, "The Case for Publicly Owned Internet Service," *Bloomberg*, February 14, 2012.

17. Susan Crawford, *Captive Audience: The Telecom Industry and Monopoly Power in the New Gilded Age* (New Haven, Conn.: Yale University Press, 2013), 11.

18. National Roper Poll from 2007. Also see, Craig Aaron, Candace Clement, Josh Silver, S. Derek Turner, "New Public Media: A Plan for Action," Free Press, 2010, www.freepress.net/sites/default/files/fp-legacy/New_Public_Media.doc.pdf.

19. For a recent account of the kind of censorship that results from corporate underwriting and high-powered donors, see Jane Mayer, "A Word from Our Sponsor," *New Yorker*, May 27, 2013.

20. There are smart proposals for publicly funding journalism that ward off concerns about centralization and congressional influence, such as the "citizen's news vouchers" that would allow taxpayers to allot a prescribed sum to the news-gathering organization of their choice outlined by Robert McChesney and John Nichols.

21. While people often worry that publicly funded art will be bland, it has in fact come under fire for being too controversial, as in the notorious case of the NEA Four. People also worry about art and culture being dictated by bureaucrats on high, but the funding process can be decentralized and democratic, for example by putting together panels of creative peers and engaged citizens to determine how resources are allocated. For more on the peer-panel process once used by the NEA, see Michael Brenson, *Visionaries and Outcasts: The NEA, Congress, and the Place of Visual Arts in America* (New York: The New Press, 2001). For a great essay on these themes, see Lewis Hyde, "The Children of John Adams: A Histori-

cal View of the Debate Over Art Funding," in *Art Matters: How the Culture Wars Changed America* (New York: New York University Press, 1999).

22. Many techies and hackers would likely prefer an ad hoc, DIY approach to the dilemmas described here: community "mesh networks" instead of national or municipal broadband, locally installed open source social networks instead of centralized ones run as public utilities, personal encryption tools instead of counting on federal privacy regulations, and so on. This perspective should not be entirely discounted, but my belief is that these efforts ultimately won't scale and risk leaving large portions of the population out.

23. The $1 trillion figure is from the Consumer Electronics Association.

24. Jesse Drucker, "Google 2.4% Rate Shows How $60 Billion Lost to Tax Loopholes," *Bloomberg*, October 21, 2010; Nelson D. Schwartz and Charles Duhigg, "Apple's Web of Tax Shelters Saved It Billions, Panel Finds," *New York Times*, May 21, 2013, A1; and Brian Faler, "Jeff Bezos Plays Active Role in Tax Fights," Politico.com, August 6, 2013.

25. The extension of copyright also incentivizes the production of films with licensing potential, such as sequels and prequels and toys and video games.

ACKNOWLEDGMENTS

Thanks to friends and family, movement comrades, and writing and film colleagues for insightful conversations and endless patience and encouragement as I worked on this book. There are too many folks to name everyone who played a crucial role but Jeff, Tara, Sunaura, Laura Hanna, Colin Robinson, Beka Economopoulos, Jason Jones, Elizabeth Stark, Josh MacPhee, Rebecca Solnit, Rebecca Gates, Bretton Fosbrook, and Sarah Resnick deserve to be singled out. Two friends and passionate activists, Dara Greenwald and Aaron Swartz, engaged with me about material that made it into these pages, and both passed away, leaving the world a poorer place. I'm grateful to Blue Mountain Center for space to think and to the *Baffler* and Thomas Frank for giving me a forum to test some of my early ideas in essay form, much of which has been woven into this book. The support of editorial teams at 4th Estate in the UK and Random House Canada has been invaluable; profound thanks are due to Mark Richards, Katy Whitehead, and especially Anne Collins and the always insightful and understanding Amanda Lewis. Without my agent Mel Flashman's guidance and wisdom every step of the way this project would not be. Last but not least, boundless appreciation for everyone at Metropolitan Books, a publisher I have long admired from afar, with special thanks to Sara Bershtel and Grigory Tovbis. My editor, Riva Hocherman, is simply a master of her craft, a wrangler of tangled sentences, twisted logic, and overwhelmed authors. I shudder to think of what this book would be without her intervention. Credit goes to these kind folks and many unnamed others (including all who have written perceptively on matters of technology, culture, and politics before me, and whose work I was inspired by and dependent on), while responsibility for any omissions and shortcomings is mine alone. Thank you all.

INDEX

ABOUT THE AUTHOR

ASTRA TAYLOR is a writer, documentary filmmaker, and activist. Her films include *Zizek!*, a feature documentary about the world's most outrageous philosopher, which was broadcast on the Sundance Channel, and *Examined Life*, a series of excursions with contemporary thinkers. Taylor's writing has appeared in *The Nation*, the *London Review of Books*, *n+1*, *The Baffler*, and other publications. She is the editor of *Examined Life*, a companion volume to the film, and coeditor of *Occupy!: Scenes from Occupied America*. Taylor helped launch the Occupy offshoot Strike Debt and its Rolling Jubilee campaign. She lives in New York.